The Berkeley Literary
Women's Revolution

Contents

Foreword

by Robin Tolmach Lakoff

In July 2001 Katharine Meyer Graham died suddenly at the age of 84. As perhaps the most influential woman in Washington and in media at the time, she received a great deal of attention. Her many obituaries traced the pattern of her long and full life, noting that the transition from society wife to powerhouse had come, not of her choosing, in middle age when she took command of *The Washington Post* and subsequently a whole media empire. This may strike today's young women as no big deal. But in 1963, women didn't run major urban newspapers. It just couldn't happen.

Her youth as a daughter of privilege; her marriage to rising megastar Phillip Graham, who became publisher of the *Washington Post*; her adulthood as wife and mother and society figure—this pattern doesn't require explanation. But then, in 1963, her husband (who had suffered for years from bipolar disorder) shot himself; and with that tragedy the "normal" story of Katharine Graham dissolves into an *aporia*: a point at which a formerly coherent narrative ceases to be intelligible.

The obituarists all tell how Graham, shakily at first but with ever-increasing confidence and competence, took up the reins that her husband had let fall at the *Post*, and became (many would argue) a greater force and a better publisher than he had been or would have become. But they skirt the hard questions: how did this happen? What occurred at the moment at which Graham made her decision to hold onto the *Post* (for her son, she said at first) rather than sell it? This moment of courage, confusion, and finally transformation in the life of a woman who had been living by the conventional rules is both infinitely moving and totally inexplicable—yet we have to understand it.

As I was digesting those obituaries, Olivia Eielson called me. I had known her for a long time, and had last seen her, in fact, a year or so earlier, at the meeting that brought this book into being. Although I was

1

not a member of the group, I found their project exciting and important. So when Olivia asked me if I would write the foreword, I accepted the assignment as an honor and a challenge.

In the late 1960s and early 1970s, a number of graduate student women in comparative literature at the University of California at Berkeley experienced moments of transformation, together and separately. The rise of the modern women's movement during those years was a source of hope and inspiration, but also the beginning of uncertainty, self-doubt, and painful self-examination for women who had grown up according to the old rules. Over the next quarter century the questions and experiments would lead to immense changes in the way a research university works: what constitutes "valid" and "valuable" research; what "collegiality" is; how a teacher should behave toward her students; and much more, more than we are fully aware of even now. At the time, none of us saw clearly where our doubts would lead, and often we were simply scared. Yet the women writing here persevered. They changed.

What brings Graham's story together with those collected here is two words: *courage* and *transformation*. As with Graham, for them to change, something first had to die: in their case, the old sentimental understanding of the university as the camaraderie of males, investigating male concerns, giving answers mainly meaningful to men, training the next generation of males. Even in coeducational institutions, women were seen by their professors as decorative at best, at worst as irrelevant distractions to the real work of the institution. Certainly they could never do scholarship equal to that of any competent male; almost certainly, with the rarest of exceptions, they would never take the places of eminent male scholars to achieve eminence in their own right. Women didn't hold major university positions. It just wasn't done.

But then something happened. And one of the places where it started to happen was in the minds of the women represented here. What I find glorious and significant about this collection is that it pulls open the curtain that, in Graham's case, must remain closed. These memoirs offer answers to some of the most important questions we can ask: How does social change start? What is required to produce a new world order? Someone might demur (there's always that straw person lurking around): the ideas and events described here occurred thirty or more years ago. Can we take these middle-aged recollections of youthful indiscretions as valid? We know how unreliable memory can be.

But the passage of time also brings clarity. Age (we must hope) offers wisdom. The reasons for choices made long ago may not have been apparent then; the battles of a generation ago can be seen more perceptively once the passions behind them are tempered by time. Now it is possible to look back and see what the struggles accomplished—what is here now that would not exist otherwise. At the time, it would have been hard to see through the chaos what the university could become. But now we have at least a glimpse of what a modern university should be, and what women have accomplished to make it a reality. We also understand the relevance of alternative solutions. Several of the writers here decided, after long efforts to play according to the rules, that the university was not where they could do meaningful work. Certainly their leaving was a loss for all of us who remained within the system. But they found ways to contribute, new paths to alternative creativity.

The memories remain vivid. I remember working with Gloria Bowles to create the U.C. Berkeley Women's Studies Program (later to achieve departmental status). Gloria's vision was to make something completely different from the university in its very midst: different governance, different standards, different relationships. As I look back on it, it still seems shockingly, daringly revolutionary. And in a university—as conservative as most institutions—it could not survive as Gloria had envisioned it. But Women's Studies still continues, if in different form, and generations of women students have had a more meaningful education as a result.

I remember team teaching a course with Deirdre Lashgari in the late and lamented Strawberry Creek College. It was the first time in my career that *teaching* was foregrounded. What worked with undergraduates? What was the instructors' relationship to their students ideally, and their relationship to each other—in the classroom and outside? How were power differences to be negotiated? How, in short, was feminist teaching different from the traditional kind? In the conventional universities in which I had been educated and in which I taught, those questions were not even askable, much less studyable or answerable. But we could examine them, since feminism had given us the vocabulary and the grammar to do so.

Other close friends, Catherine Rodriguez-Nieto and Joanna Bankier, were involved in one or both of the women's poetry translation projects, and from them I learned to ask other forbidden questions. What could that mean—"women's voices"? Weren't women just supposed to *shut up?* (It was a subversive idea back then that women could have as much of worth to say as men.) We had to learn how to listen differently, even as we were learning to talk differently (or at all), learning the language of university and profession, and doing what we could to mold it to our needs. Language was changing around us and with it our perceptions of the world and the world's perceptions of us. Utterances that had been dismissed as trivial could be reexamined, the literary canon reformulated and judgments reformed.

We were beginning to understand that control of language, of meaning and interpretation, was a power that had always been denied to women, creating an evil circularity: no power—no interpretive rights— no power, and so on eternally. By changing the standards of "literature," changing the questions that research could bear upon, we broke that circularity and began to take the language back.

But that was long ago! (the straw person interjects again). Is this story still worth telling? And the answer has to be: all the more so because victory seems assured. The new generation of women scholars all too often takes that role as unproblematic, the more or less equal position of women in the university as a given. Of course women's voices are part of the discourse! Yet they must be reminded that their participation is not a matter of course. What their elders fought for is still very new and deeply controversial. What many sacrificed so much for could still be snatched away. So it is crucial that these stories be told, that their context be appreciated.

Finally, the memoirs collected here represent a remaking of narratives, reassessment, and a reassertion of control, of meanings and understandings. The story of women within the university is not the story that academic men have told. Nor is our university theirs. But by making and telling these stories we define the university as a place for us, a place and a role rightfully ours. Without women's voices, the university is necessarily incomplete. Women do not experience the university as men do, and the university we would create is not the one that was created without our presence. Through the experiences shared within these pages, women have changed the university, making its name more truthful: a place of *universality,* a place where all of us belong.

Preface

How did Women's Studies come to Berkeley's Comparative Literature Department? It all began in 1969, when Marsha Hudson put up notices on bulletin boards all over Berkeley, proposing a feminist literary salon. All interested women were welcome. The object was not only to read the (few) women writers in the standard academic reading lists; it was also to discover and bring to light the many fine women writers hitherto hidden and forgotten.

Marsha's Salon, which continued over many years, nurtured a group of women who went on to several kinds of activism in the Comparative Literature Department. The politicos researched discrimination against women in the department, lobbied for funds to get women's courses taught, signed the letters, met with administrators, initiated and participated in the comparative literature women's caucus, and founded a Women's Studies major at Berkeley. The translators created the first groundbreaking anthologies of women's poetry and got them published by prestigious publishing houses. And then there were the teachers—those who taught the Women's Studies courses, and those who eventually carried the feminist message into literary and other academic disciplines, as well as into administration. And there were the writers of feminist dissertations. Some women were all of these things, and all were finding the truth in the saying, "The personal is political."

When we completed our Ph.D.s, we scattered and took off on a variety of paths, academic and nonacademic. Then in 1999, Bridget Connelly and Joanna Bankier organized a grand reunion in Berkeley. More than fifty women got together for lunch, champagne and reminiscences about what we had accomplished in our activist years on the Berkeley campus. By the end of the afternoon, we knew we wanted to write a history of that time, a collection of personal memoirs—this book. Five of us volunteered to get the book together. In the inclusive spirit of the '70s, we put out a call for any other interested co-editors, but as none came forward, we five proceeded on.

It's been fascinating and rewarding to read our colleagues' essays, to
see how they remember the days of women's liberation ("Sisterhood is
Powerful!") and what their paths have been through the less idealistic
times since the 1970s. And in the process of working together, we five
have come closer together, sharing our current lives as well as memories
of our time together on campus. It has been a rediscovery of words like
"sisterhood," which we began—a bit shyly—to use in e-mails to one
another.

A few years ago, the editors of *The Feminist Memoir Project* called
for collection and publication of the histories of local women's groups
across the country. Our book is such a history, and brings that history
into the present with the essays by Hosek, Kaye, and Bankier. By sharing our experiences, we hope to strengthen the memory of how much was
achieved (and what it was like before), and help rehabilitate words such
as "sisters" and "feminism." Although each generation has its own styles
and concerns, we hope also to inspire a younger generation to keep working actively towards true equality for women.

Acknowledgments

The editors owe a debt of gratitude to all the women graduate advising assistants of the Berkeley Comparative Literature Department. The Committee on Research at the University of California, Berkeley, provided funds that partially supported the *Marsha's Salon* project.

We particularly thank several husbands, Hank Massie, George Shackelford, and Dale Jensen, for their extraordinary support of the project (including Hank's catering and George's computer services, and Dale's patience).

We thank our teacher and graduate school advisor, Joseph J. Duggan, for agreeing to be the sole male author in this piece (see his letter in the appendix); and we thank Hal Reynolds in the Student Affairs Office.

Warm thanks to Lisa Gerrard for her helpful comments on the manuscript, and for her generosity with documents from her personal archive.

We are also grateful to several daughters for offering the younger generation's perspective; Kate Massie and her friend Maria Pecot gave excellent advice in their evaluations of the manuscript.

Carson Jeffries, Jack Burki, and Shirley Lovejoy Hecht we thank for their caring support always.

The Marsha's Salon Editorial Group
Berkeley, Fall 2004

1

Dancing in a Cage

Marsha Hudson

The bar smells of beer, peanuts, and sweat. Darkness obscures the expressions on the faces of the men watching me. My naked body above them, however, is well lit by lights along the perimeter of the little stage and by a crude spotlight that beams down from the back ceiling so that the men, crowded and shoving each other on the floor of the bar, can see me clearly as I dance to the loud music. Dancing is a welcome respite from selling beer. I have ten minutes to relax into the music. Spinning a tapestry of erotic, artful, and suggestive movements, I retreat into my mind, sink into my own thoughts. The music ends. As I descend the stairs to the floor, a customer blocks my exit, leans into my face, and asks with a conspiratorial leer, "What do you think about while you are up there dancing?" Always honest, I respond, "I'm conjugating Greek verbs."

At thirteen I decided I would be a college professor when I grew up. It fulfilled all of my requirements for happiness. First, it was a job that indubitably had a lot to do with books, and books were just about the most important thing in the world to me; second, it was a job that commanded a lot of respect, and respect was something I saw as accorded to few people, especially people like my mother; and third, it rewarded intelligence, and I craved to be valued for my mind. Furthermore, it was within the realm of possibility for me as a female since it was one of the five jobs, other than housewife, I understood to be allowed (white) women: secretary, waitress, nurse, prostitute, or teacher. Of those five it required the highest education, which for me translated into more books, more respect, and more intellectuality. From my youthful perspective, college professor was the perfect job for me.

9

So I set out to do what I could to make it happen: continue to be a good student, make good grades and get scholarships.

This, however, despite intelligence and motivation, didn't prove to be easy. My family life was chaotic. My mother was the sole financial support of me and my two little brothers and older sister, and she was not good at it. The culture of the fifties expected mothers to be at home with their children; God help them if they had no husband or other family to provide an income. Except God didn't help us, and my mother, becoming increasingly alcoholic and irresponsible, moved from job to job and moved us from town to town and from school to school. We were intensely poor, but what was worse for me and my academic ambitions, we were unknown and unnoticed. By the time I applied to college I had a respectable grade point average but no champions among the high school administration or faculty. I went to UC Berkeley with a few small scholarships, enough to pay my room and board for the first year. Years later I had an opportunity to ask one of the high school counselors why I hadn't been awarded more scholarships. "You didn't smile enough," she said, "and we didn't think you would be a good representative of the school." I didn't point out to her that the boy who received the most scholarship money was respected for his high seriousness. He rarely smiled.

I remember my undergraduate years at Berkeley (1963–1968) as a large block of hard work punctuated by political activity. When my freshman year scholarships ran out, I worked fifteen hours a week during the school months and forty hours or more a week during breaks and summers. I studied, I worked, and I marched in demonstrations: Civil Rights and then against the Vietnam War. In my sophomore year I was arrested in the Free Speech Movement demonstration. The decision to risk arrest was a major one for me: I had no one to support me emotionally or financially should the arrest have any disastrous consequences, and none of us knew how the arrest might someday affect us professionally. As far as I knew, it put at risk my dream of being a college professor. When the trial resulted in a $166 fine, I had to take a semester off from school to earn the money to pay the fine.

I began my college career as a double major in English and Cultural Anthropology, the former because I adored literature and the latter because I hoped the questions I had about the "human condition" could be answered through a cross-cultural study. At the end of my undergraduate years, I realized that language was essential to an understanding of other cultures and I transferred to Comparative Literature, a field which I believed would give me the language mastery I needed to understand others as well as the chance to study literature, my true love. Politically, by the end of my fifth (senior) year, I was becoming more involved with the feminist movement and less with the male-dominated New Left.

I didn't know why the Comparative Literature Department at UC Berkeley accepted me as a graduate student. My grades were respectable but not spectacular and I had rarely spoken to a faculty member outside of the classroom; I was too intimidated and they were rarely available to undergraduates. However, I was delighted: my dream of being a college professor was now truly possible! All I had to do was persevere and do what I did well: work and study.

Until I finished the master of arts and began teaching in the Comparative Literature Department, I had been a self-supporting student at Berkeley for eight years, balancing a full course load with working part-time during the academic year and full-time during the summers. When my freshman year scholarships ran out, I worked as a domestic (what some might call an *au pair*), as a volunteer coordinator for the YWCA, a legal secretary for Legal Aid, a legal secretary for a corporate law firm, an engineering secretary, a bibliographer for Southeast Asian Studies, an editor for a classics journal, and a topless dancer–barmaid.

The latter job spanned my senior year and the first year of graduate school and was one of the most lucrative jobs I held, more lucrative even than being a university instructor (a job for which I wouldn't qualify until I had completed my master's and passed the Permission to Proceed to the Doctorate). The bar I worked in was in San Jose, a forty-five minute drive from Berkeley. I commuted in my first car, a 1954 Chevrolet station wagon, affectionately called the "Yellow Submarine." The job involved serving beer to the customers and dancing on a small stage ten minutes out of each hour. We wore the same attire serving beer as we did when dancing: a "clamp" (a patch of cloth, usually of satin and of a size to completely cover the pubic region, sewn over a wire base which hugged the crotch and extended to the buttocks) and heavy mid-thigh boots which were essential to crossing the peanut shell-strewn floor as we navigated among the customers carrying four beer mugs in each hand. We were permitted to kick customers in the shin if they touched us inappropriately and encouraged to call a bouncer if a kick wasn't warning enough. More than once I poured mugs of beer over the head of a customer who harassed me. The management, however, frowned upon this.

I viewed topless dancing in much the same light as I viewed being a secretary or typist: in either capacity, the men perceived me in terms of my utility to them and related to me according to their projected fantasy; in either capacity, I was rarely seen as a full person with an outer and inner life; in either capacity, I experienced sexual harassment and devised ways to protect and defend myself. As far as I could tell, patriarchal stereotypes prevailed in respect to woman's work whether I was clothed and behind a typewriter or unclothed and carrying beer. If being a topless dancer was pandering to the male ego, then so too was being a secretary. In either capacity, my female co-workers provided the humanity and support that the male bosses and male customers withheld.

My feminism evolved over these years through a fusion of the personal and the political. In early 1969, my first year in graduate school and while I was still a topless dancer, I began participating in a women's liberation group which met once a week and averaged seven women. Most of my profound discoveries occurred in this group. With these women I read books, articles and poetry written by emerging feminists such as Robin Morgan, Kate Millett, Elaine Morgan, Judy Grahn and Alta, as well as writings of our foremothers such as Mary Wollstonecraft, Lucy Stone, Simone de Beauvoir, and of course, Betty Friedan. We told our life stories and examined our current lives in the light of our emerging feminist perspectives. Influenced greatly by these readings, existentialist thought and humanistic psychology (especially gestalt), and by the small group experience, I developed a radical feminist code to guide my actions. I held that each person was responsible for herself and for her choices, and that our choices affected the wider community. For me this translated into a fierce commitment to self-reliance and to activism. Ultimately, this perspective dictated that the bedrock of assumptions and expectations that underlay the structure of culture and society itself needed to be transformed. I believed that as each one of us worked to transform ourselves in the ways we lived our lives, and strived to transform the specific institutions in which we lived and worked, we could change the world.

For many years this "consciousness-raising" group was my primary reference point. Its members gave me support when I launched the literary salon and provided me with a sounding board and insight when I started the Women's Caucus and as the Comparative Literature women struggled to establish a course on women in literature.

Alas, less than a full year into graduate school my feminist consciousness created a major obstacle to my academic ambitions. I had become painfully aware just how patriarchal were the assumptions underlying my academic endeavors and, most specifically, how male was the literary canon. This awareness was political and personal at the same time: I experienced the lack of women writers as an affront to my gender and as an affirmation of the academy that women and their experience didn't count. The anguish was so profound that my ability to continue to study a literature written by and for men was called seriously into question. Thus, too, was my desire for a literary and academic career called into question.

My solution to this impasse was to invite other women faced with the same excruciating dilemma to join with me in reading and discussing works by women. The solution was a personal one: if the academy would not provide a forum for this intellectual inquiry, I would provide it to myself and interested others. I put up notices on bulletin boards in the various humanities departments and made announcements in the seminars I was attending that a group to discuss women and literature would meet once a week in my apartment. At first we were a group of three: myself, Doris Earnshaw (then Ribera) and a woman named Virginia, who was not from the university. Soon other women began to hear about the "Salon" and the numbers swelled. The group would choose a book to read for the next week and I would notify absent members and facilitate the discussion. We kept the group fluid; some people came only once, while others came to stay. Because of the literary nature of the discussions, literarily inclined women began to dominate, and soon the group was predominantly students of literature and language. We were forging an international feminist literary criticism.

This was, of course, also a time of national turmoil generated by the Vietnam War. In Berkeley, along with the ongoing Anti-War Movement, there was the community struggle over People's Park and the Third World Strike on campus, in all of which I participated—marching, demonstrating and serving on the speaker's bureau for the strike. In the spring of 1970 the anti-war sentiment resulted in a virtual closing down of normal university functions in what we called "reconstruction." Many classes were canceled or met off campus. My class on the Greek New Testament met in the home of the professor, a visiting scholar from Germany who was disapproving of the events and hostile toward me as the only one in the class who was actively involved. Students and faculty generated leaflets, pamphlets, and manifestos; they organized cadres to hold community meetings and go door-to-door to engage citizens in discussions about the war.

In response to the "crisis," the Comparative Literature Department held a joint meeting of faculty and graduate students. People were crammed into a small room, crowded on the available sofas, sitting on the floor and lining the walls while the department chair, Philip Damon, a rather retiring and soft-spoken medievalist, attempted to conduct an orderly discussion. At one point, someone making an attempt at humor observed that what with blacks and Chicanos and students and all manner of groups complaining endlessly of oppression, what would be next—women? People laughed, some wholeheartedly—such a ridiculous notion—and some uneasily.

A "ping" went off in my head, my chest tightened in anger, and a mysterious power lifted me onto my feet. I addressed the crowded room. "People do not speak of their oppression, do not jeopardize their livelihoods and even their lives, out of frivolity or whimsy. They do so because the conditions of their lives have become so intolerable that they must speak out against injustice and seek redress for the wrongs done them" (or some such words). "If women are speaking of oppression it is because they are wronged and feel it in their lives. I suggest that you, men and women both, look at your lives and your experiences. In your hearts you know that women's liberation is a just cause" (or some such words). I sat down, my heart pounding, and I knew that I had made an impact. No other comments deriding women occurred during that meeting.

Many graduate women asked what we might do to further the cause of women in the department and we formed the Women's Caucus. In this way the literary salon moved from my living room into the academy.

I continued to hold the salon gatherings for a while longer, as there were women participating who were in other departments such as German and Spanish, as well as a few non-academic women, but more and more my energies were directed to the Comparative Literature Women's Caucus. Initially the format was similar to a consciousness-raising group: we met in each other's homes to talk about our lives. We analyzed our life experiences from a developing feminist perspective as much as we talked about literature and women and our experiences as academic women. The group was fluid but I remember among the women who came that first year were Judy Wells, Jayne Walker, Marsha Wagner, Carol Urzi, Lisa Gerrard, Judy Kellogg, Naomi Cutner, Raquel Scherr, Melanie Persoff (later Kaye, later Kaye/Kantrowitz), Shelley Parlante, Susan Sterling, Ann Freeman, Doris Earnshaw, Deirdre Lashgari, Joanna Bankier, and Page Dubois.

These group meetings were exhilarating for me. Up until this time I had had little contact with departmental graduate students since my coursework had been primarily in the English, French or Classics departments. I felt disconnected from the department and even from academe. Many of the women were further along in their academic careers than I; through the stories of their struggles with identity and self-worth, of their encounters, some hilarious, some humiliating, some gratifying, with faculty, I began to feel part of the academic enterprise. A personal turning point occurred when I explained to the group my despairing alienation from academe and Jayne Walker commented that when I began to teach literature, all the hard work would begin to pay off and make sense. This was a new and wonderful mentoring.

The women came from a wide range of exposure to the feminist movement, but few had actually been in a women's liberation group as I had been (and still was). At the beginning, I suppose, I provided something of a facilitating role, prodding them to question and examine experience from a feminist perspective, but we were soon more or less on the same intellectual footing and the personal nature of our focus began to mingle with a political focus: what could we do to better the condition of women in academe and specifically in the Comparative Literature Department? Out of these discussions emerged the conviction that the department must have a course on women and literature and that it must be taught by graduate women, so that women could control its design. We debated how to implement the demand and worried, rightfully so, that our overt political stance might negatively affect our relations with faculty who were, after all, the people who would recommend us for jobs. I don't recall how we decided who would make the presentation (which was in writing and in person), but I do recall we were prepared for a struggle. To our amazement, the department agreed to establish the course and suggested we have Melanie Kaye, who was highly regarded by faculty, teach the first class. I was chosen to teach the course second, in the fall of 1972.

With the woman's course successfully under its purview, the Women's Caucus set up a selection procedure: All graduate women were invited to present proposals to all other women at a quarterly meeting for discussion and a vote. The procedure we institutionalized is still followed. Comparative Literature 40 continues to be a regular course offering and today is still taught and administered by the graduate Women's Caucus.

After I passed my master's exam and the Permission to Proceed to the Doctorate, the Comparative Literature Department hired me as an instructor to teach freshman composition. Even though Janette Richardson, my advisor, offered me the job with the explanation that it would help me improve my writing which she, having read my master's exam essays, felt was quite poor, I struggled successfully to focus on the gratitude and relief I felt at receiving the appointment rather than the feeling of inadequacy I had hearing her negative judgment. Graduate students at any one time in the department numbered 200 or more. A few had grants or fellowships and the rest of us had to provide our own means of support. Those who received an appointment as reader, teaching assistant, or instructor were the chosen few. There was no guarantee that I would be asked to teach more than one year—four was the maximum allowed; but I felt lucky, I felt honored, and for the first time, I felt acknowledged by the department.

And Jayne Walker was right. Teaching literature and writing made all the preceding sacrifice, hard work, and isolation worthwhile. If the salon and the Women's Caucus had made it possible to remain a student of the traditional literary canon in my first three years of graduate school, teaching gave purpose and context to the next four years. Finally I could share my first love, my life really, with students and be witness to their deepening understanding of the truths and beauties of literature. I taught my classes, of course, according to feminist principles of non-hierarchical participative learning. I prodded the students to become engaged with the texts and encouraged them to challenge each other's statements and opinions, including mine. Women authors were always included on my reading list and I incorporated a feminist perspective into our discussions. I made time available for my students outside of my office hours and had to discipline myself so my teaching didn't interfere with the time I needed for my doctoral work. Of course I had students who were not responsive to my teaching methods and I worried about this, but my overall enthusiasm for the classroom never waned.

In my second year as an instructor, I taught the women's course, designing it around the theme of women artists. The reading list included Sappho, Virginia Woolf's *Mrs. Dalloway,* and Kate Chopin's *The Awakening.* For the final exam, the students presented their own artistic creations to the class. There were sculptures, paintings, drawings, stories, poems, and skits; I, too, participated by reading some of my poetry. I was breaking up with my boyfriend of seven years at the time and interrupted my reading with choked sobs. I am still astonished at the memory. Even more astonishing is the memory of assigning the final grade by lottery: each student drew either an A or a B out of a hat.

By the time the caucus was recognized by the department as a source of instructors, some of the caucus women had begun a project of translating women poets of the world, most of them unknown in the U.S. and many of them obscure even in their own countries. Doris Earnshaw, Deirdre Lashgari, and Joanna Bankier from Comparative Literature spearheaded the project (and were among those who brought it to completion) and were joined by several others of us, including myself, along the way. The project meetings were filled with the joy of discovery and the excitement of sharing the "renderings" of unheard voices. But my involvement was short-lived. I became dismayed that the group turned, on occasion, to men as translators and though I did not doubt the competence of the male translators, I believed that this was a unique opportunity for women, and only women, to translate and present the work of other women. I wanted the project, which was quickly becoming a marvelous anthology (and published by Norton in 1976 as *The Other Voice*), to be entirely a woman's project. But I didn't speak my reservations. I was tired. I was weary of advocating for women and being seen as a man-hater. And even though that might not have been the case in this instance, I didn't have the stamina, or the heart, to find out. I quietly ceased participating, citing the weight of other pressures as the cause of my withdrawal.

One of those pressures was the dawning knowledge that teaching positions in the humanities were dwindling. In the sixties and early seventies jobs were abundant, so much so that doctoral candidates were often hired in tenure-track positions before they had completed their dissertations. They were informally referred to as ABDs, "All But Dissertation." But by 1974 the "boom" in higher education had slowed down, departments were fully staffed and, particularly in the humanities, faculty positions became available only in the rare event of a retirement or death. The word spread throughout the discipline, as more and more we heard stories of well qualified Ph.D.s who were still unemployed.

It was generally acknowledged that the doctoral program in Comparative Literature at UC Berkeley, based on the nineteenth century German model of the Ph.D. granting process, was the most rigorous of any department in the U.S. Very few graduate students completed the program and those few rarely completed it in fewer than ten years. Indeed, the department over the twenty years since its establishment by Alain Renoir in the late fifties had maintained an average of 200 graduate students in any one year, yet I was only the ninety-ninth to be awarded the degree. For the qualifying exams, the student was responsible for everything written in her major literature, and for all literature in a 150-year period of her two minor literatures. In addition, she had to show proficiency in four languages other than English, one of which had to be a classical language. After passing the qualifying exams the student took a prospectus exam, an oral exam with a committee of five reviewing the merits of the proposed thesis. Upon passing all these exams and writing the dissertation, the final dissertation defense still remained.

I took my Ph.D. qualifying exams in 1974, my sixth year in graduate school. To get to this point, I had completed as many course units as I had as an undergraduate, most of them in the English, Spanish, French and Classics departments, had demonstrated proficiency in Italian and Portuguese, and had studied independently for at least a year in exam preparation. I was examined in English literature from *Beowulf* to the present, in French and Spanish literatures from the French Revolution to 1945, and in comparative methods. The exam involved writing five essays, each of which took a day, and a three-hour oral. I passed the exam, and half a year later I passed the prospectus exam.

In spring 1975 my teaching appointment ended and I was faced with finding some means of financial support while I wrote the dissertation. This was a natural point to examine my commitment to completing the degree, especially in light of diminishing academic job opportunities. Moreover, my primary area of specialization, modern poetry, was overly represented, and my secondary area, women's literature, although becoming recognized, was still considered marginal. My chances of getting an academic job were slim. But after so many years of hard work it seemed to me wasteful not to finish. What was one or two more years of my life, even if it didn't lead to an academic job, in the scheme of an entire life? I convinced myself to continue, and decided to apply for a fellowship.

I had off and on applied for grants and fellowships in my graduate years but had been unsuccessful. This was a good point to try again, I thought, using my prospectus for a study of Muriel Rukeyser's poetry as the selling point. But first I needed to know more about the art of grantsmanship. I consulted with other women in the department and Judy Wells encouraged me to talk to Bridget Connelly, who had received several fellowships. I met with Bridget in the Doe Memorial Library on a late afternoon. The bench we sat on, just outside the women's bathroom in the main entrance, faced the sweeping marble stairs that led to the second level; as we talked I watched scholars climb and descend those stairs in the waning sunlight. Bridget explained to me her success: first, she was a scholar of an uncommon literature, Arabic; and second, she had come to graduate school with an outside fellowship and "once on the gravy train, it is easy to stay on." I, on the other hand, was a scholar of the most common European languages and I had never had a fellowship. "But I am so obviously a serious student since I have supported myself thus far. Doesn't that give me an edge?" I remember how the sun danced in Bridget's red hair as she explained how it worked: "*Au contraire*, Marsha. You have demonstrated that you will finish with or without a fellowship. They don't think that you need their help, whereas some other bloke obviously does.

They'll give the fellowship to the one who needs it, not the self-reliant who can get along without it." The cynical logic stunned me. I didn't apply.

The three years it took me to write the dissertation were difficult. The ongoing problem of income loomed especially in 1975 when the whole country was plunged into a recession. While I qualified for unemployment benefits, the income was not quite enough—even for a self-reliant one—for subsistence; I needed $28 more a month for basic needs. Loel Dudley, a non-academic from my consciousness-raising group, had a full-time job. She offered me $28 a month as a "grant." I still think of this generous stipend with deep gratitude. I wrote the first draft of my dissertation in this year of unemployment. In the last two years, I worked at a variety of part-time jobs: secretary for a recruitment firm, house-cleaner, adjunct lecturer at the University of Santa Clara, and legal secretary.

Isolated from academe, I had little reason to be around campus other than to meet with my advisor every six months or so, to visit the library occasionally, and to attend a dissertation writers' support group sponsored by the Counseling Center. But most important in terms of support, I had little contact with other feminists. I no longer attended the meetings of the department Women's Caucus. It was the domain of the new graduate women and even though I had helped to launch the caucus, I believed it was important to let others shape and direct its course. Further, most of my academic colleagues were as absorbed as I was in finishing up their doctorates, or were leaving the area to find work, academic or otherwise. And finally, my consciousness-raising group, which had been a critical source of support for many years, had ceased meeting altogether.

What did sustain me in those years was the dissertation itself. My first draft explored Rukeyser's use of classical mythology in her poetry, but when my advisor lost my only copy (I have no idea why I didn't keep a second copy!), I switched my focus to tracing the evolution of Rukeyser's imagery from anger at the patriarchy in her early poetry to a serene dedication to change in her later poetry. Muriel Rukeyser's poetry engaged me on many levels. She was international in her perspective, socialist in her politics, an activist, and a feminist (although she never used the word). It was exciting to draw upon all of my academic training in classics, languages and literature, but especially exciting to be articulating a feminist criticism developed over the years through the many exploratory discussions with other women in the salon and on campus. And even though I was isolated in my writing, I felt connected to women and to the consolations of literature. The time I spent researching and writing the dissertation was time I spent in communion with all that I valued most. It was a profoundly self-affirming experience.

However, as the dissertation progressed, so too did my disaffection from academe. Like an old warhorse, I sent applications out to all academic jobs on the planet for which I was qualified in 1976, 1977, and 1978. Of course I knew that getting a job was a long shot given the feminist nature of my dissertation and my lack of any specific faculty backing. But the results were still devastating: out of 75 total applications, I received no invitations to interview, and for most applications I didn't even receive a postcard of acknowledgment or letter of rejection. I also knew that the profession was still woefully retrograde in advancing women and that the UCB Comparative Literature Department, despite the efforts of the caucus, was definitely not in the vanguard. My own inquiry into the hiring record of the department's graduate students found that while women comprised 60 percent of the students advanced to candidacy, only 40 percent of the women had found tenure track jobs in the previous three years, whereas 60 percent of the men had. (Modern Language Association employment statistics for 1979 to 1980 show that, although Ph.D.s were granted equally to men and women in foreign languages and English, 48 percent of the men and 42 percent of the women secured tenure track appointments in English; and 45 percent of the men and 37 percent of women secured tenure track appointments in foreign languages.)

Hindsight makes it possible to see the historical irony in which I was caught—between the Charybdis of inventing a feminist critical theory and teaching method, and the Scylla of an academy that was still fearful and unaccepting of that approach. We who participated in the salon, the caucus, the translation project, and the women's course in the years 1969 to 1974 were pioneers. We stumbled and struggled, suffered and triumphed, as do all pioneers; and we were misunderstood, reviled, and rejected, as well. Today the feminist approach in literary as well as other studies has not only become respectable, but has been institutionalized, even reified. Sadly, many of us who laid the foundations of Women's Studies were not included when Women's Studies burgeoned and flourished in the academy.

With no academic job offered to me, I decided to leave academe. Like a rejected lover, I felt humiliated, hurt, and angry. It didn't matter that I had known all along that it was a depressed job market and that I was one among many, men and women both, who wouldn't have academic appointments; it didn't matter that I knew my dissertation was truly original and made a major contribution to the field; it didn't matter that I knew the department was old-fashioned and stodgy and enough perplexed by my antics to be unable to endorse my candidacy. I would just walk away. It would not suffice for me to hang on the fringes of academe, hustling a course here and a course there, still living at subsistence level, still on the outside looking in. The minute my dissertation went to the typist, I began a search for a new career. I was heartened by all of the strides women had made in all corners of society. Surely whatever work I did, I would join with women in that industry to make changes. I resolutely set my eyes ahead and willed myself to not look back. Twenty years after I had vowed to pursue the "life of the mind," I left that life to find purpose in Corporate America.

Only once did I look back. I was already working in the San Francisco financial district when Deirdre Lashgari called to invite me to a women's poetry reading* that would be given and attended by former colleagues in the Comparative Literature Department. I accepted the invitation but left before the reading was over. The poetry touched a deep yearning inside me and the familiar faces of former colleagues, women I had worked with and loved through many struggles, reminded me of what I had renounced. I stumbled out of the room close to tears. In the years to follow, the only tie I allowed myself with my former life was an anthology of modern poetry that I kept in a side drawer of my desk at the office.

---

*The poetry reading was a celebration of the publication of the first of three volumes of translations of international women's poetry that ensued from the projects spawned by Marsha's Salon. *The Other Voice* (Norton 1976) is dedicated to Marsha Hudson.

2

Daddy's Girl Goes Mad: Ten Years at UC Berkeley, 1966–1976

Judy Wells

"Would you like to sit in this chair or in Mr. Bjørnson's* lap?" said Professor Foxy,* ushering me into his office for my Ph.D. Permission to Proceed exam. I suppose he was trying to put me at ease, but neither Mr. Bjørnson nor I found it funny. After nearly a half year studying for this important exam, I hardly expected this to be the first remark from an eminent professor of the Comparative Literature Department. About halfway into the exam, I think Pierre Foxy and Michèle Hammer* got a little bored. After all, my specialty was the modern period, and Foxy's was medieval, Hammer's the Renaissance, but they had both read *Le Rouge et le Noir*. Was it only my perception or were they actually flirting as they played Julien Sorel and Madame de Rênal with each other, and I sat and watched? Fortuitously, I passed this exam even if at times I felt like an afterthought. Perhaps I was the only one in the room who had actually read Nabokov.

I relate this incident to illustrate the atmosphere of the Comparative Literature Department of the late sixties. The second wave of feminism had not yet raised its lovely head in 1968, the year I took this exam. Foxy, an early proponent of Comparative Literature, had a reputation for telling salacious jokes, scratching his crotch, and having an affair with the secretary in another department. All was well in the groves of academe.

---

*As memory speaks, I have heightened certain scenes and fictionalized characters in this essay for comic effect, in the tradition of my favorite French authors, Rabelais and Molière. An asterisk (*) indicates a fictionalized name, and it will be used only the first time the fictionalized name appears.

Unwittingly, or perhaps wittingly, he was steadily building up in the Comp. Lit. Department an enormous graduate student population of highly intelligent, multilingual, attractive women who would serve as research assistants, instructors, teaching assistants, readers, and secretaries for his department, but who would ultimately form the Comparative Literature Women's Caucus in the seventies and challenge his entrenched sexism.

I came to UC Berkeley from Stanford in 1966, completely naive about the workings of graduate school and how to succeed in it. I had no real plan for my future. An "engaged-to-be-engaged" boyfriend of three years had broken up with me at the end of my senior year at Stanford, so instead of going to the University of Wisconsin to be with him, I accepted the slot at Berkeley. I was totally confused by "the Berkeley scene." My new roommates were all Mills College graduates who closed the doors of their bedrooms after dinner and disappeared. I was not used to this sense of privacy and thought they were somewhat cold though they had chosen me, in my navy blue sleeveless dress with the red piping and my red button earrings, over two other contenders for a small, sunless back room.

On the night of my first poetry seminar in Comparative Literature, a Professor Randy Rathbone* declared we would not meet on campus but at his house on southside. Little did we know it was because he wanted access to his liquor. His grayish weathered face was the mush of booze. He was divorced, his house was in disarray, and we sat around a large seminar table in his front room where he bombarded us with questions about poems that seemed unanswerable. "What does *sometimes* mean?" he bellowed at one terrified woman. She actually began to cry. "It means 'In my best times,'" he finally answered himself.

We felt we were in the presence of a crazy, drunken genius. Early in the evening, he might read us Greek poetry in Greek, though none of us knew the language. Pindar was his specialty, and athletics was on Rathbone's mind, though health was hardly one of his personal considerations. He had a whole system of poetics he based on *The Iliad* and *The Odyssey*, though he only conveyed it in bits and pieces through barely controlled drunkenness. Terms like "Priamel structure" and "adynaton" stick in my head. Epic derives from lyric—"Sing in me, goddess"—and the whole of *The Odyssey* is based on "going home" and the themes of fire and water, or something like this.

Rathbone assigned us a paper on "Fire and Ice." Look at poetry in terms of these themes, but he didn't tell us what poetry, what century, what languages. We were on our own. I met a befuddled classmate in the Bear's Lair, and we talked. He was as confused as I but secretive and competitive, so little knowledge was shared. Surprisingly, one woman in Rathbone's class seemed to understand what he was talking about, writing beautifully about his theories with examples and using his terms eloquently. A lot of us were still trying to figure out how to spell them!

Lulu Marvell,* a wondrously tall woman with a long blonde braid down her back, was having an affair with Rathbone. I guess it was her undies we saw in the bathroom, her diaphragm. She would whisper to him in the middle of class, "Shall I get the roast out of the oven?" and would disappear. Lulu subsequently got a fellowship from the department and didn't have to TA. We whispered, I wonder why, knowingly. A few years later, her politics transformed, Lulu would become a women's studies instructor in Comparative Literature. I asked her many years later when we both showed up at a women's music festival in the late seventies, post Ph.D.s, why she had an affair with Rathbone. "I didn't think I could make it myself," she said. "Having an affair with a professor was the closest I thought you could get to success in academe." Of course, she meant, the closest a woman could get. And now, here she was, years later, a bare-breasted Amazon at a women's music festival in the California outback.

I was prepared for academic feminism by belonging to a series of women's groups which started in the very late sixties and early seventies in Berkeley. A dropout from the Comp. Lit. Department and a former member of Rathbone's class had asked me if I wanted to join her women's liberation group. I balked at the idea the way some women still bristle today if you ask them if they're a feminist. But I decided to give the group a try. I came home elated. Somebody passed out a paper called "I Have Orgasims at My Cliterous." Both key words were spelled wrong, but who cared? I had orgasms at my clitoris, too, however they were spelled, and I was dismayed that a previous boyfriend had tried to wean me away from this proclivity and have orgasms solely through intercourse. Click! I think the light bulb went on for a lot of women about the controlling nature of their relationships and how they could be responsible for their own sexuality and pleasure. I still remember how on one of my first forays onto the UC Berkeley campus, I stopped at the Sexual Freedom League table and asked the woman "manning" the table where you could get birth control. She didn't know! It seemed sexual liberation in the late sixties had given men and women access to lots more sex, but women's concerns—mainly pregnancy (God forbid we knew anything about sexually transmitted diseases)—were neglected.

My first Berkeley women's group had scattered concerns. One woman was a girlfriend of a Ken Kesey Merry Prankster, some women were artists, others were businesswomen, teachers, grad students, wives, and at least one, my good friend Xenia Lisanevich, also a dropout from Comp. Lit. and whom I met in Rathbone's class, was a struggling single mother. The focus of the meetings centered around complaints about men, the beginnings of our consciousness-raising. One night we discovered the Merry Prankster boyfriend was secretly taping our meeting.

Enough of these shenanigans. Another friend of mine, Eva, and I went on to form my second women's group with our various friends. Bridget Connelly, a flaming redhead and my first close friend at Berkeley and whom I met in E. Kerrigan Prescott's Comp. Lit. class on modern poetry, was one of the original members, but we had non-academic members also. Emily* worked in a Berkeley massage parlor after applying for work unsuccessfully as a telephone lineperson. She told us all about the massage parlor, and we eagerly pumped her for details. She tried to stay legit, but the temptations were great. The men all asked for "locals" and were willing to pay for it. A few times Emily made "out calls," which paid more, and was once asked to put on tiny thumb cuffs for beaucoup bucks. She and her friend Stella* eventually went to Japan as "dancers" and were sent to two different bars in Tokyo. Emily was miserable and wired her parents for money to send her home. Stella, a diminutive woman with a master of arts in anthropology from San Francisco State, stayed till she had enough money to buy a Japanese car and then shipped it and herself home. God knows what she had to do to make the money.

I know this all sounds like odd behavior for women who were beginning to call themselves feminists, but we were all affected by sexual liberation of the sixties one way or the other. I fed myself a diet of Henry Miller, starting with *Sexus*, *Plexus*, and *Nexus*—"literary sex" I could get my hands on and marvel and laugh about. I loved reading about an American writer in Paris and the outrageous fucking antics of the "Henry" persona Miller created in his works. It was Henry Miller who led me to Anaïs Nin, not vice versa, and I devoured her diaries and fiction, trying to piece their lives together. Details of her outrageous sexual life would only emerge much later in the eighties and nineties. For us budding feminists in the early seventies, Nin was a mysterious, ethereal shadow woman, but by God, she wrote and published and knew everyone in Paris, and that's what I wanted to do, but didn't. I was in graduate school.

To the credit of graduate school, through the English Department, not Comparative Literature, I was introduced to the first woman poet I could sort of identify with: Sylvia Plath. Horrors. *Ariel* had recently been published, and Alex Zwerdling, in his class on modern poetry, handed out a badly mimeographed copy of "Daddy" which electrified our class in the large lecture room of Dwinelle Hall (which I fondly refer to as Dwindle Hall).

You do not do, you do not do
Anymore, black shoe
In which I have lived like a foot
For thirty years, poor and white,
Barely daring to breathe or Achoo.[1]

This said it for me more strongly than any of the articles I would ever read in the bibles of early second-wave feminism: *Notes from the Second Year, Woman in Sexist Society*, and even the *SCUM Manifesto*[2] by Valerie Solanas. And it was said by a woman poet, who committed suicide in her early thirties, who was clearly a genius with language, and who was rapidly becoming famous. As I came to know Plath's life and work, at that time, I was convinced that had she had women's support groups, as we were beginning to form, she would not have committed suicide. Of course, this is mainly projection; nonetheless, Plath's "Daddy, daddy, you bastard, I'm through"[3] became my battle cry.

During the time of my second women's group, I wrote an article, "Daddy's Girl," for a newly emerging women's magazine, *Libera*, which had its office on the UC Berkeley campus. My essay begins with an epigraph from Anaïs Nin's *Ladders to Fire*: "A little girl, full of innocence and indulgence. And then this madness..." I strongly identified with Nin's preoccupation with herself as a "little girl," due partially to her slight stature and small breasts, which I too shared. My essay, "Daddy's Girl," describes a psychological pattern I fell into when I asserted myself before the people I considered "the big daddies" of the world: real fathers, boyfriends, husbands, psychiatrists, and of course, the big bad professors of academia who held the threat of pass/not pass over my head for a gauntlet of Ph.D. exams. The gist of my article was whenever I did assert myself or rebel against the Daddies, I felt momentarily strong, but then rapidly catapulted into a wimpy state for fear of retribution. And of course, there was some real danger in saying fuck you to every dick who crossed you, which, once I was in touch with my anger, happened quite often. (All this was said much more delicately and professionally in my essay.)

I even took karate with the Cal Karate Club to overcome my physical "You're a ninety-eight-pound weakling, and we'll kick sand in your face" state, and I became quite strong in six months due to our Japanese instructor often telling us, "You do twenty pushup!" for faults he would not explain to us. I began to get very angry at him for his militaristic approach and at the men in the class who ever so slightly did not hold back their punches when they aimed at my chest. Making punching motions raises your anger level tremendously if you have it in you, and I realized if I hit these guys back, they'd probably deck me in no time. Black eyes and bruised toes abounded in the older members of the class, so I quit. I was afraid to really fight, though there were one or two women in the class who were excellent. And perhaps I was afraid of my own anger.

"Daddy's Girl" did not cure herself in that class. My article, however, was a big hit and was picked up by Marlene Griffith and Charles Muscatine for several editions of the *Borzoi College Reader*; in the fifth edition, I was sandwiched in between essays by Virginia Woolf and Maxine Hong Kingston and felt quite pleased. One little thorn I've never revealed continues to bother me over the years regarding this essay. I agreed to a major editorial change with *Libera* to get that article published. I had originally written I had wanted Daddy's approval because he had *power*, not that I identified with Daddy himself. Somehow the word *power* had not emerged as the key word in the budding women's movement yet. The editor wanted to substitute *identity* everywhere I used the term *power*, so the essay was slightly distorted: For example, as published, the article states, "Since the Little Girl's only previous sense of *identity* stemmed from approval from her Daddies, cutting these figures out of her life will seem like cutting out the core of herself."[4] But *power* was the original term I used. As a little girl, I read books with girl characters and identified with them, especially tales about three sisters; being number three in a family of three girls and one boy, the long-awaited son, I saw privilege going to the boy child, and I wanted that *power*.

I must admit, though, I did identify with Henry Miller, the grandiose but poverty-stricken writer fucking his way through Paris, even after reading Kate Millett's *Sexual Politics* with her scorching analysis of masculine sexuality in Miller's works. I wonder if I read Miller now whether I'd hate him. For a Catholic girl back then, reading Henry Miller at every opportunity was certainly a cheap thrill.

What, you might ask, happened to grad school? No, I wasn't reading this book list in any of my literature classes. After a couple of years of required classes reading Medieval French, the French symbolist poets, and my favorites, the French avant-garde playwrights, then passing my Ph.D. Permission to Proceed exam with the infamous Foxy, I launched into my own book list. I must give credit, however, to the gutsy, young, independent Assistant Professor Alexandra Katz*, who introduced me to Djuna Barnes' *Nightwood* in her course on the anti-novel. Barnes was another woman author I had never heard about whose wonderfully poetic novel was built on an unusual structure; the climax of the book, mighty Matthew O'Connor's monologue, was in the center of the novel, rather than at its end. I studied Barnes' imagery in this novel of lesbian love and wrote, as I recall, on the symbolism of "birds and turds." No, I am not kidding. Read it yourself and see. I also sat in on Katz's poetry course occasionally. Here she put Randy Rathbone's methodology to work in discussing poems.

In an odd and unusual pep talk Professor Foxy once had with me, he revealed this personal tidbit about Alexandra Katz. When he hired her, he said to her, "You can either have your affair with Professor Rathbone, or you can finish your dissertation." Katz had the affair with Professor Rathbone. She was only 24 or 25 years old when it started and she later married him. Probably to her detriment, but to the benefit of us students, we studied poetry à la Rathbone. I remember discussing Randall Jarrell's "90 North" for several weeks in her class, and it was the first collaborative dissection of the meaning of a poem I had experienced. In contrast to Rathbone's intimidating tactics, Alexandra Katz was expansive and welcomed all points of view. She was a role model for me when I began teaching in Comparative Literature as a teaching assistant and later as an instructor. And she did eventually finish her Ph.D. despite Foxy's pronouncement.

I must mention another behind-the-scenes woman who gave me a break I probably never would have gotten from the big daddies of Comparative Literature—Mary Gordon, the Comp. Lit. secretary through thick and thin. Mary knew my sister's husband, and when she got wind I needed a job one summer—my alternative was the Pancake House where I would have to load three hot plates of pancakes up my skinny arms—she got me a job as a reader for Robert Alter's course on the modern novel. From that position I was able to move on and become a teaching assistant in Comparative Literature for three years, 1967–1970.

The stage was set. I had my money, I had finished my required classes, passed my Permission to Proceed exam, and Bertrand Augst would sign for six units of independent study each quarter or semester so I could qualify as a grad student. I had my Cowell Hospital health insurance, and I was free, I thought, to do what I wanted.

Enter Marsha Hudson and my third women's group, the Comparative Literature Women's Caucus. Marsha was the biggest influence on my life in terms of feminism and reading women's literature. Finally, I was in a women's group which had a larger agenda than complaining about individual boyfriends. Marsha taught us to read women's books and take on the patriarchal world, starting with the Comparative Literature Department. Chair Phil Damon hid out and let the Vice Chair Joe Duggan take on the contenders who eagerly leaped to Marsha's leadership.

Marsha was a strange bundle of contradictions, as we all were in those days. She was living in a triangle reminiscent of Simone de Beauvoir's tribulations with Sartre and his younger mistress. It was Marsha, Peter*, and Beth*, who lived down the street. Marsha approved as long as Pete was in Marsha's bed every night. She had a gynecology table in her house as joke, and once told a story about greeting a man nude at the door, then sitting down and chatting with him as if she were fully clothed and nothing was amiss.

I remember her best sitting on a table in Dwinelle Hall, conducting a Women's Caucus meeting, swinging her long legs in a pale blue leotard outfit which matched her eyes. She had a little growth which stood out of her forehead and she told stories about dancing topless and bottomless in the Ore House in San Jose, reciting Greek verbs as she danced. She told us she started working with no makeup on and her long Berkeley hair flowing down her back, and the men were touching her like crazy. Some of the seasoned dancers took her aside backstage and told her to slather on the makeup, put up her hair, and lacquer it down with spray, and the men would be too intimidated to touch her. It worked. Often the men would put their tips in their not-quite-empty beer glasses, and Marsha would have to fish out the wet coins. From my perspective, Marsha really lived on the edge, but the money, she said, was good. And hadn't we already discussed, in our women's groups, that sex workers made a lot more money than secretaries?

Marsha had already started her women's literary salon at her house. I wasn't in the group originally, but soon the book lists started circulating. Was every budding feminist woman in Berkeley simultaneously reading Doris Lessing's *The Golden Notebook*, supplemented by Anaïs Nin's early journals, and starting her own writing notebooks? Did we all read Lessing's entire *Children of Violence* series, and follow Martha Quest from South Africa to London? I know I did, lying on my bed in my $85 studio apartment on Dwight Way near People's Park. My reading list included Ella Leffland's *Mrs. Munck* (a fine tale of feminist revenge written by an author from my home town, Martinez); Dorothy Bryant's *Ella Price's Journal* (about a community college re-entry woman screwed by a professor), more Djuna Barnes, Sylvia Plath, Carson McCullers, Mary McCarthy, Virginia Woolf (OK in academia, but she certainly let the patriarchy have it in *A Room of One's Own* and *Three Guineas*), Monique Wittig's *Les Guérillères*, Charlotte Perkins Gilman's "The Yellow Wallpaper," Charlotte Brontë, Emily Brontë, George Eliot, Kate Chopin, Simone de Beauvoir's *The Second Sex*, several volumes of her early memoirs and novels, Erica Jong, Margaret Atwood, and for good measure I threw in Flaubert ("Madame Bovary, *c'est moi!*"), Rabelais, Gide and Knut Hamsun (recommended by Henry Miller).

But for a long time, I concentrated on women writers. I had lots to catch up on, since lit courses often ignored them. For example, I audited James Breslin's huge lecture course on contemporary American literature and read only males—no Miller, but a good deal of Mailer.

Something was building inside me about wanting to be a writer myself which all my female reading fortified, even if Doris Lessing's female characters sometimes seemed like masochists, and you wanted to yell at them: "Get away from Saul! He's bad for you!" More than this reading, however, some real live women poets from the Berkeley women's community were making their way onto campus. Judy Grahn and Susan Griffin were showing us real live women could write, not just dead women poets. I had previously taken one poetry writing course on campus during my first graduate student year at Berkeley from Josephine Miles, who was severely crippled from arthritis. I felt extremely uncomfortable when her male attendant carried her into class and placed her at her desk. I feared, irrationally, this was the price women had to pay for imaginative genius. Both her teaching assistants were male: Ron Loewinsohn and Ross Sheidler, whom I later TA'd for in Comp. Lit. IA. Ross, as my poetry TA, was an encouraging man. He felt sorry for women intellectuals and felt they had a hard time in academia, but I think what he also meant was it was hard for them to find boyfriends.

I was like a fish out of water in Miles' class. I tried to do my assignment each week, write a poem on this or that, but I was terribly self-conscious, striving to express myself and be literary. I remember Miles putting a tiny little check on images she liked, and once in a while I'd get a check or two. At our only personal meeting, she pawed through my tiny stack of poems to the one on the bottom I didn't want her to see. It was based on my work on a geriatric ward in a mental hospital and ended:

> Paper skin crackles softly
> As strong arms reach out to turn
> Us over in our beds.

I feared that's what people had to do with her and didn't want her to see it, but she liked that poem the best.

Still, I did not feel particularly encouraged by Miles' class. How did I know I would eventually find my subject through feminism, that rage would be my territory, and rhythm my weapon? I was a scared girl poet in Miles' class. I remember best the encouragement from one of my peers, another young woman poet. "I like this," she said about my poem about a tightrope walker. For some reason, that woman's statement was important to me and stuck to my bones.

The Comparative Literature Women's Caucus, under Marsha's leadership, began to focus my energy on the possibility of women being both feminist intellectuals and writers. I attended the caucus regularly and though not by any means a leader, I was determined to teach the women's course which the Comp. Lit. women had persuaded one of the chairs of Comparative Literature to let us design and teach. The caucus selected my course proposal, "Madness and Madness: An Exploration of the Themes of Anger and Insanity in Literature by Women," for spring 1973, and the course had such a large enrollment that we needed two sections. Mary Stoker became the second instructor. Our course was actually listed under the title "Women Writers in the U.S. and Abroad: Comparative Literature 175 (191D)" and was the first upper-division women's course taught in Comparative Literature.

My idea for the course crystallized after reading Phyllis Chesler's recently released *Women and Madness*, in which she posited that women's madness stemmed largely from their female socialization. Chesler's nutshell definition of madness is the following: "What we consider 'madness,' whether it appears in women or in men, is either the acting out of the devalued female role or the total or partial rejection of one's sex-role stereotype."[5] If a woman adhered strictly to the female stereotypical roles of weakness, dependence, passivity, and so forth, she could end up labeled mad and institutionalized, or if she rebelled against the female stereotype, acted out, was angry, aggressive, or heaven forbid, became a lesbian, she might also be deemed mad and institutionalized. I wanted to explore this concept in women's literature, how women writers depicted the mad woman against this newly emerging feminist analysis of women's mental illness and psychology.

The course had an ambitious reading list: Charlotte Brontë's *Jane Eyre*, Ella Leffland's *Mrs. Munck*, Carson McCullers' *Member of the Wedding*, Hannah Green's *I Never Promised You a Rose Garden*, Sylvia Plath's *Bell Jar* and *Ariel*, Christina Stead's *The Man Who Loved Children*, Virginia Woolf's *Mrs. Dalloway*, Doris Lessing's *The Four-Gated City*, and the anthology, *Woman in Sexist Society: Studies in Power and Powerlessness*. Phyllis Chesler's *Women and Madness* was strongly recommended as well as Mary Barnes' *Two Accounts of a Journey through Madness*, Janet Frame's *Faces in the Water*, and a string of articles including Cynthia Ozick's "We are the Crazy Lady & Other Feisty Feminist Fables," from *Ms.*, spring 1972. I also threw in some R.D. Laing for good measure.

What I remember most about this class, however, was not the academic content, but the dynamics of teaching it. It was a discussion class, and we all sprawled on the floor of the main room at Unitas House. A crazy woman from the streets would often come in and observe the class, occasionally putting in her two cents. Two women students, budding lesbians, sat holding hands and distracted me with their attention towards each other. One had a perpetually expressionless, yet somehow defiant look on her face, daring me to say anything to her and never contributing anything herself. The madness theme unfolded before me.

I talked with two other Comp. Lit. women who were jointly teaching the 40C women's course. (This must have been a boom year for enrollment in Comparative Literature!) From my journal, May 14, 1973:

> I met with F. and D. today. I almost didn't want to go—another session of telling people what I think and then the inevitable sensation of feeling extremely vulnerable. Turns out they are having the same problems I am—not knowing exactly what to do in class, seeing that sea of blank faces. And of course, the lesbian question that looms over everyone's head. F. said, get this, that her students wanted a clarification on what her relationship with D. was, and they seemed disappointed when she said she wasn't having an affair with her! In my class Camille* indicated she wanted me to say the opposite when I was telling Alice* that it was unrealistic to think that you could go on existing never relating to any men. Not wanting to tread on any lesbian toes, I stated that women have to deal with men when they are "doing business," i.e., men have the power in this society and if women want to get some of this power, they have to deal with men. Camille told me in small group she wanted me to go further and state my position on relating to men socially. But I'm certainly not going to talk in class about my "dates" with men. Nobody else does, and I don't want to expose myself any more than anyone else does at this point. Camille certainly hit the nail on the head when she said, "All this new openness is supposed to be so great, but it's just making everyone feel guilty." D. said that her students agree with a separatist stand, but she knows damn well a good number of them are living with men.

I struggled with my role as instructor, only seven years older than most of my students:

> A few mornings ago I threw my sleeping bag over my head when I was having a few painful thoughts. Should I ask them to evaluate the course through anonymous written papers? Should I confront Liz* in public or private and ask her to contribute to the discussions, not sit there, a judgmental "man" figure for the others in the course? Should I ask Jill* to stop doing the touchy-feely trip with the girl who lies on

her stomach in the midst of our discussions and hides her head? Who is that girl? Should I have a private discussion with the painfully silent Asian woman? Is she alienated because she is the only third world woman in the course or because she is so painfully shy—she looks like a fragile doll who will break with that beautiful black hair covering most of her face. And I wish white-haired Susan* would come more often; she reminds me of Mrs. Munck, my image of Munck, not the Ella Leffland we saw on the cover of the hardback edition of her book.

I invited Ella Leffland, author of *Mrs. Munck*, and formerly from my hometown, Martinez, to speak to our class. I was thrilled when she came, a soft-spoken woman, most unlike her vengeful character Rose in *Mrs. Munck*, brought to life through her torture of old man Leary, her former boss and tormentor in the tale. Once, after a class potluck, we went to see Kate Millett, who was invited to the UC campus to show her new film. It did seem everywhere I went my course theme followed, madness in all its definitions:

Nora* [one of my students] told us that at the reception the English Department had given for Millett, our superstar breezed in and asked "Where's my job?" Dead Silence. Apparently, Millett started rapping with Flanagan and when she heard what his name was, she said "Ugh!" The Irish got to her, I guess. He started doing an urbane English Dept. trip on her, and then started talking to her in Gaelic to which she uttered, "You're way beyond me." He ended by correcting her grammar. The whole scene sounded totally bizarre, but Millett must have known what she was doing. No one comes out of the university scene and can go to a reception and say, "Where's my job?"—not even Kate Millett. Nora said she felt embarrassed for her, but I have a hunch Kate did that to embarrass everyone else. She came at least a half hour late to her own film showing that night and talked as if she were stoned. Big-breasted, brown-grey flowing hair, horn-rimmed glasses, shapeless long dress over her body, and a stoned tongue and mind—that's how she was, rapping about collective films and doing in films for women what Woodstock did for hippies. She was both charismatic and crazy—utterly loony with her insistence on sitting next to the projector, wading knee deep through people to get next to that precious machine. Lights out, and then Kate booming out for lights, and "I want this projector moved back and that giant screen to come down instead of this tiny one." She claimed the janitor refused to give her an extension cord or lower the huge screen. Women scurried like mad for her madness; Channel 6 came up with an extension cord, and somehow miraculously, the giant screen slowly came inching down. Lights out again, and Kate's film was rolling—a tiny square on this huge screen, and everybody shrieked and moaned claiming she moved the projector the wrong way. And Kate was yelling we needed a bigger room, that's what was wrong, but she conceded this point, and the film finally got rolling. Charismatic and crazy—the crazy male artist has been accepted for centuries, but get an eccentric woman artist in front of a crowd and she really comes off badly. So few women ever get that artistic power that each one becomes subject to intense scrutiny. I guess we'd all crack under that pressure.

This was all long before Millett wrote *The Loony Bin Trip*.
We went to see Bergman's *Cries and Whispers* and I wrote in my journal:

> I feel harsh towards Bergman for his representation of women in this film. Perhaps my course is getting to me, but I am sick and tired of women who are "interesting" because they suffer. Bergman is merely presenting stereotypes of women and perpetuating these stereotypes as real images of women in society. Women need a revolutionary cinema—artists can influence women's attitude toward themselves by presenting positive images of women. Christiane Rochefort attempted to do this in *Stances à Sophie*, and I saw this movie twice. Bergman's movie was assault on my being, seeing it only once. In Sylvia Plath's *Bell Jar*, Esther says, "Who but a man would devise a drug to make women forget the pain they actually experienced." I say about Bergman, "Who but a man could devise the self-torture Karin puts herself through—cutting her own vagina with glass." The old "vagina dentata" myth surges forth, man's fear a woman's vagina will bite his cock off, and here's Bergman's Karin inserting glass in her own vagina which could accomplish that. Women's self-destruction when they are furious with someone else—when will we stop doing this? Let's stop seeing it in the movies under the guise of a serious psychological treatment of women. I want to see the red of anger—righteous anger—rather than the red of self-destruction.

My journal continues:

> What is marvelous about Sylvia Plath's poem "Ariel" is her transformation of herself into pure motion and energy in her self-consummation—the fusion of her "I" with the red eye of the sun. Here is anger and energy and power—not impotence. But suicide is not woman's solution to her oppression. You can't convince me of that, no matter how seductive Plath's poems are. The other reality is the daily bell jar we all live in, and the fact that women can break glass if we try. Sure it's going to be hard, but we can. And we don't have to use the glass to kill ourselves if enough of us break through.

Although teaching Women and Madness was difficult for me, both because of the course content and the teaching problems, many good things came out of this experience. First of all, I was assigned to be an instructor for Comparative Literature IA-IB for the following year. I don't think I would have come to the administration's attention if I hadn't demonstrated I could design a junior-senior level course and teach it. I certainly wasn't on any chair of Comp. Lit.'s personal favorites list. Second, I was formulating my dissertation topic in the back of my mind without really knowing it yet. And last, I was learning to speak my own mind, along with my students, coming "unhidden," as I wrote in my journal, like Deborah in *I Never Promised You a Rose Garden*, though feeling quite vulnerable in doing so.

My experience as a Comp. Lit. IA-IB "feminist" instructor was also challenging. I wanted to deal with women's themes in all the books I chose. We had to read *The Odyssey* in IB, so that was a given, but I also chose Flaubert's *Madame Bovary*, Kate Chopin's *The Awakening*, and Virginia Woolf's *To the Lighthouse*. Little did I know, as I was teaching two sections back to back, that both my teaching assistants were furious with me. Though I had let each one teach a book which was more their specialty (the guy, Homer; the woman, an additional German book, her language), they still felt I had too much power and was doing too much "women stuff." Imagine my surprise, going from viewing myself as walking around on tippy toes behind hermetic male professors in the Comp. Lit. Department to being a Comp. Lit. woman with too much power. I can't remember how I sorted that one out, but I do remember being very angry with my TAs, particularly the woman, and realizing all women weren't going to be happy identifying with feminists. On the contrary, some women would hate us.

Somewhere, amidst all this "too much women stuff," I had actually passed my Ph.D. written and orals for which I had studied intensely for at least a year. Bertrand Augst was my advisor for many years and had let me sail where I bobbed, but one year Foxy advised me. I can remember exactly what I was wearing—a long lavender skirt and an orange gauze Mexican peasant blouse embroidered with bright blue flowers on the yoke. I still had my long black hippie hair. Foxy looked at my record: "You haven't taken your Latin! You haven't taken your Spanish!" I diligently promised to sign up for the outstanding courses. Foxy helped design the program; he knew how to get you back on track so you could actually get your Ph.D., while Augst was charismatic and fun and encouraged you to go to surrealist films. This was the same meeting in which Foxy detailed Alexandra Katz's flaw in being fatally attracted to Randy Rathbone and not finishing her dissertation. And he added for good measure, "It used to be women grad students weren't the kind you'd want to peek up their skirts." In my newfound feminism I replied, "Were the men the kind you'd want to peek into their fly?" He replied with a straight but slightly abashed face (at least I'd like to think it was abashed), "Yes." Then he proceeded to tell me a story about primitive birth control methods, how they got rid of girl children—exposure. That got me out of his office on the double.

When, in 1976, UC Vice Chancellor Heyman asked for anecdotal evidence about sexism in the university, Lisa Gerrard and I gathered evidence from women students in our department, and Lisa presented our group protest of Foxy's and other professors' sexism to Eve Appleyard*, the chairman of Comparative Literature at the time. She dismissed our claims as nonsense and declared the writing in our document was atrocious. I was personally insulted by this claim, as Lisa and I had written the document, and Lisa had meticulously edited it. Of course, we had the wrong audience for our complaint. Eve herself was an early protégée of Foxy's and would hardly be receptive to an attack on his character. Our document also brought to the administration's attention how few women professors there were in contrast to all the women graduate students in the Comp. Lit. Department. Of course, our department was not alone. For years, all language and literature departments of our era were stuffed with female students and male professors the way the Catholic Church has been stuffed with devout female churchgoers and male priests.

Per Foxy's advice, I did go on to take my Latin and Spanish classes. In my nineteenth and twentieth century Spanish drama class, I met a wonderful woman professor, Mrs. Dorothy Clarke Shadi, who made me feel as if I had a special gift for writing, and I am indebted to her. I then went on to study intensely for my Ph.D. written and oral exams, a tortuous rite of passage in academia. I would not have passed these exams without the help of Shirley Lovejoy Hecht, a psychologist at the university's Cowell Hospital and later at the Educational Counseling Center. Counseling was not something I had ever thought about until I met Bridget Connelly my first year at Berkeley. She was seeing someone with her husband, and I thought I might give counseling a try too, considering my maladjustment during the first year of my graduate life in Berkeley and my struggles separating from my nuclear family and becoming an adult.

Shirley became my mentor. I can't say how many times she picked me up emotionally and lit my inner flame, though I was totally bewildered by psychotherapy when I first started seeing her. I used to stare at the big medallions she wore and think she had magical powers of some sort. Also, her hair was going through interesting changes with blond dye and streaks of grey—the beauty issues of middle age I would know only too well later, but thought of as strange signs at the time. Therapy was a complete mystery to me and frightening until Shirley began a new approach with me. She decided she had to build people up, give them confidence before she went to work on their weak points or explored their dark side with them. She explained her process and that demystification helped me a lot.

I spread the word of Shirley's gifts as a counselor and soon many of us Comp. Lit. women were seeing her. She also had a very pragmatic approach. "The Gifted Simplifier," Bridget's soon-to-be-ex-husband called her, half with respect for her following, half with contempt for her non-psychoanalytic (for the most part) approach. Shirley knew the MO of all the professors, all the bad boyfriends, and how to manipulate the academic system with an emphasis on "The Man." For a long time, I would consult "my inner Shirley" when I had a problem, and a big boom-ing voice would reply inside me. Gradually, it faded and I had the inner Judy to rely on.

Shirley started the Ph.D. Exam Group at the Counseling Center. A group of us from various disciplines—Comp. Lit., English, and History departments—gathered together under her leadership to strategize about setting up our exam committees, studying our disciplines, and making it through the grueling writtens and especially the three-hour oral exam for us Comp. Litters. Choosing a friendly committee of the "big bad profes-sors" was crucial, and for the most part I managed it with the group's sup-port. I also figured out it was impossible for me to read the mammoth invisible book list we Comp. Lit. students were supposed to know—every-thing in our main literature from medieval to modern (for me, French) and everything in two more literatures in our period of specialty (me, English and Spanish in nineteenth and twentieth centuries).

I learned about "negotiations" in our Shirley group before that term became a corporate buzz word. I went around to each of my professors and negotiated a reasonable list with them; actually, to give the term *every-thing* some specificity, I brought my own list of works I wanted to be examined on. To my surprise, most of the professors were quite friendly and seemed happy to have a list. Underneath it all, they didn't want to look like asses as examiners who had to know everything. When I pre-sented my French list to the chair of my committee, he did seem taken aback at first. I'm not sure anyone had ever presented to him "her list," but he agreed and was immediately on the phone to one of his favorite students, whom he had probably told she had to know everything and now she didn't.

The exam group kept me focused on my task, and eventually, indi-vidual members brought me to the orals door in Dwindle Hall and picked me up after the ordeal was over. My committee chairman told me I was doing quite well at half-time, and I was heartened. I too felt I was doing great on my own period, nineteenth and twentieth century questions from Alex Zwerdling (English Lit.), Richard Terdiman (French Lit.), and Dorothy Shadi (Spanish Lit.). During the final half hour or so, the sixteenth century French professor tried to quiz me on a book of criticism I hadn't read. When I said I didn't know the book, he replied, "Imagine what's in it from the title." Wearily, I replied, "I feel like you're leading me down a road and I don't know where it's going." Was that the best question he could come up with? Why didn't he ask me about the poetry of Maurice Scèves he had introduced me to? There were a few lame questions about Comp. Lit. theory in the modern period—the department's weakness; my weakness also. And that was it. All in all, I felt I had done a good job, for at least the first two and a half hours of the exam. The verdict came—You passed! I jumped for joy.

A few days later, still riding on cloud nine, I stopped in to see the chair of my committee. "You know, you really didn't do that well," he said, deflating my ego. I've been mad at him for years for that judgment, but that's academia for you. Never let a student think she's too smart, and for that matter, never let another professor think she or he is too smart. There's always a great big hole in your brain because you don't know everything.

I think this experience hurled me back into my "madness mode." I originally thought I would do my dissertation on the theme of androgyny in *fin de siècle* literature in French and English literatures. I had read Carolyn Heilbrun's book on androgyny and thought there was lots more to be said. However, on querying an important professor about the idea, I found out he didn't know what androgyny meant. A bad sign. I did have to find some dissertation committee members. I had written a proposal on androgyny, which looks interesting in retrospect, but I myself found it intimidating for more than one reason. I would have to read loads of obscure literature in French, and I would have to deal with my own sexual identity uncertainties, which were starting to arise. No, I just wanted to get my dissertation done fast, not torture myself.

I scrapped the androgyny proposal and chose my former course topic: "Madness and Women: A Study of the Themes of Insanity and Anger in Modern Literature by Women." I wrote my proposal one paragraph per day while spending the summer in what I called "The Mini International Flop House," actually the Canterbury House across from the UC track, where I spent the rest of my summer chatting, flirting, and playing with grad students from India, Peru, Russia, Germany, England, and Northern Ireland; and from America, Mary Stoker, the Comp. Lit. sister who had co-taught my Women and Madness course. Even Mary did not know about the wonderful clandestine affair I was having with a Peruvian man in the house. (I have not gone into the trauma and heartbreak of the romantic relationships I had during my grad student years, but rest assured, they were numerous, tumultuous, and terminal.)

Two more large distractions occurred before I finally got down to writing my dissertation. The first was teaching my Women and Madness course again at UC Extension in the fall of 1974. Maria del Drago was the coordinator for Women's Studies there, and when I presented her my proposal, she asked me if I needed the money. "Of course," I replied. I had completed the four-year maximum teaching stint in the Comp. Lit. Department, and had burned out on previous work-study jobs as secretary in the Cowell Birth Control Clinic, telephone answerer for Project SEED (an algebra for kids program), and essay reader at Merritt College in Oakland. Maria speedily got my course approved through her bureaucracy so I could teach it immediately. She also introduced me to Kate Millett, her lover, at a women's conference, and I was so bowled over I couldn't say anything.

More importantly, Maria gave me some motherly feminist advice about anger and battles. "As you get older, you don't fight every single one. It drains you too much. You choose a few which really count." I was deeply saddened when I learned she committed suicide some years later, but I learned her lesson about rage, and I still think about it. As I've aged I have severely cut down on fighting battles. Sustaining an angry posture is ultimately draining, but in my twenties, it was exhilarating. Anger was my territory after I got wind of feminism. The women's movement provided a release for this great molten rage boiling away underground for years which I hadn't acknowledged because I didn't know what it was. Now I knew. I grew up knowing it was not cool to be a girl in a family where social privilege accrued to the fourth child and only son, despite the double message my family gave its three girls that we could be anything we wanted to be. Maria del Drago knew I was mad, knew we were all mad, and wanted to help the younger feminists of our era.

The version of Women and Madness I taught at UC Extension attracted a looser, older group of working women. We had fun, even though the reading list was serious. I remember two women students in the class in particular: a physician and a future politician. The physician took her final project seriously and presented her paper to the class on Zelda Fitzgerald's *Save Me the Waltz*. The future politician, Carole Migden, former San Francisco County supervisor; former state assemblywoman; and now, chairwoman, California State Board of Equalization, got out her old high school baton and twirled it for us to our cheers. She was a major majorette then and still is.

My final distraction that school year also involved women's politics and money. A former member of my second women's group gave me a call from Napa College. She was in the Drama Department at the community college and had been involved in starting a women's re-entry program at the college. They were hiring a coordinator. Would I apply? I didn't have a car and barely drove. "Get yourself some wheels," said Jan Molen, who was once a used car salesperson when that job only went to men. I gulped, applied, got myself some wheels—a bright-orange used Datsun 510—and also the job, due to Jan's innocently plucking my resume from the stack and saying, "Look at this one!"

The job was only seventeen hours a week, two-plus days, which was OK by me, but I quickly noticed the hours were too "low profile" to really present an effective feminist presence on campus. However, I used my low profile to advantage, and I quietly got Women's Studies courses approved through the curriculum committee. I hired new instructors, one of whom was a former student of Deirdre Lashgari, Lauren Coodley from Berkeley. Lauren now heads up Women's Studies at Napa and recently won their distinguished teaching award. I also lobbied successfully to get the women's re-entry coordinator changed into a full-time position—half teaching and half administrative. A friendly dean, John Mehrens, greatly helped and encouraged me, as did two colleagues who worked in the dean's office with me: Marilyn Freund, a video specialist; and a male sociologist, who included a question, "Would you like to see a women's re-entry program on campus?" in his telephone needs assessment survey of the Napa community. Of course, most of the women said, "Yes!"

Nonetheless, I hated all the politics of my job. I didn't actually know what I was doing, and the president asked for an accounting of all my future time from the beginning of the job. I made up a fake tentative schedule of "my plan" and actually ended up following it. Sometimes intuition works! The president was satisfied. But I soon began hearing rumors from other instructors: "She's just looking out for herself," "Her program will steal our students," and other nasty tidbits. I actually did not want to continue this administrative job and was creating the full-time job for my successor. Through another Berkeley friend, Joel Mills, who was a part-time drama instructor at Napa, I became acquainted with the exploitation of part-timers who worked for the community college system. I wanted the next woman in my position to get full benefits and a full-time job.

I also felt pressured by having to be "the perfect feminist," whatever that was, in an isolated setting. I realized how valuable the support I had from the Comp. Lit. Women's Caucus was, how much it sustained me through my graduate years. In addition, I knew I'd never finish my dissertation if I had a full-time job at Napa College. My contract was for the 1975 spring semester only. Not re-applying for the new full-time job may have been a mistake in retrospect, considering the skimpy job market for Ph.D.s, but I wanted to spend the next year writing my dissertation full-time and get my degree. And let's face it—I was not ready to be an administrator.

The Woodrow Wilson Fellowship competition named me as an alternate for writing my feminist dissertation and a most encouraging letter assured me that I'd probably get a fellowship, as some of the frontrunners would surely turn theirs down for some other offer. But no one did that year. The money was tighter; the Ph.D. job market had virtually shut down. I wrote "Madness and Women: A Study of the Themes of Insanity and Anger in Modern Literature by Women" on a "governmental fellowship": unemployment checks.

My dissertation proposal was gutsy, feisty, opinionated, and ambitious. I proposed to study both the literature of the "mad woman"—i.e., crazy ladies as depicted by women writers—and the "*mad* woman"— enraged, angry women—in two separate sections of my dissertation against a background of feminist, psychological readings, primarily Phyllis Chesler's *Women and Madness*. I proposed that within a literature of great despair, one could find the seeds of a literature of revolt. What I found when I actually wrote my dissertation was not "the seeds of revolt" but the revolt itself.

After studying mad women characters in the works of Doris Lessing, Charlotte Perkins Gilman, Anna Kavan, Christina Stead, and Shirley Jackson, I found out there was no clear separation between the "crazy woman" and the "enraged woman" in the fiction of madness. I wrote:

> It is not surprising that when these fictional female characters go "mad," they are actually enraged for having nullified [and having others nullify] their selves so many times. In her rage, each female character creates a powerful persona who embodies precisely those characteristics that she lacks or has suffocated in herself through conformity to a fixed female identity. Usually these traits [of the new persona] are those associated with masculine rather than feminine identity: action, struggle, thought, mobility, and pleasure.

My one semi-regret as I look over my original proposal and my actual dissertation is that I pragmatically took the advice of my thesis director

Carol Christ (an early proponent of women and literature courses) to get my dissertation done. I eliminated the strong first-person voice which was emerging in my writing and switched to dull third-person academic voice as my thesis director wanted. She read the first chapter of my dissertation and basically told me to take the politics out of it. My proposal committee had already told me to leave out the "polemics." I put a lot of my feminist theoretical material in my footnotes and kept to a well-crafted textual analysis of my material. It's a much more restrained dissertation than I had previously envisaged, but I figured nine years was enough—time to leave school. My goal was 1976, the bicentennial year. I had been at UC Berkeley since 1966.

After adhering to my thesis director's advice and getting approval for my new chapter one, I spent the next nine months cracking peanuts in the Anthropology Library, writing three pages of dissertation before the library closed at 5 P.M. after stalling as long as I could, typing up the pages at night, and watching *Mary Hartman, Mary Hartman* go crazy on TV. My Comparative Literature dissertation group also kept me going—Marsha Hudson working on Muriel Rukeyser, Marsha Wagner working on Wang Wei, and Barbara Quevedo working on Augustín Yáñez.

I had one serious job interview during this time. I received a request to interview for a Humanities Department position in Modern Literature and Women's Studies at Arizona State University at Tempe. A limp male hand greeted me when I stepped off the airplane. The chair of the department immediately attempted to impress me with Arizona State University's football team and the fact that Judy Chicago had actually visited the campus.

My potential job was to co-teach a large lecture class in the humanities with two men and to submit all my lectures by August, as they would be used for the textbook of the course. My mind was shrieking, "You've got to be kidding! It's late spring, and I'm exhausted from writing my dissertation. I'll never be able to produce a textbook by August!" but I kept my mouth shut to see what else the chair had in store for me. The other major course was teaching Women's Studies, something I knew I could handle. I was scheduled to give a talk to "my future colleagues" about my dissertation, and a handful of men and women dutifully showed up for my presentation. I gave a lively talk on my women and madness research, and they all asked questions and pumped me for more information.

The chair then allowed me to chat with the woman who was vacating the position I was interviewing for. He gave me this vague message that he was proud she had acted so maturely during my visit. She and I met in her small cubicle, two young women with long hair facing each other. "They're horrible here," she told me emphatically. "They don't know what Women's Studies is!" She'd been canned and was leaving for Berkeley to join the Blake Street Hawkeyes, an experimental theater troupe where Whoopi Goldberg got her start.

I had one final interview with either a dean or the president of Arizona State University—I can't remember which. He queried me about my feminist leanings, and I naively told him exactly where I stood, only realizing much later Arizona had not even ratified the Equal Rights Amendment and was a conservative stronghold. After this final visit, the Limp Hand bid me *adieu* and lit up a cigarette. I was surprised, as he had never smoked in my presence during the two days I was tagging along with him. He was no longer trying to impress me, and I instinctively knew I would not get a job offer. Sure enough, he phoned a week or so later to tell me the bad news. As much as I thought I might loathe the job, I would have preferred turning him down. When I asked for specifics why, he was very vague and wished me luck. Some time later, in Berkeley, I saw the young professor who'd been canned. "You really freaked them out," she said. "They flew out a woman from Utah as soon as you left. She wore a white tailored suit and Coro jewelry and had never taught a Women's Studies course in her life! Her specialty was John Donne."

Though I did not know it at the time, the Arizona State University interview was the first and last one I would ever have for a tenured position in academia.

I rushed to meet my own June 1976 deadline on my dissertation and wrapped up my conclusion:

> The modern fiction of madness by Jackson, Lessing, Gilman, Kavan, and Stead illustrates the fact of female powerlessness and asserts women's desire for more power over their lives. That these authors' fictional female protagonists must resort to madness either to escape from the female roles which keep them powerless or to express traits (independence, activity, assertiveness, aggression, etc.) deemed masculine by our culture (those of a "she-devil" as Stead's Louie well knows) indicts the rigid patriarchal culture out of which Lessing, Gilman, Kavan, Stead, and Jackson write.

Carol Christ signed off. Co-director Eric Johannesson asked me what Carol thought about it. "Fine," I said, and he signed, adding he thought all the good stuff was in the footnotes. Ann Smock signed.

I was *DONE*. All that was left was the big bash at Lisa Gerrard's where an old friend gave me a cap and gown he had bought at a second hand store—a funny green flowered hat and a cheesy pale-green nylon nightgown. I had my Ph.D. regalia, finally.

Gloria Bowles, Olivia Eielson, and Neil Forsythe all finished in the same year, and somehow the Comp. Lit. administration hadn't ordered enough hoods for the graduation ceremony and I didn't have one. Perhaps I only decided to go at the last moment. Professor Rosenmeyer lent me his red one from Harvard, so there I was, walking across the stage in UCB Wheeler Auditorium with my scarlet hood getting applause for my Ph.D. with my Women Studies dissertation on women and madness. It was a rare high before my fall into chronic underemployment and my new career as an impoverished, enraged, but powerful poet, encouraged once again by Shirley Hecht and my new fairy tale writing group, Marjorie ("and the blue wind blew") Feder, Deirdre ("A Witch on Her Head") Lashgari and Bridget ("Gunslinger") Connelly.

The Woman Who Wanted Too Much

Olivia Eielson

Back in 1963, at a breakaway art school in Harlem, Holland (in a cold, light-filled building that once housed Napoleon's horses), my teacher made one of his rare classroom visits. He looked over my paintings and said, with the weary disdain of the European to the American, "You want too much."

Want too much? I was puzzled. What should I not want? The art world seemed cracked wide open, and a whole realm of possibilities was available to every painter: Pollock or Picasso, Matisse or Rauschenberg, Op or Pop, Diebenkorn or Raphael. It was like knowing twenty-one languages, with the possibility of exploring the thought processes that lie curled up in each like superstrings. It could also, of course, be like the Tower of Babel, but that realization came later. I wanted to be able to want. Contemplating my teacher's breath as it hung in the frosty air, I threw in my lot with Faust. Yes, I wanted everything. If I had to pay at the end, so be it.

Thus when feminism appeared, it was the answer to a simple question that had been lurking in my mind for years, but which I had not had the words to ask. That simple question was, "Why can't I too?" So many parts of life had been off-limits to women—or at least off-limits to those of us not brave enough to look behind all the curtains labeled "men only." Even for the most courageous and able women, there were some absolute limits, glass ceilings like the those still so firmly in place.

But of course, feminism's advent didn't mean that every woman was suddenly magically transformed, Cinderellas at the hearth one moment and the next descending the royal staircase like Prince or Princess (Un-)

Charming (every choice was theoretically open to us). It did mean that a lifetime of anger, hurt, and bafflement could come out into the open, with whatever speed a woman could handle, and it meant suddenly being part of a huge confederacy of women. We were coming out of hibernation, trying out our wings and beginning to think about where we wanted to go. To be part of that movement, in the midst of things, comparing notes, learning from one another, finding out that we were not alone after all—it was incredible luck to be there.

All my life I had been a reader, but I'd always secretly identified with the male rather than with the comparatively dull female, who was usually waiting someplace for the hero to arrive and give her a life. Who could identify with Sleeping Beauty? (We don't hear anything about what her dreams might have been, in that long sleep.) But while inwardly my thoughts were free and went anywhere they liked without asking permission, outwardly I was in disguise, looking like the sweet and docile Midwesterner I had been raised to be. In the stereotyping of the time, strangers often assumed I was an elementary school teacher. Actually, as a job that would have been better than the few other work options women then had: nursing, which was too physically demanding for me; or being a secretary without the slightest hope of advancement. Until I encountered feminism, there had been no way of acting out or being the person I was in my thoughts. There seemed to be no acceptable place for that person, and unable to *be* myself, it was hard even to know who I was or might be. Some of my early paintings show a wary-looking woman behind a bouquet of flowers. She is in hiding, and doesn't know how to get out.

Like so many readers, I tried my own hand at writing. In my teens I wrote countless poems, all of which ended suitably (profoundly, I thought) with the word "death." In my undergraduate years I wrote better poetry, won some prizes, got published here and there. Thus I came to think I would be a writer. I had a yearning for something, for some intensity, for some approach to what was truer than the confining conventions of my upbringing.

With my poetry prize money, I bought art books—picture books. The truth was that the visual world pulled me more strongly than anything, yet painting seemed impossibly difficult. I had no idea of how I could ever move from my primitive first efforts to some approximation of what my eye registered. In high school I walked home in a private ecstasy at the elm trees that then lined our streets, blazing with green life force in spring, and in winter stiff, angular, and dark against the sky. How could anyone paint such things? Only in the last year of college did I chance on a drawing and painting course which gave me a technical foundation and a hope of somehow rendering what I saw onto canvas. One of my paintings won a prize at one of the men's dormitories ("houses"), and my reward was dinner with the headmaster and his coterie of male companions. Unfortunately the headmaster was also a professor of English whose courses on the "New Criticism" I had followed faithfully—and faithfully I had fallen asleep midway through most of his fine but monotone lectures. Did he recognize me, or was he just annoyed at the idea that a mere girl had unexpectedly invaded his all-male turf? As if I weren't there, he and his companions carried on a learned conversation about literature; sometimes they lapsed into French, which I had not yet studied. I sat in silence, eating the dull food and looking at my painting on the dining room wall across from me. It definitely was the work of a beginner, but still—someone had thought it worth the prize.

Maybe it was during that dinner that I decided I would become equal. Someday such men would have to let me in on the conversation. In 1960, "feminism" was not in my vocabulary, but feminist rebellion was brewing in me nonetheless.

At graduation time, I avoided adding the "Mrs." degree to my B.A., though there was plenty of pressure: in 1961 it was odd for a girl to stay single past age 22. But the idea of children didn't much interest me; I wanted to define myself before I married, so that I would have a clear identity and path of my own. I felt sure that otherwise my life would be quickly subsumed into my husband's, as I became the helpmeet wife, cooking, cleaning, bearing children, and making it possible for the family to have a pleasant life while my husband made money and had both family and a life outside the home.

The idea of art school began to seem more and more logical, so after working and saving my money for two years, I went to the only art school I had heard of: Oskar Kokoschka's *Schule des Sehens* in Salzburg, Austria. This was a two-month course, and seemed like a kind of art boot camp. From 9 A.M. to 6 P.M. we did watercolor sketches of nudes, who changed poses every fifteen minutes. We worked and worked, and so did the models, tough wise-cracking local women with great furry pelts of hair at armpit and crotch, and the stamina of Amazons. Kokoschka's aim was to strip us of painterly tricks we might have adopted and force us to see (*Schule des Sehens*—school of vision, or seeing) exactly and only what was in front of us, as areas of color rather than outline.

On his classroom visits he had his pockets filled with hard candies, which he gave as rewards to students whose work he liked. I had a small stash of these; it was years before I could bring myself to eat them. One person got far more candies than anyone, an Englishwoman I'll call Edith.

She was older—in her fifties or sixties, and she was really good. One day she said to me, sort of out of the blue, "Don't get married. You know that expression—being tied to the apron strings. It's true, I have been, tied to the stove, tied to the children who always need things. I think it's too late for me, but you—you're young. Don't let it happen to you."

I never forgot her—her gift, and her belief that she had missed her chance to use it. Another sibyl came to me later, at a crowded flea market outside Paris. I was there with my second husband, a man who exuded a masculine life-force like perfume, making both women and men glance at him again. He could also be extremely annoying (I suppose I was, too—yes) and we were quarreling—our wills set against one another. Out of the crowd came an old gypsy woman. "Madame, I will tell your fortune," she offered. I gave her a franc. "More, Madame," she commanded. "It's all I can afford," I told her, while my husband turned away impatiently. The gypsy woman put her hand on my arm and hissed, "You must keep your life for yourself. For yourself! You must lead your own life." And that was it—that was my fortune.

But that was later. After Kokoschka-Schule, I found my way to that wintry classroom in Holland. Edith had already prepared my mind for my Dutch teacher's comment. And eventually, after making my way to as many as possible of Europe's art museums, I wound up back at my parents' house in Minneapolis, broke and unsure about my next move.

It's still a mystery to me why I didn't go to New York, where *the* art scene was happening. Probably I didn't even know it existed. In any case, I don't think I had the self-definition needed to survive in that macho milieu, any more than I had it for marriage. Thus I let my parents persuade me to stay at home and earn a master of arts in English at the University of Minnesota. It was the easiest path, and I naively imagined I would be able to find a position teaching my favorite authors while also painting seriously.

While at the university I had many wonderful, encouraging professors; but I also had two encounters that today would simply not have happened. In a seminar of five people—two women and three men—the male professor secretly invited the three male students (none of whom was especially outstanding) to join him in a study group at his home, thus giving them extra instruction and an advantage in the regular class. The women were simply ignored and excluded. I found out about it by chance in talking with one of the male students, who had no idea that the women had not been invited. Then at the end of the program, when I had received the highest mark on the Permission to Proceed exam, and had a record of A's, my adviser told me that I should not try to get a Ph.D.: "You really aren't up to it." It was lucky that those other (male) professors had been kind and encouraging, so that I wasn't entirely crushed; and at the time, I was more interested in a paying job than in a Ph.D.

Thus I went off to Boston and rather miraculously found a position at a small school, Calvin Coolidge College. CCC had lost its accreditation a few years earlier (selling Ph.D.s had been profitable but unwise) and it was at the very bottom of the heap. We had no admissions requirement except ability to pay tuition. Thus our 104 students lacked self-confidence. They weren't Harvard or MIT. They also weren't Brandeis, Tufts, Boston University, or any of the other 34 well-regarded colleges and universities in the Boston area. Many of our students were the first in their family to go to college. Though they ranged in ability from competent to extremely bright, they didn't think they were entitled to read, say, poetry. They thought such things must be impossibly difficult, and not for the likes of them. So I had a mission. Not that I taught down to them. They got everything full-strength, and they handled it. We read, for instance, Chaucer in his own language; we had a full year-long course reading all of Shakespeare's plays; we read Joyce's *Ulysses*. I was always just a step ahead of the class; and as for teaching, they taught me. "Uh, Miss Eielson, would you let us ask some questions in class?" (I was furiously lecturing away.) In the second year I went half-time and painted; it was almost ideal, except that the school was clearly headed towards bankruptcy, and I was too aware of my own lack of knowledge. Thus I applied to graduate schools for a Ph.D., thinking that I would eventually find another post like that at Calvin Coolidge, live cheaply on a half-time salary, and be able to paint.

When I arrived in Berkeley in 1968, the Free Speech and Civil Rights movements had shifted into the anti-war phase. It was like a set of musical themes with variations and key changes. Feminism was part of all this, but I had no easy way to connect with it until *Ms.* magazine appeared in 1972. By then I was deeply involved in graduate school, and in the environmental movement. In addition, I had married, seeking a safe haven from loneliness and the stresses of the dating and sex game.

My marriage, however, proved to be a port with lots of waves and hidden rocks. My husband and I thought of marriage differently. He wanted an accomplished but subservient wife, an entertainer, soother-of-brows, always on tap for his needs, conveniently out of view at other times. I wanted a union of equals, a companion and lover, someone with whom love and trust could grow over a shared lifetime. With the warnings of Edith and the gypsy woman in mind, I also wanted to avoid the old exhausting contract: he works, and his work is important. He has the money and thus the power. She does all household work and social arrangements, none of which is deemed important. Necessary, but not important; without clear limits and thus unending. Our contract was, instead, an equal allocation of household chores and exactly equal contributions to all joint living expenses. That my husband agreed to this contract is a tribute to his sense of fairness. However, conscious ethics and unconscious assumptions were on a collision course.

The first warning signal in this marriage came early on, when I decided to keep my own name. I was 32 years old, had used that name for my bachelor's and master's, and had signed my paintings with it. It was mine. I refused to be subsumed into my husband's identity. This question, on which I refused to budge, was our first important disagreement, and it was then that I learned he believed in the old adage, "In marriage, two people become one, and that one is the man."

Still, the marriage lasted for five or six years, and it gave me a dependable place to be—full of difficulties, but nonetheless a place, and a way of closing the door on the chaos of Berkeley, where mobs stormed through the streets shouting "Power to the People!" or "Revolution Now!" and the National Guard stood with rifles on the street corners as we walked uneasily past them to class. Often enough, classes too were disrupted, either by protesting students or by helicopters spraying tear gas in wide, misty swaths across campus.

I organized buildings in the rent strike, and I worked against nuclear power, which at the time most people thought meant the Bomb. I got together a small band of students for an organization and set out an information table on Sproul Plaza, where every crazy in Berkeley came, staring intently at a spot an inch or so above my eyes, confessing that he had found a source of infinite clean energy: just put a stick into the ground, take some string, and then.... I initiated and produced a small weekly radio program, *Nuclear Follies*, at the local Pacifica station; and I read and read and read: Homer and Mann, Shakespeare and Goethe, Balzac and Horace—and those few women in the canon: Austen, Eliot, the Brontës, Woolf and Dickinson. And whenever possible, I painted. Marsha was having her salon and I had no idea that what I needed so much was happening just a few blocks away.

As Marsha's Salon went on, it became the Comparative Literature Women's Caucus, and I began to hear distant reports: they were demanding more women authors on reading lists; they wanted a course in women's literature and women's issues. At first I wasn't sure such a course was needed. Why not just enlarge the old structure? For some reason what I could see easily in the environmental area, I had trouble at first seeing in the feminist arena. Maybe it was because of being, as they say, "invested" in the male point of view. After all, I had identified with the male in my reading since childhood. I had never hung out with men as "one of the boys," but nonetheless I felt myself to be a sort of honorary male. What else was there to be? Womanhood meant having no identity of your own, no thoughts or opinions worth hearing, no accomplishments worth mentioning (unless, like good cooking, they were in service of a male or his offspring); it meant spending all your time and money on items like hair and clothes, shaving various body parts, teetering on painful and limiting high heels, and learning how to make men feel important so that one might deign to have sex with you or even to marry you. A woman "caught" a man; he was the desired object. She was the spider in the web. To want more was to "want too much." A whole generation, it turned out, had wanted. Men, too, in a different way, were breaking loose from old definitions of what they were supposed to be. Sex, drugs, rock and roll; tune in, drop out.

It was only in my last year of graduate school that I was able to face the fact that most of my favorite authors were male; and all had been, to some extent, "male chauvinists." At first this devastated me. Even Shakespeare was suspect; but how much weight should I give *Taming of the Shrew* as compared to all those plays of his with feisty, independent and entirely lovable heroines? Or what about old John Milton, whose very style was patriarchal, with its (undeniably magnificent) roll, its calm assumption of the right to speak from on high and explain the nature of God? (And what about God, for that matter? Always a he, and the creatures that mattered shaped in his image.) Keats seems to have had a terribly idealized view of women; it's hard to say whether it is more debilitating to be on a pedestal, or to be excluded by definition from "mankind." I guess it's an exclusion either way. All my beloved authors were flawed. I couldn't have been married to any of them (my private question, at that time, on encountering a man in print). That being so, how could I spend my life with them, as a teacher of their texts?

The two subjects of my thesis helped resolve this question. I chose subjects that were challenges—that said, I was now in the major leagues and deserved to be heard. (Somewhere the voice of my adviser at Minnesota still reverberated.) Thus even though Walter Pater and Friedrich Nietzsche are, of course, male, it was in a way a feminist choice. Each man advised readers to "follow your bliss" (as Joseph Campbell put it later). Pater commanded that one "be present always at the focus where the greatest number of vital forces unite in their purest energy ... to burn always with this hard, gem-like flame" of consciousness (with no apology about wanting too much). Nietzsche commanded, "Become who you are!" (*Werde, wer du bist!*) I thought they were right, and while I found it bliss-ful to read and think about what I'd read, my greatest bliss was to be the maker—mainly of paintings, though sometimes also of sentences. This realization, helped along by my disillusion with the mostly male world of writers (which I still loved) and by therapy associated with the breakup of my marriage (and I still, painfully, loved my husband, but realized that he could not love me), led me to opt out of academia in the year that I actually achieved my Ph.D.

My last act in graduate school was to teach the course so coura-geously wrested from the department by my more active feminist col-leagues. My Comparative Literature 40 course was titled "The Myth of Romantic Love." It was about the myths I had grown up on, the ones that seemed to have led me into that painful marriage and divorce; the linch-pin myth which, I believed, kept most women down. (I ignored the impor-tance of sheer sexual lust; but that's another story.) The class was the most exciting I had ever taught, because the students analyzed the sexual pol-itics of the texts, then laid the patterns of their own lives and feelings over the texts, and compared. Students were involved in this course in a way I had never seen before. They read and re-read the texts. They sat on the edge of their seats; they talked and they talked; their eyes were bright. I felt that their lives were being changed.

And with that I was launched into a new life: no husband, no career, no money, no context. I became a half-time secretary at the UC Law School. That meant going from the prestige of teaching to the invisibil-ity of the ubiquitous "girl"—though my boss, a deeply civilized man, a World War II Jewish refugee from Eastern Germany, insisted on calling me "Doctor Eielson." I shared a cheap flat with a woman who became one of my dearest friends, and I recovered from it all.

It took time. My support system was my therapy group. If I'd known about Marsha's Salon, and been part of it, maybe things would have been easier. When my marriage ended, I had realized that I had no intimate women friends, no one who could give me the love and support I so needed. I'd mistakenly depended on my husband for that; graduate school, plus my environmental and political work, hadn't left me time to develop strong friendships with women. That was one of the things I set out to remedy, in that bleak post-graduate-school, post-marriage time. Art and friendship became my primary goals. Both took time—a lot of time. I'm still working on them both, through and after two more marriages—lov-ing marriages (that ended in deaths, not divorce) which I never let get in the way of either painting or friendships with women.

I now paint daily, and tend and am tended by my friendships. The academic side, though, has languished. My precious books surround me, and I dip into one now and then—a little German, a little French, new and old English novels and poetry. But it's rare that someone else is reading the same thing that I'm reading. There are few chances to share and compare notes, to put into an historical or history-of-ideas context with someone who can contribute equally. I miss it. For that part of my brain it's like being an athlete forced to sit all day, waiting, waiting. Gradually the muscles grow flaccid. I forget more and more of what I so eagerly learned; connections, that were so very interesting, fade out of view. It's a partial dying process.

I'm also, however, amazed at my luck. I have time—that most precious thing. My life is serene, independent, and above all, chosen. I still want too much; but at 64, and having nursed two husbands—both originally so full of energy and life—through their dying processes, I see my own mortality now, and am more willing to compromise. I pray for ten years, as that seems a request modest enough not to anger the gods or call their attention; but really I hope for twenty good years of work time. Goddess or whoever, grant me enough years to test all sides of my painting work, and I will die content.

I don't think I'll marry again. It's tempting: a companion, a warm easy presence in the house, a warm and sometimes sexual body to curl up around at night. Someone to do things with—movies, walks, an occasional trip somewhere. The need to share my life, to know and be known, seems so strong. But when I think of loving again, I think also that caring for another beloved husband through his dying would kill me. And I have this thing to do which is not human loving. It is that wanting too much, which I think is the essence of what drives an artist. I try to paint the painting that will "answer" perfectly. That I-know-it-when-I see-it combination of subject, color, composition, and divine grace is a seductive will-o'-the-wisp, appearing flirtatiously just enough in individual paintings, but never completely, so that I am driven to paint again and again, a dance with a Protean or even invisible partner, trying to make it visible. In a way art has been my partner, my first lover, from the beginning, so that my husbands were—though intensely and thoroughly loved— not perhaps as primary as they might have wanted to be. Comparative Literature, too, was not quite primary.

Sometimes I wonder whether it would have been better if I hadn't gone to graduate school at all, but had just painted full time from age 22 on. I certainly would be much more developed as a painter than I am now. But I wouldn't have met the two men, both of them intellectuals, who have meant so much to me; and we were compatible because the book-loving, reasoning, analytical side is also essential to my being.

I think more charitably now of my Dutch painting teacher. He was struggling with his own demons, and doing it as I do, through his work. Probably his comment was, at least unconsciously, misogynist: after all, would he have thought it a problem for a man to want too much? But he couldn't help being of his time and place. I have accepted all those male authors, too, with their varying degrees and modes of male chauvinism. I'm just glad I wasn't around when they were; and, taking the hedonist view, I'm equally glad I was granted the chance, years-long, to read and absorb their work. It is now a part of me, along with memories of my students at Calvin Coolidge College and Berkeley, many of whom I will never forget.

To be completely fair, there is one sense in which my Dutch teacher was right: it was wanting impossibly much to think of having a career as an academic or scholar, and also another career as a serious painter. Marriage would be a third item. But if I hadn't wanted and tried—buttressed by Edith and the gypsy woman and all the women like them, feminists before the word was rediscovered—I would have missed too much. Perfect equality for women will be a continuing effort; there will have to be many Marshas, many Marsha's salons. For myself, I wanted only what was legitimately mine, though it too has to be won and re-won: I wanted my own life.

"You Are Very Well Qualified, Madame, but We Don't Accept Married Women as Graduate Students in the French Department"

Doris Earnshaw

UC Berkeley, 1951.

These were the words of Professor Percival Fay, chair of the French Department, and undisputed God in my life. Neither my young husband nor I had any thoughts of protest or of application to another university. Why not, I wonder now. We had graduated from the same New Jersey high school and from Middlebury College in Vermont. As for qualifications, I had studied French for years, lived for two years in the French house at Middlebury and had taught at the College Cevenol in central France. Only later did I realize that the French Department at the University of California, Berkeley rejected *all* women, but because I was so clearly qualified, the "marriage" excuse was used.

Well, the Philosophy Department accepted my husband and I took a maid's job in a wealthy home on Roble Road across from the Claremont Hotel and Ashby Avenue. We settled into a small apartment over the garage. I wore a gray uniform for day work, and a green sateen one for evening dinners and parties. I cooked and cleaned and tamped down hopes of an intellectual career for myself.

In non-work hours, I undertook a methodical study of the complete dramas of French classical dramatists: Racine, Corneille and Moliere. I also enjoyed taking classes at the Christianson ballet studio in San Francisco. I had formerly studied ballet in New York studios, and had a small collection of Russian ballet teachers' texts. In our 1933 black Chevrolet, I would drive up steep California Avenue to the studio, and one day had the thrill of being in class with the great dancer Alexandra Danilova. Two years passed. I was biding my time, by birth or insanity an optimist.

When my husband finished the master of arts in mathematics (an M.A. in an "other field" was required for the Philosophy Ph.D.) he then decided that his real calling was to be a playwright, and he would need me to continue to support him. He did not want children. For some reason, which I cannot recall, we decided to move to Washington, D.C. Another trip across the continent, this time in the 1933 Chevrolet. We rented a room in a large old house with other Berkeley students, and I continued as cook and housekeeper. Saturday mornings found me at the Farmer's Market shopping for our group dinners. I was now supporting creative work with my labor as I had supported the M.A. at Berkeley.

This time, my amusement came in the form of a fine old violin I inherited from my grandfather. I studied with the concert master of the Washington Symphony, a strict German teacher who put me over his knee and spanked me once when I made a stupid mistake of not having spare violin strings when one broke in class. As I practiced songs and scales in the basement, the marriage and the old friendship turned sour despite the many shared adventures—touring Europe on a little British BSA motorcycle, hitchhiking from Florida to California. But now, I rebelled at the prospect of another year in that big house on Highway One in Washington, D.C. Clearly, a change was required, even for this optimist.

After a Las Vegas divorce, I accepted a proposal to marry one of the California men living in the house. We were married in the historic Federal period Unitarian Church, where we both attended. I found a job at the Library of Congress checking in new Russian periodicals. We lived in a large house near Rock Creek Park where you could hear the lions roar from the back yard. After a year, we made new plans and returned to Berkeley via Canada where we visited my relatives (Oh! those long cross continent car trips!). He studied landscape architecture at Berkeley while I happily began a family with my first child, a beautiful girl. His career designing parks and gardens prospered. With a friend who had been a fellow student, they established a thriving business. Their work won a national award, given by Pat Nixon in Washington. The firm occupied a large old building in Oakland.

I loved the role of mother, wife and housewife for many years, fashioning small links to my former studies, still firmly convinced that the old dream of further education was closed. I taped Russian vocabulary lists to the wall beside the kitchen sink, and gave the older children responsibility for the little ones as I watched Russian lessons on the TV. But the hunger for academic life still smoldered.

The turning point came in the mid–1960s when the last child was still a toddler. Somehow *The Feminine Mystique* came into my hands. Like so many others, I realized clearly, suddenly, that "my case" was not unique. I was part of women's history, both in its long-term custom which I had accepted and in the short-term economic strategy of postwar "get-the-women-back home" movement. The consumer ethic had never impressed me—the joy of matching the mop handle color to the dustpan, the need for Saran wrap, Dacron and all the new allurements offered to women—but I had not recognized or resisted it.

"The long road back" began with an extension course in Russian at Santa Rosa Junior College, near the home we then occupied in western Sonoma County. I remember seeing a new Montgomery Ward store "Coddingtown" with majestic pillars and hanging baskets of flowers at its grand entrance and "getting it" that this was the new American temple. It has now morphed into the international Wal-Mart empire. Our few years in the country ended as we moved back to suburban El Cerrito, just north of Berkeley. When the youngest child began kindergarten, I would stand in the kitchen of my now empty house and scream as loud as I dared. As this behavior continued, the rational part of me understood it to be an extreme case of personal, perhaps "suburban" distress. Years before, during World War II, I had been part of a Quaker volunteer group working in a large public mental hospital in the Philadelphia area. I knew very well the possible consequences of my solitary screaming.

Obviously, some action on my part was urgently needed if I wanted to avoid a very nasty fate. I thought through the problem alone, which now does not surprise me. Self-reliance was an early habit. I had been advanced in grade school, did well in high school and left home for college at sixteen, probably too young. Both mother and father died when I was twenty-five. Now, at age forty-five, I looked around for an effective cure. I thought, "Why not become a high school teacher? Surely they will accept me." With this step in mind, I applied to the Education Department at UC Berkeley and was accepted for a one-year program to qualify to teach political science in high schools.

It was winter 1968 when the miracle happened and shackles of twenty years fell away. One day I walked across the Berkeley campus from my north side Education Building to the south side's massive humanities building, Dwinelle Hall, to look up an old acquaintance in the Speech (now Rhetoric) Department. Standing in the wide lobby, I scanned the list of departments on the wall plaque. In amazement, I stopped at the words "Comparative Literature." What could that mean? Curiosity impelled me down the hall to the nearby office where a beautiful woman professor, Louise George Clubb—pink suit, garnet brooch—welcomed me warmly. She outlined the program, saying somewhat sadly, "But for our Ph.D., you need to know four foreign languages." "I have four foreign languages," I said, and told her of my studies and travels. She invited me to enter the program with one course, "to be safe," and advised me to finish the high school credential. Then she said firmly, "I think you belong with us."

That spring quarter, I was a very excited—giddy and sleepless—forty-five-year-old "returning student." The informality and brilliance of Robert Alter's novel course was thrilling. And that was just the beginning. Assuming the freedom to study what I wanted to know, I audited and took for credit as many courses in Medieval Studies as I could. It was the sweet and natural tone of voice in the poetry and epics that drew me to the period. I attended seminars on Augustine in the History Department given by the brilliant Professor Caspary and, one year, a seminar by Peter Brown, from Oxford, author of an important biography of Augustine.

One September morning before classes started, I woke up with the question, "How can I be a medievalist without a grounding in Dante?" It was well known that the founder of our department, Alain Renoir, despised Dante and favored the northern epic literature. Well, I found my way into a year long study of Dante in the Italian Department, taught that year by the visiting Cambridge professor Barbara Reynolds, a friend of Dorothy Sayers, the novelist and translator of Dante. Professor Reynolds' teaching inspired me deeply, and with other students we formed a Dante Club. Right from the beginning, however, I sensed that something of major importance was missing in my studies. Each day I moved from a full home life to school classes, seeing my husband off to work, and four children off to school with their lunches, permission slips, homework done. Then I would drive to Berkeley to learn literary values. Often I would set an alarm to study from 2 A.M. to 5 A.M. to fit school work into my busy life.

The problem was that nothing in the works I was given to read talked about a the reality of a woman's life. We new students were required to attend a "get-to-know-your-professors" evening series in which faculty members lectured for three hours on their special interest. I became uneasy. A tremendous gap existed between what I was studying and what I knew about life. I would walk around the campus saying to myself, "There must be a voice of women somewhere in all this, but no one mentions it and I will die with this secret knowledge." I had asked the teacher of a poetry translation course for a woman poet to translate, and he said, "Doris, women don't write poetry; they write letters and journals."

Imagine my feelings when Marsha Hudson stood up after one of Ruby Cohn's summer drama seminars to say, "I am starting a student group devoted to research on women writers." The heavens opened! I quickly said, "Count me in."

We met for several years, building strong friendships as we began to discuss one work after another in the only line of women writers we knew: Jane Austen, George Eliot, Virginia Woolf, Djuna Barnes. Gradually, some of us moved into the lesser-known area of women poets—we had language skills and could do the research. As a body of poetry grew in our hands, we conceived the bold idea of publishing this newfound women's poetry.

We were just the right group to do this work. Financial grants from the National Defense Education Act were supporting the study of "exotic" languages. We had specialties in Tamil, Urdu, Hindi, Classical Chinese, Farsi, pre–Islamic Arabic, Provencal, and ancient Greek. In addition, we were becoming familiar with cultures much older than ours, whose literary treasures included women poets unknown in the limited western European curriculum. We organized translation workshops, critiqued each others' work and compared various translations of the original poem. Joanna Bankier went on to teach translation classes at several universities.

Help for our project arrived from an unexpected source. One day, after my M.A. exams were over, the department chairman asked me to meet him in his office. "Would you be willing to put aside your studies for two years to help the department? We need an office secretary for the graduate advisor, and we have to make it an unofficial appointment." He explained that a university-wide budget crunch forbad new hires, but the current secretary was about to take a two-year maternity leave. The department needed someone to hold the job while they kept the official secretary on the payroll. "Certainly, I accept," was my instant reply. I knew that the department's lively environment had rescued me from what had been a serious threat to my mental stability, so I was genuinely glad to help.

My new position as graduate secretary turned into a wonderful advantage for our group research. For the first year, I worked for Janette Richardson, a professor of Medieval Rhetoric whose specialty was Chaucer. She gladly and generously supported our group and our research, incidentally teaching me the fine points of successful business letter writing. She quietly loaned money to needy students, and allowed me to keep our files in the office and to pursue research as I worked. The second year, my boss was Professor Joseph J. Duggan, an outstanding medievalist and writer on Roland and medieval epic, who later became a dean. Both professors took pride in our poetry project, giving me moral encouragement and lots of drawer space for our expanding files.

I took advantage of their generosity and worked for the project on department time. While planning M.A. and Ph.D. examinations for our several hundred students, I could ask professors, "Are there any women poets in your language?" How naive we were! They all would light up and say with enthusiasm, "Ah, you couldn't possibly go to press without poems of _____, our great woman poet!" The tall, elderly, very distinguished Paul Alexander, authority on Byzantine Greek, made certain we knew the poet Kassia, whose secular, witty poems are delightful, and whose religious lyrics are sung today in Greek Orthodox churches around the world. In the same way, we learned of Mira Bai, whose "bajans" are sung today in India.

And so we found our pantheon of poets: Murasaki Shikibu, eleventh century Japan. ("Our Shakespeare is a woman," the Japanese professor said.) We learned of Li Ch'ing-chao (China), Auvaiyar (Tamil), al-Khansa (pre–Islamic Arabia) and dozens of others whose voices reached us across centuries and cultures. As the collection and our translations matured, we sought advice from two poet-professors we admired: Josephine Miles, English Department, and Leonard Nathan, Rhetoric. In separate interviews, they said, "Limit your first publication to modern material, and leave the historical project for a later time, as there is plenty of excellent, unknown poetry in the twentieth century collection and you are not really ready for a universal anthology." We took their advice, and six of us jointly shared the authorship of *The Other Voice: Twentieth Century Women Poets in Translation*. We were four from Comparative Literature and two from the English Department.

To our delight, Adrienne Rich wrote the foreword in which she used the metaphor of archeology to describe our work: "As women, like a tribe long ago conquered and dispersed, we have our buried cities, our pictographs on the walls of hidden canyons, our anonymous songs, our lost arts and tools, our secret sharings, our inscriptions which are only beginning to be deciphered." We found a willing publisher in W.W. Norton, and gained experience dealing with a veteran New York editor, John Francis. Deirdre Lashgari and I prepared lengthy biographies of the poets, but John insisted we pare them down. In exchange, he agreed to print their published works in the original languages. He would not allow us to discuss in our introduction the ugly fact of the many suicides among the modern women poets: Karen Boye of Sweden, Violeta Parra of Chile, Alfonsina Storni of Argentina, Marina Tsvetayeva of Russia, as well as our own Sylvia Plath, among others. The sobering knowledge of those suicides increased our sense of the importance of our work. When the book appeared, the department gave a party at which Joe Duggan, one of my favorite faculty members, presented me with a gift, volume four of *The History of Mankind*, a UNESCO-sponsored, global world history, the first of its kind.

That lovely book, *The Other Voice: Twentieth Century Women Poets in Translation*, never rewarded us financially, but we all felt victorious. While meeting the demands of our individual doctoral programs, we pioneered the unknown field of women poets. And then the group of six fell apart. Are you surprised? An enterprising member of the group, not from Comparative Literature, signed a contract with a publisher for a historical book of women poets. Much material was part of our collection, but we were not consulted, informed or invited in. The excuse was given that "You would be too involved with your dissertations to be able to work on an outside project." "You" filed a lawsuit, claiming appropriation of intellectual property. Our lawyer was Robert Truehaft, a colorful, Oakland-based civil rights champion, husband of Jessica Mitford, and a long-time acquaintance of mine. He laughed at our falling-out story, and amused us in his office interviews with stories of wearing the wig and gown in British courts. He managed to have our names appear on the title page of the offending book as "associate editors." Again, no financial reward. To be sure, I was concentrating on my dissertation research, but two of our six editors, Joanna Bankier and Deirdre Lashgari, forged ahead with the wonderful *Women Poets of the World*, published by Macmillan in 1983. That book, along with our *Twentieth Century Women Poets*, is now out of print.

Always a member of the Women's Caucus, I proposed and taught two courses of Comparative Literature 40, first on women songwriters, and then on women poets. Songs as a subject intrigued me—I had sung in choirs in high school and college—and so I also studied bird song and found fascinating research about bird song and gender—only males sing, except in tropical forests, where both genders sing to find each other in the dark. My course on American Women's Songs (as far as I know, a first) was taught in the summer of 1979. We met in Morrison Hall, the music department building. I visited the campus radio station, high up on the hilltop behind the campus where some of the early atomic research was conducted. My students were examined on one hundred songs by a surprising (to me) number of women lyricists. Alberta Hunter, Buffy St. Marie, Joan Baez, Bernice Reagan, Holly Near, and Deborah Harry were among the many women who created and recorded their own songs.

My second 40 course syllabus was drawn from our own group research on women poets of the world. I was supposed to limit the class to only twenty, but when eighty students signed up, I couldn't bear to turn any of them away. After all, this was a voice that had been so painfully missing in my first graduate study years. I welcomed everyone, dividing the class into four groups of twenty, making sure that each group had leadership from the more advanced students. At the close of the first class, one student remained in her seat in a back row, not willing to leave or to speak to me. I took a flower from some I had brought in and laid it on her desk. When the ice was broken, she told me she had grown up in poverty in Appalachia, in a remote valley. She was a poet and wondered if I would look at her poems. Within a few weeks we had a selection of her poems ready to submit to publishers, *Six Ears of Corn*, about her childhood experiences of poverty. Teaching those classes had the heady excitement of newness and bold discovery.

After the two years of "office secretary" work were finished and I had returned to student activity, the dreaded qualifying examinations stood in the way of my progress toward a degree. The written exams came first. For preparation, you agreed with your professors on a reading list that covered each century of your main language, in my case, French, with limited concentration on certain centuries in your other languages. The reading list meant you concentrated on the authors' works, but you also were to know criticism on the works. Each question had two parts: a translation test and an essay question. You wrote one question a day, from early morning to midnight, doing the translation and then "a publishable essay," Professor Alain Renoir was known to say. Like the characters in folktales who have to spin straw into gold overnight, students sweated through the ordeal. I had seen them many times in my graduate secretary days.

I put off my exams for six months at a time, not once, but several times. Finally, I took advantage of the university's mental health provision of ten free hours of psychiatry at the Student Health Center. My psychiatrist was an older man, an artist whose works decorated the office walls. He wore hiking boots with bright red laces, and for the first two of the ten hours I did nothing but look at those boots and sob, unable to talk. After that, I talked about my life, and by hour six, I was ready to face the music. Of course, we were all overprepared for exams. We were so conscientious, more deeply learned than most of our examiners; but we felt so much pressure, I think, because we knew we were breaking new ground, trespassers in the all-male intellectual tradition. Also, comparative literature as a subject was on trial at Berkeley, having been started by Alain Renoir, and had to prove itself.

With the exams finished, I enjoyed a sense of success, and a compliment from a Spanish professor still rings in my ears. He said, "You taught me something about the epic poem the Cid." My most difficult moment in the exams was on the day of the French renaissance period question. After finishing the assigned translation—a poem of Du Bellay, "Si nostre vie est moins qu'une journee"—with sheer delight, I could not make my mind turn to analysis, which had to be done but was so "against the grain" of the morning's imaginative work.

Once the written exams were passed, the oral exam loomed: three hours in the classroom with five male professors, not quite so strenuous. Professor Duggan was in charge of mine, and we knew each other well from the year when I was his secretary in the Graduate Office. Also, I had help from two sources in particular: a German student friend gave me a "mock oral" in which I had to answer questions aloud to her. She tested me on what to say if you can't answer the question. You say "That's a very interesting question!" (Buys you time.) Fashion advice (yes!) was contributed by an artist friend, who suggested a navy blue silk blouse and black long trousers.

During the intense time leading to the exams, I had been staying at the Berkeley City Club, a great stone building near campus, designed by Julia Morgan, the architect of the Hearst Castle. There I learned to swim the crawl in the beautiful pool with her aqua flower medallions decorating the edges. I read for hours in the grand reading room with a 60 foot Persian rug and fine old furniture covered in blue linen velvet, the original fabric and rugs from the 1920s.

I was very attracted to the tone of some medieval works in which people call one another "dear sweet friend," and so I was hooked on medieval studies in the romance languages. Professor Philip Damon, my kind, conscientious and unassuming dissertation director, suggested a dissertation topic that would connect with our group research on poetry, as well as with my special interest in Rhetoric and Medieval Studies. We met in Palo Alto while he was teaching at Stanford for a few years and settled on the "chansons de femme" or women's songs in medieval literature as an appropriate topic. He insisted that I study the lyric poetry of all five medieval romance languages: Old French, Old Italian, Provencal, Mozarabic Spanish and Galician Portuguese.

I combed through ten thousand poems in these languages to identify the poems with direct speech of a woman, noting its location as the whole text or part of the song, and describing the character of the speaking woman. With my twelve-year-old son as companion, we went to France on a research project. I pored over manuscripts and scholarly studies while he taught skateboard riding to French boys in open spaces near the Trocadero. He also had a job demonstrating skateboards outside a store and came home loaded with shirts and gifts.

After isolating the direct speech of women characters in this body of medieval dramatic poetry, an "aha" experience came. Comparing the speech and character of the rustic women speakers in romance language poems, similarities emerged in the womens' speech style and character. Typically, she protests her situation against a man who wants to make love to her, or to make fun of her. She seemed to be an ancestor of Eliza Doolittle, I thought, whose uncouth speech style forms the subject and plot of the modern musical comedy *My Fair Lady*, derived from George Bernard Shaw's play *Pygmalion*. Eliza protests her situation as an impoverished seller of violets in the famous lyric: "All I want is a room somewhere, Far away from the cold night air With one enormous chair Aw, wouldn't that be loverly."

Like Eliza Doolittle, the speaking woman of many medieval comic songs was a social outsider, smart, funny, articulate, protesting her personal situation or the general social scene. Her song becomes a voice of protest and a contrast to the silence of the socially acceptable and adored love object, the lady.

Not every poem had this characteristic in the female speaking voice, but I found enough of them to indicate a pattern of how the voice worked for social control. A lady is silent, she wouldn't want to talk like that (Eliza is marked as a poor speaker by her word "loverly" for "lovely" in her famous song). I learned that Eliza's composer, Alan Jay Lerner, had studied medieval lyric at UCLA. Also, in the technical sense, Eliza's song uses the A-A-A-B rhyme scheme typical of the woman's voice in the old lyrics. I felt I had discovered one way that worked to narrow and define the voice of a speaking woman. One can find the same characteristics, for instance, in the "Crazy Jane" poems of W. B. Yeats.

The concentration on my dissertation was so complete that I was surprised after I finished and someone said, "Just think, the Vietnam War is over!" But the Vietnam War in Berkeley could not be missed, and it had affected us all. One day a frightened fellow student ran up to me in Sproul Plaza, terrified because she had just seen, from her apartment window, a woman being shoved into the trunk of a car. She was ready to leave town in fear for her life. It was the Patty Hearst kidnapping. Early one afternoon (the war between Oakland cops and Berkeley students always began after lunch) I was caught under the tear gas being sprayed from a helicopter. We all ran into the Student Union to look for water to wash our eyes. Then the Cambodian invasion crisis drove classes off campus, and we met students in our living rooms.

With the dissertation done and my degree in hand, life began to assume a more humane dimension. I had moved south to the community of Laguna Beach to be near my younger children. Teaching jobs opened in the local community college and at the new University of California campus in Irvine. I applied for teaching positions, and was accepted at both schools. The classroom always feels like a holy place to me, although I keep a light touch and speak of literature as "the best gossip." I learned from students, recently arrived from troubled places, about their experiences of modern political turmoil, stories of Thai, Hmong, Vietnamese and Tamil youth now safely away from the fighting. Foreign students were not the only ones who melted my heart. One student was a "valley girl" from Fresno. She failed several writing courses, and was failing my course when she came to the office. She said she was afraid she "would have to return to Fresno." There were no independent ideas in her papers. When I suggested she apply what she was learning in her psychology courses to her literary analysis, she said, "You mean, it matters what I think?" I replied, "Yes, indeed, it does matter what you think," and she turned an essential corner in her academic life.

With the late-blooming teaching career has come an economic change. After years of dependence, I found myself working at the instructor's salary of $700 a month. For the first time, I became interested in how the dollars come and go. Each year I have kept track of my earnings: first $7,000 as a graduate student teacher (no income in the summer); then up to $14,000 as a part time "freeway flyer" in southern California; then over $20,000 as a full time lecturer at UC Irvine and as high as $34,000 at the University of California, Davis.

Publishing has been part of both my student and retirement years. After the publication of *The Other Voice* in 1976 and *Women Poets of the World* in 1983, my dissertation was published by Peter Lang in 1988: *The Female Voice in Medieval Romance Lyric*. Reviewers noted its originality, and said that only one European scholar had attempted such a broad study. One said that if I had translated the poems into English, it could be a widely read book. I did have a lovely moment at UC Davis, when a graduate student in the English Department said to me, "You mean you are the Doris Earnshaw? We all read the theory chapter of your dissertation."

What can we conclude about the publishing effort we students made as feminists at UC Berkeley in the 1970 and 80s? You could say we were "co-opted" by the women who researched and published women poets in English only. They have enjoyed huge financial and professional successes with text book adoptions in colleges and universities. Their limited scope was more easily managed by thousands of teachers trained exclusively in the tradition of British and American literature, not to mention editors, publishers and sales staff all unfamiliar with non–English traditions.

Our group's global expertise and thirst for learning put us ahead of our time. We felt capable of encompassing the whole world at a time when a "one world" view could be called "globalony." More and more today, however, students from Asia, Latin America and Africa find respect for their traditions, many of which are much richer in depth of history than the English language tradition. On the other hand, English language dominance affects those students as well as native speakers of English.

Now teachers at all levels know that a worldwide view is essential to "diversity minded" departments and curriculum designers. I look back on twenty post-doctoral years of teaching literature with university students in Ohio, Colorado and California. I have never again felt as I did before that unplanned visit to the Comparative Literature office. I never attained a rank above lecturer, but the teaching years have been a joy. Recently I was pleased to learn that the Internet lists about fifty of my book reviews.

In retirement since 1993, I have been called back to teach works new to me, particularly Chinese and Japanese classic novels. I started my own small press, Alta Vista Press (altavistapress.com) with three books in print. They are collections of biographies, photos and talks by political women at the state, national and international levels. Their titles: *California Women Speak, American Women Speak* and *International Women Speak: the Emergence of Women's Global Leadership.* The third book is dedicated to my six grandchildren, who, with their parents, are the joy of my life. These books bring together my original concern for government and world affairs with my love of good writing.

While it is naïve to think that gender balance in democratic legislatures will solve the problem of war, still it is obvious that gender balance in democratic legislatures will alter the focus of attention towards issues of concern to women. And for me personally, the work of a press brings great satisfaction. I can and do attend major international conferences with a press pass (such a lovely scam!) including the "Beijing Conference," the Fourth United Nations World Conference on Women in September 1995. What a glorious experience that was! The only words in

Chinese I knew were the names of the characters in the great classic novel *The Story of the Stone*, and people would light up and realize that I knew something of their literature. I saw that the world's women are working together for human rights, development and peace, and there is no stopping them.

American schools no longer question the right of women to aim for the highest levels of achievement in any field. From that springboard, women will put their energies toward solving the many unresolved problems of family life, economic justice, war and peace—there is so much for women to do. As I write this, I am preparing a talk on "Gender Balance and the International Criminal Court." It is a topic I enjoy because it is such unknown material and so important. Quite like teaching a class. And for me, no more screaming!

Broccoli and Oranges:
The Caucus and the Rest of my Life

Deborah Ellis

When I first contacted Marsha Hudson about this volume of essays, she said to me, "Weren't you the one with the dog?" I've rarely been in contact with anyone from my graduate school days, in fact, who didn't begin by saying, "Weren't you the one with the dog?" I did indeed have a spectacular dog, a large black-and-white husky mix named Fletcher who was much addicted to begging on Dwinelle Plaza (where I scattered her ashes some years later, having flown her remains from Cleveland). My dog was my main way of staying grounded during many frustrating years as a Comp. Lit. graduate student. One of the only other ways was the Comp. Lit. Women's Caucus.

Formally speaking, the Comp. Lit. program must have been one of the most impersonal academic deployments at Berkeley. Every faculty member's primary loyalty was to his or her home department, where the real decisions were made. The university's essential alienation and anonymity, qualities I welcomed thankfully as an undergraduate but which were a liability to a graduate student, could not be overcome within the unstable perimeter of Comp. Lit. In my memory, no Comp. Lit. professor in my time as a graduate student actually stimulated me to think. In addition, the nature of the qualifying exams—five days of written essays at eight hours a day, followed by a three-hour oral (and this, of course, represented the humanitarian reform of the 1970s)—chilled anyone's desire to learn. We all sought merely to pass.

The exception to this bleak intellectual landscape was the Comp. Lit. Women's Caucus. I became a reader for one of the first women's literature courses taught (perhaps the first course), and I remember the excitement in our discussion of Shirley Jackson's *We Have Always Lived in the Castle* and the symbolism it may or may not have been working from. (For some reason, the way someone in the class—the teacher?—said "Blue is Mary's color" and the enthusiastic surprise of class members glimpsing the underlying dimensions of a novelist's imagination has always stuck in my mind.) The class also drove me crazy as students and teachers kept grappling with the question of shaving their legs. I had no context for seeing this as anything but trivial; I had no understanding at all of feminism, and I merely stared at the assertion that the personal is the political. Nothing I had ever studied or read prepared me for Women's Studies, despite my radical family background. But at our Women's Caucus potluck dinners, including the famous one in which everyone brought either broccoli or oranges, I was surrounded by women of my age and experience who were thinking through the meaning of their lives in ways I found unsettling and exciting.

I have only two proud memories of my years as a graduate student in Comp. Lit. One was the day I knew I was a Berkeley finalist, and therefore almost certainly a winner, for a dissertation research Fulbright Fellowship (I did go on to win this). The other was the day that the Women's Caucus elected my course proposal for our Women's Literature course, Comp. Lit. 40. In retrospect I can see how extraordinary it was for the department to grant the Women's Caucus total control over this course, even though we had initiated it. But because we did have control over staffing and topic, and because it was the single forum where our feminism intersected with our professional literary studies, the course generated great enthusiasm and a richly cooperative competition among members of the Women's Caucus. I still have many of my materials for this course from 1975, my first real literature course and the one that cemented my desire to teach for a living. As I write this, I realize I taught the class half my lifetime ago, and that teaching it shaped the way I've lived the rest of my life.

The topic of my Comp. Lit. 40 course was "Women and Violence"; I remember that other courses centered on, for instance, the female *bildungsroman,* and that most of us took the opportunity, in the best Comp. Lit. tradition, of teaching texts in translation that we had read in the original, as well as texts originally in English. I did not emphasize that aspect of Comp. Lit., but I did make a more-or-less conscious choice to cross class, race, and gender lines in my text selections: the poetry I culled from various sources, both by famous authors like Rukeyser, Plath, Dickinson—lots of Dickinson—Sexton, and Rich, and by much more obscure ones like Kaufman, Herschberger, and Reese, taken from now out-of-print anthologies like *The World Split Open;* blues songs from Ida Cox and Ma Rainey; *Wuthering Heights,* Margery Allingham's *Tiger in the Smoke* and Dorothy Sayers' *Gaudy Nights,* the latter a text popular in the Caucus; *A Room of One's Own* (ditto); *Frankenstein; The Awakening;* Carolina Maria de Jesus' *Child of the Dark;* Thomas Middleton's *Women Beware Women.* In fact, as I look over my old records, I am impressed by how much all my subsequent teaching has taken the same pattern: starting with the questions in Woolf and extending them outward into other questions in other dimensions.

My course description reads, in part:

> The anger felt by women as a result of personal and social oppression has only recently been explicitly articulated; but earlier writings channeled these feelings of anger into literary expressions of physical and mental violence, where women were usually portrayed as being either impotently angry or criminally violent.... The selections on the reading list represent violence against oneself, against others, and against society; the very act of writing can have a violent character.

My fellow graduate student, Lisa Gerrard, and I shared a fairly serious belief that everyone wrote a dissertation that was about them. If they wrote about broken marriages in literature, they were experienced with divorce; if they wrote about bestiality, well, better not to ask. My dissertation was essentially about medieval women's lack of refuge ("The Image of the Home in Early English and Spanish Literature"), and even I could see without much introspection that it reflected the broken homes of my childhood and adolescence (although I was largely unaware that I was writing a feminist analysis). Using this old guideline, I can see that the violence that drew me to this topic for Comp. Lit. 40 reflected the violence I felt towards the entire graduate program. This was not an uncommon feeling, I think; although I make frequent visits to Berkeley to visit my closest friends, I never go on campus, and the other women from Comp. Lit. that I know about never go either. The program was not empowering. Yet when I look through my dusty collection of Comp. Lit. 40 course proposals, profiting for once from the fact that I never throw anything away, I see real engagement with literature and with teaching: "Women in Industrial Society," "Women at Work," "The Female Bildungsroman," "The Devil's Handmaiden: Demonic Women in Literature," "Twentieth Century Women's Poetry," "Women with a Special Sense of Place," "Varieties of Romantic Love," "Feminism and Film," "Against the Grain: Woman as Outlaw." (These titles do not support my theme-as-neurosis hypothesis, and should not suggest any such connection.) Our discussions of these proposals were always stimulating and cooperative. My notes show that many of the texts I ended up using were first suggested in a caucus meeting where I presented my proposal, and others of us also profited from the suggestions and help of others.

The excitement and cooperation found in the caucus did not usually extend beyond it. Thus, although my dissertation advisor was extremely intelligent, well-read, and well-meaning, he was unaware that I was writing a feminist thesis and so, to my shame, was I. In my research linking medieval architecture to women's self-image, I was led to find my critical matrix in anthropology. Instead of reading Simone de Beauvoir, as I should have, I went out and read theories of kinship (which I probably also should have). In practical terms, this absence had many repercussions. I did not list the dissertation in *Feminist Abstracts,* for instance, and I did not seek to publish in feminist venues. The dissertation as well as subsequent work I've mined and refined from it lacked until recently a central articulation of its point. Moreover, every time I taught women's literature or especially women's studies, I had to reinvent my own intellectual wheels. It was only in repeatedly teaching the Introduction to Women's Studies in my current job that I finally figured out not only how women's studies operates, but also how my own work is a part of a larger feminist interrogation of "women's place"—in both its meanings. I believe that if I had written my dissertation actually in Berkeley, instead of in London where I spent two years on that Fulbright, I would have had the input of the Women's Caucus and my work would have been much stronger from its inception. (Not that I'm complaining about London.)

My archives have also revealed to me a four-page letter dated May 18, 1976, from the Women's Caucus to Ira Michael Heyman, then the vice chancellor of the university, which was included in the Comp. Lit. department's self-evaluation (I think) and which was highly critical of the department. The major complaints in the letter included hostility towards women's studies, hostility and overt sexism towards women graduate students, and the under-representation of women faculty and graduate students. The letter (see Appendix) points out that "at present only two women hold tenure in a faculty of twenty-four persons," concluding that "it should be no surprise ... that in 1974–75 Comparative Literature had 15 female and 5 male doctoral candidates, but only 3 female Ph.D.'s and 3 male Ph.D.'s." There was another level of hostility towards women implied but not addressed in this letter, however, which is relevant to both of these statistics: the issue of motherhood. When a visiting professor from Israel, Mr. Hrushovsky (I think), told us in a meeting that our exams were far too strenuous and took so long that they interfered with female students' reproductive abilities, I was very offended. How dare he reduce us all to bodies? Yet the man had a point: the department, I now realize, expressed its latent hostility towards women partly through its overt hostility towards mothers. The two tenured women mentioned in the letter had no children, and it was generally assumed among the female grad students that I knew that a woman could not have children and attain a tenured professorship. I was also struck by the story of one grad student whose name I have forgotten who did have the temerity to have a baby. The day after she gave birth she was back at work, leaning against the walls of the corridor as she staggered to her classroom. This was the heroic model offered to those of us looking down at a ten-year doctoral program. I myself had children late, when I was within a few days of turning thirty-six and again at forty, and both deliveries were horrendous, the first one being so bad that my infant spent her first week in intensive care recovering from it. Of the other women I have kept up with in Comp. Lit., two had one child fairly late and the rest had no children. My current job offers a very different model to students here, with many female faculty, many of whom have chosen children, or chosen no children, or come out, or some combination of these. But I work in an undergraduate college, and I don't know what kind of a model Comp. Lit. now provides its female graduate students in this respect or in others. Meanwhile, I keep teaching the Intro to Women's Studies course, and listening to students tell me that their lives will be very different: they can have careers and children simultaneously, and their husbands will help with all the housework. They think I'm cynical. I think I'm experienced.

My experiences with the Comp. Lit. Women's Caucus changed my professional life in other ways too. Many of the courses I now teach, which I have developed at this job, stem from my twenty-five-year-old pleasure at teaching Comp. Lit. 40. I now teach Women's Literature I, cross-listed in Women's Studies and English, which goes from the Middle Ages to the eighteenth century; it starts with *A Room of One's Own* and crosses class, ethnic, national and racial boundaries. I also have a favorite course on Medieval Women, which is cross-listed in three departments. My autobiography course stresses women's voices, just as my earliest teaching in Comp. Lit. 40 did. Even my composition courses take a feminist perspective, cautious as I must be, and my regular courses on Chaucer, Shakespeare, Medieval Literature and Renaissance Literature all focus strongly on female perspectives. I helped start the Women's Studies Program at my campus, and I taught the first Introduction to Women's Studies course here (delayed a semester so I could give birth). The feminism I first came into contact with through the Women's Caucus has infused every bit of my professional life: teaching, research, writing. My two daughters are feminists, even when they're impatient with it and with me; I've tried to make sure that they learned earlier than I did, just as I made sure they learned how to swim younger than I did. I still can't go in Dwinelle Hall without an anxiety attack, but I am very grateful for this one part of my experience there.

6

Stealth Feminism

Bridget Connelly

"My dear young lady, you are overly ambitious. You overestimate yourself," the distinguished professor admonished as he rose from his chair to stand a good foot above me. He looked over my impertinent red head toward the door, dismissing me—and my plans for doctoral study in French and Arabic leading to a career as a college literature professor.

The "ambitious" one—that was me in the Comparative Literature Women's Caucus letter to the vice chancellor (see Appendix). Not that I signed the letter or even saw it back in the seventies, when the caucus accused the professors of languages and literatures at Berkeley of subtly and not so subtly discouraging women from pursuing scholarly careers. During the years that the caucus' brave group was successfully introducing Women's Studies on campus, I was variously researching Arab oral epic tradition in North Africa; teaching Arabic, French and Comparative Literature at Cornell; and turning my dissertation into published articles. Hence, I did not see the letter that cited my interview with Professor K. as just one case history of egregious gender discrimination.

That fall day in 1966 when Professor K. accused me of ambition, I almost quit. After telling the good professorial gentleman whose advice I was seeking about my previous study of Arabic and French as an undergraduate, after (vaingloriously it seemed) parading my multiple fellowships and awards as a good student and being told I overestimated myself, I walked out of Dwinelle Hall humiliated. I sat in the courtyard and was about to cry before dragging myself up Sproul Steps to resign my fellowship and withdraw from graduate school; before I could do either, my friend Judy appeared at my side to ask me what was the matter. When I told her, she was outraged. She expressed great indignation at what she saw as the masculine arrogance that so readily dismissed my professional dreams and accomplishments. Getting angry hadn't occurred to me. Neither had a feminist perspective.

Thanks to Judy's suggestion that I was not bad but plain mad, I walked back into Dwinelle Hall twelve years later as an assistant professor, only to leave it permanently in 1996 as an emerita professor retired early from a twenty-year teaching career. My career, it turned out, would be an anomaly in my generation of graduate students—both men and women.

While everything else changed before my eyes as I sat in my own professor's chair in Dwinelle Hall, the one thing that remained constant was the dismal job scene. The graduate students I advised in Berkeley's Rhetoric Department always imagined that, unlike the ordeal they faced in the eighties and nineties, a booming job market awaited Ph.D.s back in the seventies. By 1974, however, the bottom had fallen out of the academic market and when my generation went job hunting, very few college teaching positions were available. Both my graduate-school friends and my graduate student advisees, for the most part, ended up either changing career paths or piecing together a hectic schedule as part-time teachers working quite literally out of the trunks of their cars as they drove from one campus to another, paid a meager hourly wage with no benefits.

A few of us lucked out. My study of Arabic oral traditions had marked my dossier as somehow "special." That, combined with some very good friends who formed a sort of underground old girls' network brought tips and eventual job offers to me so efficiently that I ended holding positions at not just one but two institutions of higher learning.

The first one came in the spring of 1974 via a telephone call from Cornell Dean Alfred Kahn. Had my buddy Hazel Cramer reached me first to warn me about what she had just had the gall to do at the dinner table of the Cornell dean of humanities, I would have been less flabbergasted when I picked up the telephone. Hazel, a State University of New York (SUNY) French professor and friend from our Fulbright fellowship days in France, would later recount how she raced home from an informal dinner party to grab the phone and tell me how her friends' dad had come home unhappy with the situation of Arabic studies at his university. Hazel piped up: "Why don't you hire Bridget Connelly? She is just finishing her dissertation out at Berkeley on Arabic hero tales." Thus, before Hazel could alert me, the phone rang in my one-room, cockroachy apartment and I had a job teaching Arabic in Cornell's Semitics Department.

The winter of 1974–1975 was a long cold one in Ithaca. Lonesome for my California boyfriend, with chilly visions of a spinster-schoolmarm's life overlooking Cayuga's waters, I decided not to continue my professorship at Cornell. I was unhappy with the complexities of Middle Eastern politics in a Semitics Department chaired by Ben Zion Netanyahu; mainly, however, I wanted to be in California near the man I had met and fallen in love with while writing my dissertation. By the end of spring semester, just as the crocuses dared poke their heads through Ithaca's frozen turf, I returned to Berkeley, broke but in love. I wanted it all—not just an academic job, however prestigious. I wanted a teaching job, a marriage, a family.

My friends, faced with bleak job prospects, greeted my impetuous flight from the Ivy League with dismay. They thought I was nuts. Indeed, I counted for a while among the newly forming jobless corps of "independent scholars." Needing to earn a living, some of my graduate-school colleagues had turned to doing housework, gardening or taxi-driving. I chose paper-pushing and worked for a while as the lowest category of clerical worker in the basement of the Graduate Division. An earlier interview for a much higher paying job at an engineering firm with contracts in Saudi Arabia and elsewhere throughout the Arabic-speaking world—a company whose personnel director assured me that his firm appreciated former teachers and would put any talents I had to good use—convinced me I would rather push paper for an educational institution than for a global company that built nuclear power plants and laid oil pipelines.

Yet another friend saved me from my paper-pusher career when Doris tipped me that the Rhetoric Department was looking for someone to teach oral traditions in a comparative perspective. "They must be looking for you!" she joked encouragingly and sent me to another Comparative Literature friend who was working as a Rhetoric Composition teacher; Susan Strong generously briefed me on what the department sought.

While my serendipitously successful career owed its very existence to old-girl networking, I was never a member of the Comparative Literature Women's Caucus. My field was never Women's Studies. I studied macho myths in what was at the time the very masculine field of Arabic studies. In 1971, when my classmate Consuelo Lopez-Morillas and I delivered papers at the Middle Eastern Studies Association conference in Denver, we were the only women registered, except for Laura Nader and Janet Abu Lughod, two well-connected, emergent stars. Mere graduate students, Consuelo and I dared be there thanks to our very supportive Professor James T. Monroe, who encouraged his students to read papers and publish them while yet students—something virtually unheard of at the time.

If my teacher earned his sobriquet of St. James of the Latter Day Feminists, as a graduate student, I certainly deserved the epithet of Stealth Feminist. Having elected Arabic as my field of study and having married a Sicilian in 1967, I had to be a bit sneaky about my feminism in the last half of the sixties and early seventies. My life was steeped in Romance. Judy Wells' poem, "The Kiss of Death," took inspiration from one of my Ivy-League-educated Sicilian husband's more notable quotes: "For a woman, the Ph.D. is the Kiss of Death." We guessed he meant the Death of Romance and Happy-Ever-After Endings. Fortunately, my other romance—my love for Arabic poetry—saved me from the Sicilian stew I had cooked up for myself on the home front. A financially dependable suitor, Arabic studies offered me fellowships for four years of course work and exam-taking, followed by two years of support for my dissertation work: a field trip to North Africa in 1972 to collect living oral traditional poetry.

Only one book assigned in graduate seminars had kept me up all night reading. The book was Albert Lord's report of the research on oral epic poetry that Milman Parry had done in Yugoslavia in the thirties and Lord had continued into the fifties. This was exciting stuff. Not some abstruse philosophical notion about literature, here was a real theory, a hypothesis about how traditional bards such as Homer or Turold could have composed long, heroic epic songs improvisationally in performance without the aid of writing. This book kept me up all night because I couldn't wait to finish it and read it again. Excited over this thesis that made sense of the special relationship between the oral and the written, between performance and composition, between tradition and the individual, I wrote a long seminar paper and handed it in to both my Arabic Literature and Comparative Literature professors.

The paper won the Folklore Prize at Berkeley; an excerpt from the paper received the A.J. Arberry Prize at Cambridge University and was accepted for publication in a British journal. The news about my paper's success came to me in Tunis in August of 1972, arriving in the same mail delivery as my final divorce papers. This Ph.D. really did seem to be the "Kiss of Death" to my student marriage.

From the vantage point of my various campus desks over thirty years, I pretty much saw it all. Sometime in the late eighties or early nineties, the notorious Naked Guy even paraded down the hall and into my Dwinelle office where I held advising hours for Rhetoric majors. The student advocating nudists' rights gave new meaning to demonstrating for a political or social agenda. I must admit, a stark-naked man in my office did make me blink, even though I had managed to avoid the pitfalls and perils Berkeley's many distractions offered throughout my graduate school years—1965–1974. I avoided tear gas on the way to my qualifying exams and tried to keep focused on academic goals during a time when the university and all its institutions and affiliations were in turmoil.

In the youthful folly of our student days, some had found my pragmatism hard-nosed. I was the farm girl who took on a boy's academic mission and went off to North Africa to find myself a Singer of Tales. My dissertation project had garnered three major extramural dissertation fellowships. After the astounding success of my grant applications, I went to thank the faculty members who had helped my project with their recommendation letters. Most of my mentors were pleased with the results of their sponsorship of my dissertation proposal; however, one professor (the very American chair of Near Eastern Studies) greeted the news with the admonition that I "shouldn't be so greedy," that I should "leave something for the other students." I felt ashamed and humiliated, much as I had the day Professor K. accused me of being too ambitious. Once again, I stood blamed for being successful—guilty of some kind of overweening ambition and megalomania.

Actually, I probably did overreach myself. Professor K. had probably been right when he point-blank challenged my outrageous ambition. I really had no cultural or social background to do what I proposed to do. I was just a kid from a farm out to see the world, a western Minnesota prairie high school valedictorian whose dad—with only a grade-school education—sat on the local school board and whose mom was a teacher. When Professor K. had dismissed my career goals, he challenged something very profoundly ingrained in me. I had always known I would be a teacher like my mom and the other smart women in the class-leveling prairie community where an uneducated farmer could marry the town schoolteacher because he liked smart women.

Still, you had to be a bit hard-nosed to get off the farm via high test scores and great expectations. You had to have a bit of a megalomanic vision to read a book that passed for theory and then run off to see if it worked. Lady literature students usually kept their noses firmly stuck in their books and did not traipse off like some latter-day Margaret Mead to commune with Arabian bards. This baby had come a long way.

From a rural, farming community, I did my bachelor of arts at the University of Minnesota. My class had 6,000 at entrance in 1959 and

2,000 at graduation in 1963 (Bob Dylan was among the dropouts). Growing up in the Midwest, I had heard the conventional middle–American wisdom of the late fifties regarding sex roles. Sunday newspaper features seriously questioned whether it wasted educational resources to give women university educations—since they would all marry a breadwinner and never work outside the home. In the contrarian way of rural western Minnesota, our extended farm family had a long tradition of educating its women to be teachers, accountants, nurses, and businesswomen so they could be self-supporting and self-reliant.

I remember being chagrined in graduate school to read the conventional attitude still prevailing in the late sixties as the eminent psychologist, Theodore Reik, summarized it in a popular self-help book; the concluding page pronounced the formula for successful achievement. In order to be judged a success in life, a man needed to achieve three things: happiness in work, home, and love. A woman's success as a human being involved only two parameters: happiness in home and love. From this gender-biased perspective of happiness and success, it looked as if I were trying to be a man! Surely, that's what my Sicilian husband had thought. My natural drive and ambition to him felt like unseemly competitiveness that usurped him—even though I had carefully, intuitively gravitated to "female" fields; I wouldn't have dreamt of going near a history department—it was purely a man's domain. Literature seemed more girl friendly, especially poetry.

Although academic fields—unlike jobs listed in the newspaper want-ads at that time—were not labeled in university catalogs as "male" or "female," it was pretty clear to me that there were men's fields and then there were fields of study that would tolerate women. Applying to graduate schools, my undergraduate Midwestern girlfriends had been variously informed that history departments did not admit married ladies; we were uniformly counseled against trying to become doctors since a woman's admission would only deprive a man of his spot in medical school. When I arrived at Berkeley as a teaching assistant in the French Department in 1965, most of the students were women. The profs, however, were male, save Mlle. Marie-Louise Dufrenoy, who was on crutches. The only other woman professor I noticed that first year at Berkeley was the English Department's Josephine Miles—who was wheelchair-bound. Scary, I thought. Discovering two other women—Professors Louise Clubb and Janette Richardson—the next year in the new Comparative Literature Department came as a great relief. Professor Renoir, chair of Comp. Lit., recruited me into his department, promising that not only could I continue to study both Arabic and French, but that a National Defense Fellowship in Arabic would pay my way. I transferred happily.

Even though Professor K. would soon let me know what he thought of my abilities and my aspirations, I couldn't think too much about all the obstacles—lest they overwhelm me, lest they become too real. Best ignore them and do what had to be done was my philosophy. The Women's Caucus wasn't formed until I had been in graduate school for a good four years and was busy passing my doctoral qualifying exams and applying for fellowships for field research in North Africa. It never occurred to me to join the caucus. Bent on succeeding, I managed to remain determinedly oblivious to the kind of confrontational tactics necessary at the time to open up the curricular canon. Radical I was not, just liberal and determined—a rugged individualist Judy had called me once.

As I saw it when I was in my twenties, if you were ambitious and a feminist, you'd just better be sneaky about it: look feminine, wear lipstick and girly stuff, all the while talking straight, serious, tough intellectual stuff—guy stuff in whatever terms they had set up.

Ambivalence and conflict about women's definitions of "success" was general. It manifested itself in the dilemma of how to present ourselves. Some of my friends, who turned out to be extremely successful in their academic careers, confessed to slipping *Cosmo* magazine surreptitiously into their grocery bags the minute it appeared each month. *Ms.* magazine only became available as counterfoil advice to all of us academic "Cosmo Girls" in 1972—I read the first issue of *Ms.* on the plane to Tunis as I took off on my first research adventure.

When I arrived in Tunis that first time in May 1972, many women in traditional sectors of the community still wore the *safsari* to cover themselves outside the home. When I tried donning the head-to-toe white wrap, my Tunisian women friends howled with laughter. Trying to look neither silly nor conspicuously foreign, I followed the lead of the dear woman who adopted me into her family, a secretary at the Bourguiba Institute of Modern Languages; Sarra advised long sleeves and a scarf to cover my red hair when I was working in the medina. Sarra herself wore mini-skirts to work.

But how to dress was not just a problem in Muslim countries. When we went off from Berkeley for job interviews or to read conference papers, what should we wear? Pantsuits? We didn't have a uniform—a dark suit, white shirt and necktie. Some of us just wore jeans, blazers, and silk blouses that blew the budget; others dresses, hose and heels; some even showed a tiny bit of cleavage. Francoise, going off to accept her assistant professorship at the University of Chicago, expressed our fears to a T: "Ohmygod, I'm afraid I'll go off and become a professor and grow cobwebs under my armpits!" Exactly my sentiment.

I feared my ambition and my early success as much as I thrived on it. What if my drive ended me up a stereotypical old maid school teacher—a professor at Harvard or some other Ivy League pinnacle of success? Would I climb the academic ladders of success blinkered by ambition, tied to the tenure clock's tick, with no time allowed for some of the juicier things in life: love, children, family? Doing it all, having it all seemed hard, but I, for one, could not have one without the other.

During my last year or so in grad school, the time Marsha's Salon moved out of her living room and onto campus to become the Comparative Literature Women's Caucus, I could participate in the informal off-campus feminist support and consciousness-raising groups, the anthology translation projects—the Sunday evening gatherings to which we brought food to share and a poem by a woman, translated from one of the languages we were studying. I brought Old Provencal poems debating the merits of marriage versus the nunnery and pre–Islamic women's battlefield lamentations on the loss of a father, brother or son (husbands for some reason seemed not to be mourned in this elegiac tradition). All this I could participate in, but not the caucus itself—the formal organized political wing of our "movement."

Neither could I read the groundbreaking feminist literature of the time—books that were to become the foundational canon of Women's Studies and the academic feminism that would sweep the academy and profoundly change it, heralding as it did the era of post-colonial studies, deconstructive readings of canonical literature, and the eventual dominance of cultural studies in the postmodern humanities and social science departments.

At the time—even though I had devoured Simone de Beauvoir as a twenty-year-old studying in France—I could not bear to read Friedan, Millett, even Virginia Woolf. Thinking about it all just made me mad. I knew too well what they were talking about and if I dwelled on it too much, it would make me feel overwhelmed and powerless to do what I had set out to do—which was hard enough in itself: to poach on what was then pretty much a men's club.

And I did end up in several men's clubs. One was the Cornell Semitics Department. It felt great to have a job at an Ivy League college, the students were very smart, and Ithaca was gorgeous, but I was indeed the only woman (and the only Arabist) in the Semitics Department. I held office hours in a windowless space that was a former broom closet, while my colleagues (including the visiting lecturer in Hebrew who hadn't finished his Ph.D.) sat in large offices with views of the beautiful campus. My friend Jayne Walker—a Berkeley Comp. Lit. Caucus member—was hired by Cornell's English Department that same year (1974), so at least we had each other for support. We were the only women in that university's budding Comparative Literature program, which was already profoundly influenced by French philosophers like Derrida and Foucault; we soon discovered that East Coast feminism was developing in a very different way from the "human potential" type movement we were part of at Berkeley. Both Jayne and I ended up leaving our Cornell positions— Jayne for a job at Cal, me for love.

At the same time that Romance led me to make what seemed like a very unliberated career move, I continued in my scholarly work to poach on a very real male tradition: the heroic epic in living performed versions. The combat epic is a genre about men and for men, vaunting manly prowess and valor, celebrating the battlefield, boundary conflicts and violence. At the time, the oral traditional world of peasant societies and the oral epic traditions of the Arab world were unstudied—an open field. Because vernacular language folk traditions were held in contempt, literary histories maintained that the Arabs had no narrative fiction, no epic literature.

The academic field called Oral Literature was also in those days pretty much a men's club. Albert Bates Lord of Harvard had articulated the "Parry-Lord" theory of oral-formulaic composition which quickly became a theoretical orthodoxy, albeit a much-debated one. The dean of the field was jokingly referred to as "Our Lord," to whom we vassals owed fealty. I think I can say without undue begrudgery that doing research in Arabic-speaking, predominately Muslim countries was far easier than breaking into the American scholarly field of oral literature.

Westerners often assume that the overt gender apartheid practiced in many Arab countries would impede a woman scholar's work. Ironically, however, I found in both Tunisia and Egypt that the practice could open up doors for me that were closed to foreign male researchers. The traditional society in Tunisia in 1972 still dichotomized men's and women's space along public-private lines. Tunisian women, for example, did not go to cafes unescorted; the lone woman could be very uncomfortable since she was quite literally out of place. One day when I tried to get a sandwich at a brasserie near my Tunis apartment, a very pleasant maitre d' explained to me that this was *not* a good place for me to eat; he told me that his family lived just around the corner and that his wife would like to invite me to have tea. Tea with Rafiqa the next day turned into dinners for the whole month of Ramadan with very good, helpful neighbors. Women, I learned, held sway at home in the company of the extended family and household, and in the local neighborhood at community ovens and hammams. A nice, serious woman living alone, who was not a tourist, clearly needed to be taken into a family who would help her.

Thus it was that as a foreign woman-scholar, I could operate professionally in the male sphere where my academic credentials gave me the status of "honorary male," yet I also had access to the private world of the household which would not be granted a foreign male scholar. An anthropologist colleague would later put it: in Tunisia, if you're a woman researcher, the whole family will work on your project. My own academic hard-headedness made me pass over what I later realized was a treasure trove of women's lore: my friend Sarra's grandmother spent many hours teaching me—sitting on cushions at her knees—Tunisian dialect through proverbs, lullabies, and the household lore of weddings, henna parties, and children's tales.

The boundaries of what was a proper subject for a comparative literature doctoral dissertation did not extend to household tales in 1972 and I was not about to risk my career, as many of my Comp. Lit. girlfriends did, by being too far ahead of current academic trends. (A decade later, my students would take up such topics and go on to have successful academic careers.) I therefore remained fixated on the genre that was part of the literary canon: the combat epic. In early 1978, a Social Science Research Council postdoctoral fellowship enabled me to go to Egypt on my second field trip to investigate the living sung epic tradition. Just as Sarra in Tunisia had adopted me and made life easy for me while I was researching my dissertation, I was lucky enough in Egypt to be invited to stay in the home of that country's premier poet and folk-epic collector, Abd al-Rahman al-Abnoudy. He and the film maker Atiat Abnoudy helped me record a singer of tales performing the "Beni Hilal Epic" and generously taught me how to listen to the epic song and to comprehend it in the terms its audience understood it.

When I returned home from Egypt late that spring as a visiting lecturer in folklore, Albert Lord was a visiting professor at Berkeley. He came to hear my lecture to the Berkeley faculty group the Friends of Oral Literature (FOOLs). Feeling honored that Professor Lord would come to hear me speak, I was eager for his response to what I had found in Egypt—a still-living tradition of orally composed epic performed by singer-poets to the strum and tune of the *rebab*. At this FOOLs meeting, I presented the first public statement of my hypothesis about the particularly Arabic and Egyptian oral technique of poesis, demonstrating how poets use paronomasia (elaborate punned word-play) as a musical-poetical structuring and interpretive device on both the verse-quatrain level and the narrative-story level of composition—something I termed "musical metaphor." The lecture's hypothesis about audience response to puns in performance became two papers delivered at separate conferences the next academic year (Berkeley in April 1980, and Hammamet, Tunisia, in June 1980). These early papers became the key chapters of the book *Arab Folk Epic and Identity* I finished in 1984 and which appeared in 1986. The book was awarded the 1987 Chicago Folklore Prize as the "best work, worldwide, in folklore."

Albert Lord had responded dubiously to the materials I presented, fresh from the field in 1978. But respond he did, and we had a continuing dialogue during his sojourn that spring at Berkeley. Imagine my surprise when, in 1986, Lord published an article on perspectives on recent work on the oral traditional formula and no mention was made of my work—not even a negative review. Indeed (I see as I review the journal today while writing this retrospective feminist essay), the only field workers in living oral performance traditions mentioned were men. Alas, the field of living Oral Epic Studies and Oral Literature was still very much an old boys' club as late as 1986—the only women who counted were rocking-chair folklorists who applied the Parry-Lord Theory of oral-formulaic composition to medieval texts—epics long dead. I knew that the Lord of oral tradition studies wore a hearing aid, but it didn't dawn on me that he didn't hear me when I presented my hypothesis about the use of paronomasia as an oral-poetic structuring and interpretive device—an idea that introduced the notion of an aesthetics of audience response into oral epic studies.

At the end of spring term 1978, Lord returned to Harvard and that fall I started my assistant professorship in the Rhetoric Department at Berkeley. The department elders were very kind gentlemen who nurtured me well. As the last hired, however, I taught only required undergraduate classes, none of which had anything to do with my field of oral narrative. Consequently, my research and writing had to be crammed into odd moments between teaching, grading papers, and advising undergraduate majors. Fortunately, no committee work was assigned to me and all my classes were scheduled for Tuesdays and Thursdays. It hadn't hurt a bit that the department chair liked redheads (he later married a carrot-topped student) and was charmed by the fact that, when he asked why I had left Cornell, I confessed that I had fallen in love with a UC professor.

The Rhetoric elders seemed pleased that "our little mother," as the kindly, white-haired department chair referred to me, was the first professor to benefit from the university's brand-new maternity leave policy. Newly conscious of the fact that women's biological clocks and the tenure clock were not well synchronized, Berkeley had just instituted a wonderful policy, and when my baby was born in 1981, the university gave me a full quarter's leave with pay. This unexpected bonus combined with a spring quarter sabbatical leave gave me time for my scholarship.

In the meantime, I had been balancing teaching and research. I was excited about what the Abnoudys had taught me, when I lived and studied with them in Cairo in the spring of 1978, about how to listen to the Egyptian *rebab*-poet's sung epic narrative. I demonstrated it to any student or visiting scholar who cared to listen to the taped recordings of live oral performances while perusing the rough transcripts and translations I had put together as texts. Conversations with the friendly linguist down the hall, George Lakoff, helped extend my ideas about the musical possibilities of punning, story, and rhyme that we termed "musical metaphor." I was developing a full-scale hypothesis about the aesthetics of reception and transmission of the Egyptian oral epic performance tradition. Two students—one an undergraduate at UCLA and the other a discouraged grad student in Near Eastern Studies at Berkeley—along with a young visiting scholar from North Africa via a Paris all-but-dissertation doctoral degree, were eager to listen.

While on maternity leave throughout the fall of 1981, I nursed my baby and held an informal kitchen-table seminar in my home. The full potentiality of my hypothesis as a methodology for future fieldwork into the Egyptian sung epic tradition was becoming clear. My informal students and I were envisioning more fieldwork observing oral epic performances in Egypt to see if what I hypothesized from limited data was more generally true in the greater tradition. The university generously accepted my application for intercampus travel funds to enable the UCLA duo to participate in our little workshop; the Berkeley NES grad student became formally registered in Special Studies courses with me. When I met her through mutual friends in 1978 just after I returned from Egypt, her research field was contemporary Egyptian novels. I invited her to come to the FOOLs faculty group and learn about the fascinating field of oral narrative and to meet Albert Lord. I gave her my draft lectures to read. I was pretty naïve.

In the nurturing atmosphere of Berkeley's Comp. Lit. program and the projects spawned by Marsha's Salon, the students supported each other. Openness and mutual sharing were part of our ethic, part of our idealized notion of what Comparative Literature meant as a field of study. We aspired to no less than global understanding and communication through the study of the particular languages and literatures of diverse peoples. We were very much post-colonialists before the term became current. Perhaps we helped invent it.

In our idealism, however, we were probably naïve about the realities of academic success and the struggle to climb the ladder. Certainly I was. The ethics of collaboration and cooperation I learned in the Comparative Literature Department women's community would later bring me into direct conflict with the realities of careerism—the raw competitiveness of singularly ambitious people, who view one person's gain as their loss. As students in a very interdisciplinary department, Comparative Literature students could afford to be supportive and generous with each other, to share ideas, to collaborate with each other. Unlike the students in the English Department or the individual language departments, none of us had the same areas of specialization; we were breaking departmental boundaries in our scholarly interests and pursuits. We actually were not competitive with each other, since we each followed an individually tailored program. Our Comp. Lit. profs, for the most part, were our enthusiastic boosters. One of our graduate advisors, Joe Duggan, was not much older than we were ourselves and has long held our group endeavors and successes up as a model of what graduate students can accomplish. Some of us have teased him that we helped train him to become a very good graduate division dean—from the student point-of-view.

Professor K. at Berkeley was the only harbinger I had had in grad school of the negative attitudes other people might have to my professional ambitions and toward my easy assumption that I might actually succeed in them, let alone how others could respond to my actual success in fulfilling them. Small, round, and female, I didn't really look like someone who ought to make it; in short, I didn't fit the profile of the successful scholar in the field. A fellow Arabic literature student and future friend and colleague laughed about the disparity he perceived when he met me after having read an article I wrote for the *Journal of Arabic Literature*: "Bridget, can this be you? You do not look the way you write!" While this amused Muhammed, it outraged others, and raised competitive hackles in a few peers and later in a couple of aspiring grad students.

At any rate, somehow, I did succeed eventually in having it all, in achieving more than I ever imagined I could. I really did get a dream job at Berkeley—my number-one choice school—in an innovative, lively, interdisciplinary department; I had not been insane to leave a "good" job at Cornell for love and desire for a family. I had my dream job, a baby, a supportive husband. Of course, not all was smooth; there were indeed some major bumps along the way. Since my book was quickly published by the University of California Press and awarded the top prize in its field, tenure should have been a snap. But achieving tenure at Berkeley, as everyone had assured me, was never easy.

The Association of Academic Women (AAW) and the chancellor's new Title IX Assistant on the Status of Women held yearly teas at which tenure horror stories were recounted—the idea being that other women coming up for tenure would become more savvy and learn from the ordeals of their sisters. I stayed away from these teas. Horror stories only reified any latent fears I had about the tenure process. Before it was over, however, my own tenure case became pretty horrifying.

Ironically, while I was the first to benefit from the new laws assuring fairness for women with the wonderful bonus of a paid maternity leave, I was also the second person the new anti-"harassment" laws were used against. The female NES grad student whom I had introduced to the very nascent field of Arab Oral Epic studies took umbrage when I asked her to cite my 1974 article, my lectures, and unpublished papers and forthcoming book if she were going to focus on how Egyptian *rebab* poets used puns as a structuring and interpretive device while performing epic song before live audiences. She maintained that my ideas on the subject were "obvious" and needed no citation; she then wrote a letter to the chancellor accusing me of "harassment from a position of power," of attempting to ruin her academic reputation by accusing her of plagiarism (which I had not done—I had merely asked for the respectful acknowledgment due a teacher's work). A formal investigation was launched at the most vulnerable time for an assistant professor. A distinguished professor of Victorian English literature, who knew nothing about either Arabic poetry or oral tradition, was appointed as special investigator.

That year was very difficult, but it was also the year I made some important choices. My nemesis had spread scandal far and wide about what a bad, unscrupulous, unethical person I was, how suspect my research might be. She managed to do to me exactly what she was accusing me of doing to her. Caught up in confidentiality clauses imposed by both the university and my attorney, I could not publicly defend myself, nor did I really want to.

The special investigator had the habit of calling to grill me in the evenings between five and six o'clock. This may have been a convenient time for him, but at my house it was time to cook dinner for my family and to relax with my little daughter before her father arrived home. It was probably my daughter who saved me from the sheer folly of it all: at age three, she clung to my leg and cried as she heard the anxiety and tension in my voice when the university's Grand Inquisitor telephoned and pulled me away from our domesticity. I soon put a stop to the intrusive and indeed harassing telephone calls from the distinguished gentleman by telling him to talk to my lawyer.

My friends, colleagues, and mentors on the faculty had advised hiring an attorney. The American Association of University Professors provided a "professional liability" policy of $500,000 worth of insurance and asked to be kept apprised of developments in my case, as did the faculty union I had joined. All was resolved by the end of the academic fiscal year, June 30, 1985. My attorney (a specialist in copyright and defamation law who counted Larry Flynt and *Hustler* magazine as well as the University of California chancellor among his clients) was not happy with the settlement. He urged me to take action and would have cheerfully, as he put it, "made mincemeat" of the special investigator on the witness stand. Exhausted and relieved to have the ordeal finished, I had no heart for further fight.

By the time my tenure was announced, I wondered if I even wanted it. The year had been frustrating, demoralizing, and disillusioning. I felt betrayed by the institution I had always believed in and to which I had always been fully committed; and, incidentally, an institution which had always been good to me. That year, I learned cynicism, which is, I guess, the realization of failed idealism. It was also the year I realized I had a valuable life separate from the narcissism of the climb up the ladder and the smallness of academic vanities.

My family responsibilities during this time were enormous. My mother had died, leaving a large, complex Minnesota farm operation to her children. In the 1980s, with farm crop prices at an all-time low and inheritance taxes on land at an all-time high, the farm was on the verge of bankruptcy; as administrator of my mother's estate, I became the farm's CEO and had the job of dealing with the U.S. Department of Agriculture, bankers, and Minnesota tax and estate lawyers who had not yet learned the habit of talking to women in the public sphere.

Needless to say, I was pretty busy running a farm in Minnesota, professing at Berkeley, and raising a family. I made some choices. I decided I did not choose to spend my life traveling the world to repeat and claim my ideas, to promote my reputation in the mode of academicians busily climbing the "ladder" to ever higher positions and pay. I decided that the ladder was a bad metaphor. I did not have the heart for it.

At the university, this decision gave me a new kind of freedom. I taught my classes, advised my students, and enjoyed what was, after all, the important mission of the university—teaching. In my department, I served as head graduate advisor, as ombudsman, as affirmative action officer, and chaired the Graduate Admissions and Fellowship Committee. I also served on Academic Senate and faculty administrative committees I believed in: I chaired the Student Affairs Committee as well as the Committee on Prizes; I served on the Graduate Fellowship Committee and had the pleasure of working with a Comp. Lit. Caucus alumna, Dr. Jacqueline Mintz, on the program she set up to support graduate student instructors in the classroom. I also ended up a member of the Graduate Division Council, the governing body of the graduate school. (This particularly tickled some of the women on the staff in the division for whom I had once worked as a clerk in the Admissions Office.)

For the first time, I became overtly political. I served on the Beatrice Bain Center for Gender Studies' advisory committee and gave workshops on academic "financial facts of life" for the Women's Center. I joined the Association of Academic Women (AAW), the faculty women's political group organized by Prof. Susan Ervin-Tripp, and served as its vice president the year Spanish professor Emilie Bergman was president. That year we were active supporting the Chancellor's Title IX Assistant on Affirmative Action, Prof. Sally Fairfax, in the tenure stand-off of two women against the Math Department and the Law School—two very entrenched masculine bastions. We won.

I continued to publish, to develop new research projects, but now without the publish-or-perish pressure, since I never again put in for a promotion up the professorial ladder. While I might have been ambitious, it seemed I was never particularly careerist. In 1989, a volume of *Oral Tradition* devoted to Arabic traditions came out. My paper was the only one authored by a woman. In the same volume, the male authority hierarchy once again put me in my place. Just as Albert Lord in the same journal in 1986 had ignored my work, in this volume the former undergraduate at UCLA who had sat around my kitchen table in informal seminars, now a fellow at Harvard studying with Albert Lord, made erroneous statements of fact about my work and attributed my key concept to the Berkeley female student who had accused me of harassing her. Cured of my accursed ambition, I didn't bother to reply with a correction note in the next issue. I was too busy living my life—happily free from the pettiness of the ladder, perched on the modest rung I had achieved.

Validation for my scholarly work came a few years after I retired— and it came in a form unmeasurable by the standards of the university promotion criteria. It came from Cairo: an experimental Egyptian theatre group dramatized oral versions of the Hilali Epic into a stage play called *Spinning Lives*. The playwright and director of Theatre el-Warsha credited my book's analysis of the Beni Hilal Epic in Egypt as the inspiration for the script and staging of the play. A Ford Foundation grant brought Theatre el-Warsha to San Francisco and to my Berkeley home. Scenes from the play were performed in our living room and in front of our house for my students, colleagues, and former teachers, and members of the Joe Goode Dance Company; sword dances performed by turbaned sheiks stopped traffic along our elm-lined street. In an undreamed of way, the Arab Singer of Tales I had set out to find in 1972 and 1978 had come to my house.

Such good fortune was not mere serendipity; once more, it came to me through our Berkeley women's network. My friend Kristina Nelson, an ethnomusicologist in Cairo and former classmate in Arabic language courses, was the fairy godmother who handed Hassan el-Geretly, the founding director of the Egyptian troupe, my book on Arab folk epic. Indeed, the old girl network engendered by the collectivist ethic of Marsha's Salon and the Berkeley Comparative Literature Women's Caucus still lives and thrives.

For Love of Stories

Naomi V. Cutner

"She has a fairly large vocabulary, loves books, demands 'tory' before nap and going to bed at night," wrote my mother of me just shy of my second birthday. Stories have always enthralled me. How I delighted in Charlotte and Pooh, Dr. Seuss and Madeline, Nancy and Alice. Their stories were funny and sad, quirky and comforting, and they were good company. When I had an appendectomy in my teens, I was soothed by the thought that Madeline had had one too. I still prize my books and the characters they contain. They are like people—to be explored, understood, cherished. It is hard for me to let go of a book, especially if it is one that tells a story.

My love of story informed my life choices, determined my life's direction. It propelled me into the study of literature, then into journalism, and now into my work as a psychotherapist. Perhaps because I was sensitive to sounds as a child, I developed an ear for language. "She says any word she hears," my mother wrote. I took up the study of French in the ninth grade and have not stopped. My love of the language and a good narrative led me to the literature. My struggle to make sense of my own feelings made me want to know what other people felt, and why they did the things they did. Partly as an escape from my own confusions, partly out of a need to understand them, I immersed myself in the emotional conundrums of others. Though I also loved biological science, the emotional life was what ultimately held my attention. I wanted to know about people's lives and the worlds they inhabited, about their motivations and fears, the forces inside and out.

My eight years in Comparative Literature at Berkeley from 1966 to 1974 were formative. I immersed myself in many of literature's great stories and found myself increasingly curious about the intricate processes that shaped a character. Were people free to make choices or were their lives determined? What part did family play, what part society, what part temperament? What led to emotional upheaval, what to equilibrium?

It was during this time that the sisterhood of women in Comparative Literature figured prominently in my life. I was a late bloomer and I felt myself growing up in the company of my new friends. I discovered myself in relation to them. We were always telling each other our stories—of our loves and losses, of our mothers and fathers, sisters and brothers, of where we had been and where we hoped to be going. Before long we had become a part of each other's story. Perhaps what I learned about the value and meaning of friendship was the most important learning I did. The friendships I forged are strong to this day; they have sustained me through difficult times and brightened happy ones. I felt that I belonged in a way that I never had before; I was a member of a community of women searching for meaning in their lives. That search for meaning was critical in shaping my life's course.

The women of the department opened my eyes to writing by women and to the things they were saying about women's lives. The stories that were told by the writers we read—about women in particular—became intertwined with our own. A character's tears might become ours, and remind us of a heartbreak we too had felt; her journey of self-discovery might jolt us to renew ours. Our discussions about literature and life sharply challenged my assumptions about the sexes and social roles, as did the cultural upheaval swelling around us. I felt a momentous sea change taking place inside of me, a fundamental shift in my perceptions of myself, of men and women and relationships. My mother's expectations for me, which had largely become mine—that a man would take care of me—were turned upside down.

With these momentous changes I began to question everything, including the path I had chosen. I was confused about what I wanted to do and what would give my life meaning. Eventually I felt the urge to spread my wings and continue my search beyond Berkeley and academia. I needed something else, though I wasn't sure what it was. The formal Comp. Lit. chapter of my life ended, and I moved away. As I think back over that time, I can't completely make sense of the decisions I made, but I am learning to accept that some questions don't have answers, or only partial ones. Stories don't always make perfect sense. I always want them to, the way they did when I was a child, but now I know that life is not that simple.

My search brought me to New York and into book publishing, where I imagined I could put my master's degree to good use. But after a while,

I lost my illusions that the high-intensity world of trade books suited me, and I found my way into journalism. I liked gathering up information and shaping it with words, and images, to make some kind of meaningful whole. I told stories for *Life Magazine* about all kinds of people—Beatlemaniacs, lighthouse keepers, war vets, scientists, single moms. It was exciting for a time. I traveled around the country, interviewing my story subjects about their lives. Then, after seeing my stories—with all their intricate details—once too often shrunk to a few paragraphs on a page, the glamour faded and I began to yearn for a different kind of connection to others in my work. I didn't want to glide past people so quickly, but rather to stay a while. I wanted to make connections that held, just as words joined a certain way create indelible meaning.

My fascination for the intricately shaped building blocks of a life again came to the fore, and I went back to school for my master's in social work. I wanted to continue to expand my self-awareness, to look more closely at my confusions, and to help others who were confounded by their experience and yearned for clarity or comfort, or simply to be heard. I might not find answers, but I wanted to grapple with the baffling questions and perhaps emerge with new perspectives.

Over the past eight years, through my work in a community mental health clinic and more recently in my private practice, I have discovered and rediscovered the awesome power of a cultural system, a family system and a particular psychological system to shape a life. I have also known in myself and in others the healing power of telling. For most people life is disorganizing at some points, and the narrating of one's story to another generates at least a semblance of cohesion. Surely the telling of stories has been, since the beginning of human existence, about the making and sharing of meaning in the face of bewildering experience. If what has felt elusive or chaotic can be examined and at least partly understood, it has less power to overwhelm. I have heard many stories—harsh and cruel, uplifting and extraordinary. In telling and retelling, my clients gradually find their experience taking on a shape that they can grasp and hold. As they put their feelings into words, they make meaningful connections. When much of life is about separation and loss, putting things together is a relief.

As I age, I am increasingly saddened by the loss of story—my story as well as those of the important people in my life. My father died many years ago, just when we were really getting to know each other. That story is too short. And the longer the story, the more details there are, the more there is to remember and the more to lose. When my mother died four years ago, her memory having failed her, I not only lost her but many parts of her story as well as my own. I still struggle to accept that there will always be missing pieces, just as I struggle to accept that she is gone. I am sorry that I do not have (my own) children to tell stories about, or who will tell stories about me. But I rejoice in my nephew, now four years old. His story is in part a continuation of my story. He is beginning to wonder about me, about where I am going and what I am doing and why. I am happy to comply when he wants me to read him a story, or to tell me one. Gradually we are shaping and naming the experience we share.

As I shaped the story of my own life, have I followed my bliss? I have not always known how to recognize it. But now more than ever I feel it is both out there and emerging from within. It is in a sense of peace during a swim or a walk on the shore, or as I wake from a sound sleep; it is in a moment of understanding shared with a friend or loved one, a colleague or client. It is in a story that is coming into focus. Sometimes I just barely pick up its scent; at other times it hovers a while before slipping away. Now more than ever I know there is always the possibility that I will feel it again, if only for a brief moment. Then there it will be, surprising me like the words in a book that I cannot put down.

8

After 1968: Two Essays

Susan Sterling

For a long time when I thought of my after-college life, I perceived a great divide. On one side lay the years from 1968 to 1975, when I was a graduate student at Berkeley, years in which I earned a Ph.D., marched in anti-war protests, and discovered myself to be a feminist. On the other lay all the years since, after I married and moved to Maine, had two children and struggled to earn a living and find time to write.

The divide seemed to encompass and transform everything my life touched—the kind of friends I made, and what my husband and I did with our time, and how we talked about our lives. Until technology brought the rest of the world closer to this remote part of New England, central Maine was culturally ten years behind the West Coast. Now you can get cappuccino in the gas stations and tai chi is taught at the YMCA, but when I moved here the area didn't have many amenities or cultural diversions. In my first years in Maine, I found myself in the odd and not terribly comfortable position of being the only one anyone knew in our town who had kept her own name when she married. (Now my daughter, who attends the local high school, reads Maya Angelou and Dorothy Allison in her English class and writes papers on how women's relationships are depicted in literature, but you wouldn't have found that then.)

In the same way, when I was working on these two essays, I thought of them in terms of the divide—what I learned from being part of the women's caucus in Berkeley and what I learned from living in rural Maine. It's only after finishing them, in fact, that I see both are really about the same process of self-discovery as a writer and as a feminist. I didn't abandon my feminism when I came to Maine, though I had to temper it and learn to respect people who didn't share or understand my views. And while most of my writing life has been in Maine, its roots lie partly back in Berkeley, where I gained the confidence to begin to write at all and realized I had things to say that others found worth hearing. For that, as well for as the wonderful friends I have made in California and Maine, and for the excellent, if very different, educations both places provided, I remain grateful.

I. California Studies

For me, the history of the women's course and the women's caucus begins back in the spring of 1970, when President Nixon ordered the bombing of Cambodia, thereby expanding the Vietnam War. The University of California at Berkeley essentially shut down as students abandoned classes to do anti-war work. Many of us in the Comparative Literature Department spent our days going door to door, talking about the war. Our assigned territory was Marin County, north of San Francisco, and I remember being appalled by the number of women who would answer our knocks and tell us that they didn't pay attention to politics. "My husband takes care of the war," they said. "I leave that to my husband." When the canvassing was over, I transferred to the women's movement the sense of urgency that I'd felt about Vietnam. Several of us formed the Comp. Lit. Women's Caucus and began meeting to discuss concerns we had as graduate women. One of our concerns was the absence of literature by women in the courses offered by the department, and we were eventually given a course to teach in Berkeley's summer session.

The process for choosing teachers involved members of the women's caucus listening to the proposals of those who wanted to teach, and then voting. My course was the second or third to be offered, I believe. Others had been more active in establishing the class, and I suspected my proposal was selected partly because it included a look at women's roles in fairy tales, a topic we hadn't yet talked about as a group, giving it a certain appeal.

I taught the course in the summer of 1973, a summer that had become problematic for me because my boyfriend had just moved from San Francisco to Ukiah, two hours north, the distance emblematic of what was happening in our relationship. The course was, for me, a real refuge in a hard time, as I believe it was for many of the students. I don't know, really, how well I taught it, but the students were deeply committed, so perhaps I was more effective than I now judge. In a way, my role hardly seemed to matter. In the spirit of those years I envisioned the course as a collaborative effort. I saw us as a group of individuals engaged in a process of discovery about our lives, with literature as our starting point. The classes, with their free flowing discussions, were like the adult reading groups that are popular now, but with a consciousness-raising element thrown in. The atmosphere was democratic and egalitarian: although some, of course, were more comfortable talking than others, everyone was seen as having something to contribute.

The twenty-five or so students in the women's class spanned a range of experiences and ages. There were a few men and one or two mothers. Toward the end of the summer term we moved our class to the Berkeley home of one of the older students for potlucks. The reading list was eclectic and included Adrienne Rich's *Diving into the Wreck*, Emily Brontë's *Wuthering Heights*, Joan Didion's *Slouching Toward Bethlehem*, and *Grimm's Fairy Tales*. Since women's literature wasn't discussed in other classes at Berkeley at the time, in a way it didn't seem to matter what we read. For the first time we were studying how women were depicted in literary texts—their dreams and ambitions, their relationships with others, the restrictions on their lives. Texts that might once have seemed remote, difficult, or outside our own concerns revealed new insights when seen through this lens. The books led to conversations, often painfully personal, of the students' experiences, which included rape, difficult romances and marriages, the struggle to lead less circumscribed lives than their mothers.

For me, the success of the course was confirmed about halfway through the summer. I had gone backpacking for the weekend in the Trinity wilderness in northern California and planned to finish the reading when I got back, but for reasons I can't remember, I returned a day later than intended. I barely made it to the university in time for our class meeting. Still in my hiking boots and dust-encrusted shorts, I apologized for my irresponsibility, but the students appeared not to care. They leapt into the discussion—they, if not I, had finished *Wuthering Heights*—while I sat back and listened. Afterwards I was exhilarated. I thought it was one of our best classes.

Was it good teaching? I don't know. That summer and in the composition classes I taught at Berkeley a year later, I saw my role—indeed the role of any teacher—not in transmitting information and insights, but rather in creating an atmosphere in which the students felt free to explore literature and their lives. My own reticent approach to authority was so clear from the beginning that those who wanted something different dropped the class immediately. About fifty students showed up for the first meeting, during which I sat cross-legged on the desk and explained how the class would work and why I'd chosen the books we would read.

The second class meeting half the students had disappeared, but the discussion was so animated, I hardly noticed. Those who stayed appeared excited by the class and the openness of our discussions. Still, I know it didn't work for all of them. There were three Japanese students who came faithfully every day—young women who were at the university that summer to improve their English—and I can only imagine how lost they must have felt. They appeared attentive but never spoke, and the reading must have been impossibly difficult for them. I was concerned about them when we read Joan Didion's essays, with their specific cultural references, but I never found a way to share with them my concern.

During this time I was also working on my dissertation, titled "Witty Heroines and Lovely Victims: Changing Ideals of Femininity in Eighteenth Century German Drama." It was, I believe, one of the very first feminist dissertations at Berkeley, although I didn't see it in those terms then. Energized by reading women's literature, I was determined to write on a topic that had meaning for me. German was my major literature (specifically, eighteenth and nineteenth century German literature), and while studying for my Ph.D. exams I had become aware of a puzzling change in the way women—especially intelligent women—were depicted in the German dramas of the late eighteenth century. In the Enlightenment plays women were valued for their intelligence and wit and often took the leading role in courtship. In the plays of the *Sturm und Drang*, only a few years later, these same qualities in a woman betrayed a dangerous malevolence. What the hero valued then in the woman he loved was her innocence and passivity. Since I myself had been raised by a mother with highly conflicted feelings about women's intelligence (she was fiercely proud of my intellectual achievements but equally fearful they would drive away marriage prospects), I knew, even then, that I was exploring an issue with resonance in my own life.

If I express any reservations about the decisive role of the women's caucus and the women's course in the direction of my dissertation (part of me feels I should do some kind of homage to the group that I'm reluctant to do), it is because my first experiences of feminism predated them. In the summer of 1968, just before I drove from the East Coast to Berkeley for the first time, a friend gave me copies of the magazines *Off Our Backs* and *Tooth and Nail*. In the fall of 1969 I met a French priest at a party in Berkeley, and we fell into a discussion about American feminism. As it turned out, he was an editor at the French journal *Etudes*, and he asked me if I'd be willing to write an article on the women's movement for his journal. Although I was terrified—I'd never written anything but academic papers before—this was clearly too good a fortune to turn down.

Rereading the article now (it was published in 1971) I see how familiar I already was with classic feminist texts. In the article I refer to Kate Millett's *Sexual Politics*, Simone de Beauvoir's *Second Sex*, and Betty Friedan's *Feminine Mystique* as well as a number of now obscure works and groups. (SCUM—the Society for Cutting up Men—particularly startles me; I have no memory of this group with its vivid and aggressive suggestion of a program.) The article I wrote was all about politics and the roots of the women's movement in the civil rights struggles a few years earlier. I don't say anything about women's writing. Indeed, I suspect it took the women's caucus to lead me to see the extent to which women writers and women's experiences had been considered too trivial for literary study.

If it didn't set the direction of my dissertation, the women's course clearly influenced my teaching. After my experience that summer, I wanted to teach literature in a way that illuminated present life and to have students write about matters that they found deeply significant. I read Peter Elbow's *Writing Without Teachers*, and modeled my Comparative Literature composition classes after his writing groups. These classes, like those in the women's course, involved collaboration and a spirit of equality. Everyone wrote and read aloud each week, including me. I was a fervent disciple of all those who wrote about open classrooms and student autonomy and for a several years rejected almost everything about the traditional academic training I'd received. Eventually, I learned to integrate my experiences in the women's course with the more traditional approaches many students wanted and needed. Still, what gets most praise in my course evaluations are the openness of class discussions and the fact that I take each student's opinions very seriously—a style of teaching I observed in a few of my Berkeley professors, certainly, but which the women's caucus made seem important and valid.

I don't have regrets about my graduate studies, but rereading the article I wrote for the French journal, I'm aware of a sense of loss. I've often wondered what would have happened if I'd been able to take my non-academic writing more seriously when I was at Berkeley, and even earlier in my life. My article on American feminism was well-received; it was reprinted a year later in *La Documentation Française: Problèmes politiques et sociaux*, and I received an invitation from a French feminist to collaborate on a book on women's lives, an offer I declined, begging off because of geographical distance. But I saw this writing as an aberration in my life, an event with no implications for my future. It took me many years to realize that at heart I was a writer, not an academic, and more years still to break through some of the resistances I had to completing what I wrote.

Still, its clear to me now that the women's caucus and the women's course gave me something I've not acknowledged until I began work on this essay. Through these experiences I learned to see women's writings as worthy of serious study, and I disabused myself of a notion I'd unconsciously held since childhood—that language, with few exceptions, belonged to men. Without that, I'd never have discovered that I, too, had words that deserved to be heard.

II. Maine Studies

For many years there was a restaurant in central Maine called "The Silent Woman." Driving north on I-95, about three hours out of Boston, a traveler could just glimpse its lights beyond the first Waterville exit. In front of the restaurant a broad sign depicted three jolly men seated at a long, plank-like table. Behind them, carrying a serving tray, hovered a buxom woman with no head. The restaurant advertised in the back pages of *The New Yorker*. "Someday," read the ad, "you will find yourself in Waterville, Maine."

In my case, the text proved prescient. In 1974 I spent Christmas vacation in Waterville with my boyfriend who was teaching music history at Colby College, a small liberal arts college in the town. He picked me up at the airport in Boston and we drove up in the dark. As we crossed the Maine border, snow appeared in the fields and in the forests bordering the highway. The lights of towns were miles apart; even in the darkness I'd never seen so many trees.

Entering Waterville, we passed the restaurant with the offending sign. "I could never live in a town that allowed a restaurant like that!" I announced, but that principle lost out to love. The following summer, two months after I handed in my Ph.D. dissertation, we married. I had considered staying in Berkeley another year to teach at the university (which I could do as long as I technically remained a graduate student and didn't actually file the dissertation). After seven years, I had put down roots in the West Coast, and Berkeley felt like home (or, as one of my friends said, "home without the family"). But to stay another year would be treading water, and I had desperately missed the man I loved, so I took my degree and left.

The fall I moved to Waterville most of the area's employment was provided by two paper mills and a shirt factory on the Kennebec River that flowed through the town. (Since then, one of the mills has closed, and the other mill and the shirt factory have struggled to remain open.)

Colby College, which is situated on a hill and looks east to the river, together with the nineteenth century Opera House downtown, offered what culture there was. The faculty traveled ridiculous distances—often to Portland, nearly an hour and a half south—to find decent restaurants. Winter came early and lasted into April. Snowflakes sometimes fell in May. I felt as if I'd arrived at the end of the world.

I didn't want to teach that year, but we needed money, so when I was offered a job at Colby for the spring semester, a course teaching nineteenth century American literature (which I'd never studied), I took it. At Colby I included in my reading list Emily Dickinson and looked forward to discussing the painful fate of Hester Prynne in Hawthorne's *The Scarlet Letter*. But once class started, I quickly found myself in a confusingly adversarial relationship with the students. Most were English majors required to take the course, and they desired in a teacher what they had always known—indeed, what I had found helpful in my own undergraduate and even graduate professors (though I had forgotten this). They wanted an authority figure who would point out to them what was significant in the literature and help them understand how it fit into nineteenth century American history. I wanted them to come to class eager to share their individual reactions to the texts and to see the ways what we were reading illuminated issues in their own lives, as my Berkeley students had done in the women's course. Of course, these are not mutually exclusive goals, but it took me several years to understand this. When my questions were greeted with silence and anxious expressions, I didn't know what to do. Finally I resorted to lecturing in a rather nervous fashion, trying to hide my resentment. I felt I'd been dragged back in time, that the students—indeed the college itself—had trapped me there. The course was, in most ways, a failure, and I wasn't rehired. I went on unemployment, wrote out my unhappiness in my journal, and began to write fiction.

A year and a half later I found myself teaching at Thomas College, a business college also located in Waterville. The dean of faculty at Thomas was not interested in my experience at Colby, if he even bothered to inquire about it. Thomas College was in the process of bettering itself, and I had something the institution very much wanted: a Ph.D. Until quite recently it had been a for-profit college, founded by a local family, the Thomas family, and located in two rooms above Woolworth's on Main Street. It was now on its third campus (the Maine Criminal Justice Academy having taken over the buildings comprising its second). The new campus consisted of four very plain brick buildings on an unlandscaped piece of property sloping down toward Waterville's other river, Messalonskee Stream.

At Thomas I taught three sections of freshmen composition to sixty students, each of whom I saw weekly for a brief tutorial in addition to class. (This was considered part-time: the standard load was six courses a semester.) The facilities were poor. The three of us who comprised the English faculty worked out of narrow, shared offices on the second floor of the college's only classroom building. We were responsible to the chair of the Liberal Arts Division, who also oversaw the teaching of biology, history, and psychology. The more essential business faculty was located on the first floor. There was no secretarial help. I shared an office with the college's one history teacher, a man with a strong French Canadian accent who later would become mayor of Waterville. After the first year, in addition to composition, I taught American Literature, the short story, children's literature (in the night division) and business writing. I still included women writers in my syllabi wherever I could, but I had learned my lesson at Colby and no longer tried to teach in opposition to the prevailing mode of the institution—though indeed Thomas students were, surprisingly, more open than my Colby students had been and were glad when we could relate the literature we were reading to their lives.

These students came mostly from Maine. Many had hoped that by attending a business college they would never have to write another English essay. In our composition classes, to get them motivated, we asked them to write first about their own experiences. I received essays on dairy farming, on preparing a horse to show at a county fair, on deer hunting (some of these surprisingly lyrical, evoking the silence of dawn in November, frost on the ground, watchful waiting with fathers and uncles). I learned about going home every weekend to work in a pizza shop, about growing up right on the Canadian border, and about potato farming in Aroostook County, where every fall (still) children are let out of school for two weeks to help with the harvest. These students didn't share my passion for language, and I never got them to care about avoiding clichés. They loved, in the same essay, to describe clouds "as white as snow" and to depict the landscape as "covered with a blanket of snow." These were phrases everyone knew; using them made the students feel as if they belonged and were communicating well. They saw no advantage in being original. Their way of looking at the world was very practical; working with them I found myself anchored in Maine culture in a way many of my friends at Colby, still driving to Portland in search of a decent French restaurant, were not.

The majority of my students were the first in their families to go on to any sort of higher education. Their fathers owned drug stores, gas stations, grocery stores; their mothers worked many hours as seamstresses and clerks. Many of the families were involved in lumbering. A few of the students grew up on welfare and studied at Thomas under government scholarships. Many students were of French Canadian origin, and of these a few had grown up speaking French in their homes and were uncertain about their English. They were studying to be marketers, managers, medical secretaries, accountants. Each year I had one or two who I felt would have been happier at a place like Colby, where they could have majored in literature or history and performed in plays, but their parents would never have invested in anything so frivolous as a liberal arts education.

At graduation, these families, including grandparents and many aunts, uncles, and cousins, filled the Thomas gym. Some of them appeared ill at ease in their new dresses and ties, but they would not have dreamed of missing the occasion. There was nothing jaded about their pride, nothing to be taken for granted about what their children had achieved. In my own family college had always been assumed. All four of my grandparents had gone on to higher education. All but one of my many cousins graduated from college; a number of us have advanced degrees. Sitting in the hot Thomas gym with the rest of the faculty, in the cap and gown the college provided, I found myself surprisingly moved.

Eventually I returned to teaching at Colby. This, too, was a door my Berkeley Ph.D. opened for me, or rather re-opened. The college had instituted a new program for first year students, the Freshmen Seminar Program, team-taught by faculty in various disciplines. One of my friends was involved in a Great Books seminar titled "Response and Counter-Response in the Western Tradition." The previous year the course had been taught by five men, and all the texts were by male authors. The men were embarrassed by their unwitting chauvinism. Because the seminar was essentially a Comparative Literature course, and my degree was in Comparative Literature, they asked me to join them. I gave lectures on *The Odyssey* and on the short stories of Flannery O'Connor, and met once a week with the fifteen students in my seminar—an experience that I enjoyed.

The following year our family lived in England, and when we returned I began making trips twice a year to Asheville, North Carolina, where I earned a master of fine arts in Fiction at Warren Wilson College. Then I returned to the Colby English Department part-time and did what I had done at Thomas, indeed what I had done years before at Berkeley: teach sections of freshman composition. I also taught introductory literature and creative writing and, on occasion, directed the Colby Writer's Center. At times, though, I wondered if my life were fated to keep circling backwards to Berkeley and the years before the women's course—to my first section of Comp. Lit. 1A, where I graded papers and led discussions on *The Odyssey*. In Comparative Literature my field of specialization was eighteenth and nineteenth century German, French, and English literature. Since leaving Berkeley, I've never taught any of those literatures, nor ever had a chance to use the Latin, Middle High German and Old High German I spent so many years learning.

And yet I would not have missed the experiences I've had in Maine. This is a difficult place to find work, let alone decent part-time work. The state is losing population; each year many high school and university graduates, who love Maine and would prefer to stay close to their families, have to leave to find jobs. My degree has been a ticket to work that is usually interesting and comparatively well paid. And in many ways my years reading French, German, and English literature—and looking at the roles of women in them—have prepared me quite well to live in such a remote and beautiful corner of the country. In this blue-collar town where even in late March Christmas wreaths hang on the doors, I'm continuing the studies I began at Berkeley, learning about cultures quite different from the one in which I grew up. The text is the state itself. If I'm circling back, it's on a path that's also leading deeper into unexplored territory.

9

The Legacy: From Comp.
Lit. 40 to Women's Studies

Gloria Bowles

I moved to Berkeley in January 1967 to marry and to enter the Ph.D. program in Comparative Literature. I was leaving Ann Arbor behind. There I had just finished a master of arts degree and was planning to go on for a doctorate, but I fell in love. My husband-to-be had been an under-graduate in Ann Arbor, as had I, but we traveled in different circles and had never met. He was an honors student in English. I specialized in the *Michigan Daily*, famous for its coverage of civil rights in the sixties. I'd dreamed of working on the *Daily* as a teenager in Plymouth fifteen miles away. Unlike my husband-to-be, I got to class when I could. My heart, and my nights, belonged to the newspaper.

I met him first during a brief *séjour* in San Francisco after college. He visited Ann Arbor when I was back for graduate school and then it was *coup de foudre*. We both loved literature. He was working class, as my father had been, and wanted to make it. The first time he asked me to move to Berkeley I said no. The year and a half of my M.A. at the University of Michigan had been a magic period. Finally I had time to read—Baudelaire and Baldwin and Mallarmé. I got to know the professors and I got all A's. I had a wonderful apartment all by myself and plenty of boyfriends. Suddenly the English Department offered a teaching job. It was just a teaching assistantship but I was amazed that someone wanted to pay me for what I loved to do: read and write. Before then, I'd had no intention of entering academe. In 1966, about to finish my M.A., I was thinking of doing just that. The Michigan Ph.D. in Comp. Lit. wasn't too demanding. I thought I could finish in three years.

In between the assigned papers about male artists for graduate classes in French and English, I was writing another essay:

> Ann Arbor, Michigan, February 15, 1965
> "C'est malheureux d'être une femme (It's unfortunate to be a woman)," wrote Stendhal, that great analyst of "*La psychologie feminine*" over a century ago. Stendhal, like Benjamin Constant in *Adolphe*, described the beautiful, sensitive and intelligent woman of the nineteenth century who, forced at an early age to marry a man of position, rich and uninteresting, even despicable, takes a lover in her mature years. It is the assertion of independence, the satisfaction of a need. The meetings are clandestine and passionate: the woman lives from one to the next. It is, essentially, a life of waiting, and brief moments of intense suffusion of feeling. In the waitings and the meetings, there are tears of joy and anguish, words of tenderness and anger: momentous emotion in all its forms. The waitings, the meetings lead, eventually, to the separation, which is never "the clean break," but the long, drawn-out pathos of repeated farewells, the attempted rapprochements, the sobs of the loved and the ministrations of the lover who finally escapes to a war, to his work, to another mistress—and forgets. The woman, if she is grand and tragic, commits suicide, or more characteristically, resigned and quiet, spends the rest of her days in a convent. Romantics, we admire her quiet strength and endurance, her stoicism. But our cloudy vision blinds us to her real situation, a life without light not very much worth living.
>
> The modern woman, in light of the Stendhalian perception, is not as modern as she thinks she is. True, she is seldom forced to marry a despicable man because of the demands of the social order, nor does she need to prepare the clandestine meeting in the boudoir, swathed in silken gowns and perfumes, the preparation of days for the satisfaction of an evening. She is not, in fact, forced to marry at all, although her desire for neither matrimony nor children will be considered strange. It is the quietly accepted Age of the Lover, even in America.

I went on to assess a female character in James Baldwin's *Another Country*. I was interested in Cass because she had put her life into her husband's hands. He was writing a novel. Once finished, she did not like it, thought it bad even. I asked: "Grieved and disillusioned as she was by her husband's failure, would she have been able to cope with a failure of her own if it had come?"

This fragment of an essay remained buried among my papers. Yet it dealt with the basic conflicts I was experiencing in the mid-sixties: my relationship to men and to my work. There was as yet no movement to help me feel that my questions were legitimate. As editor of the *Daily's* Sunday magazine when I was a senior at Michigan, I had run a long article on *The Second Sex*. I understood the argument on an intellectual level. Now I was grappling in a personal way with a split between my ambitious self and the woman I was supposed to be. I had for years been in revolt against the example of my mother, who served her family and, despite her devotions, did not seem happy. I wanted work but I wanted to be a "woman" too, though I still did not know how to define that for myself.

Thus it was that in 1967 I fell into my Passive Period. My new husband knew I "did not want to be my mother." He wanted to be married to an "accomplished" woman. But he had traditional expectations for marriage. He expected me to decorate the apartment in Berkeley and to make meals. He was unconscious, as we all were then, about ideas we now take for granted about male and female roles. Thrust into domesticity, I was also confronting a daunting Ph.D. I had three more foreign languages to learn.

At moments I felt lucky to be sitting in a study which looked out upon the spreading branches of a live oak tree. On my desk were Horace and Hoffmansthal. I was getting a gentleman's education. I had a job teaching in the French Department. We lived in a lovely redwood-lined apartment at the top of the Virginia Street hill. There was not a lot of money but enough. We went to the movies. We took turns with friends giving dinner parties. Life was simple.

But the study seemed endless. And it was. Comp. Lit. was the longest degree; thirteen years was the average in those days. My natural dynamism got lost. I got depressed. I had an affair. Finally in 1972 I made it to my Ph.D. exams.

I visited Blake Spahr, who had just been assigned to chair my Ph.D. committee. I had never talked with him before.

"I'd kiss you but I have a cold," he shouted as I entered his office. A young faculty member passed his door. "I told her I'd kiss her but I have a cold," he yelled even more loudly.

I told Spahr I loved the lyrics of the Middle High German poets.

Spahr gave me questions on Medieval German epics, portions of which I also had to translate from Mittlehochdeutsch. He startled me with a modern question on *Death in Venice*. That was too easy, too obvious. I hadn't read it in years. But the obscure stuff I knew.

One day in the office I heard him complaining about all the pages he had to read. Students wrote answers to seven questions for as many days. I produced one hundred typed sheets.

I passed my writtens and then I got mad.

They have put us through this, for years. And for what? I went to my orals full of anger. We sat around a big wooden table like those of the boardrooms of corporations. When the kindly Scott Momady asked me about landscape in nineteenth century American fiction, about which I knew nothing, I said so. I told him I had studied *fin-de-siècle* in depth and declaimed for twenty minutes on Wilde, Baudelaire, Mademoiselle de Maupin, and theories of decadence.

After my orals, I had a dream. My husband dropped me off at a butcher shop. I walked through a turnstile and approached the big cuffing table. Suddenly the butchers threw me upon it and took me apart, limb by limb.

In the spring of 1972, Jackie Mintz and I called a meeting of graduate students. We wanted to lobby for more reasonable, less general exams. We staged a masterful presentation in Alumni House. Faculty attended, some a little alarmed to see their dutiful students speaking up. We were hopeful that things would change for the students who came after us.

Once I passed my exams, I had the courage, because I felt more powerful, to suggest to my husband that we separate. We should never have married. We did not know ourselves well enough yet. One day in the halls of Dwinelle I discovered that two of my classmates had also wrested themselves from marriage after their doctoral exams.

I had heard before about the salon organized by Marsha Hudson in 1969 to read women writers. I have a vague memory of passing the house where she lived in the flatlands and thinking about the salon. This memory is like a dream. I had a fleeting, almost unconscious sense I was not ready for it, immersed as I was in my studies and my marriage and then my affair.

But after my exams, Jackie said: "The caucus is meeting this summer. Why don't you come?" These graduate women caucuses were something new. The English Department had one as well.

We met in the sun-dappled living room of one of the graduate students. The talk was of professors and reading lists and the women's course. Some of the students were translating women poets from around the world.

Only after my exams did I realize there were no women writers on our reading lists. I had been responsible for sixty German works before the Modern Period and all of French, German, English and American literature in the Modern Period for which there was no reading list.

I got mad again, at myself for being so unaware, and at the department for pretending to mount a comprehensive degree.

In 1972, a group of graduate women had demanded a course on women writers to be taught by a student chosen by other students. They had also asked for an upper-division course and more women faculty.[1]

Comp. Lit. 40 was their first, wild success. The department loved it because it brought in students. For us, it was an opportunity to study and teach these "new" women writers.

I got to teach Comp. Lit. 40 in fall 1973. It would change my life. For the first time, I would teach women writers. Thus, for the first time, I would read and research them. The caucus had agreed we wanted the class to be small—about twenty-five students. Two-hundred and twenty-five students applied. There were very few courses on women at Berkeley at this time. Ours had become famous for its combination of intellectual rigor and personal relevance. I had to choose a few students from that stack of applications. I decided to take a preponderance of upperclasswomen, each saying with vehemence, "I want to take one women's course before I leave Berkeley."

And what a group it was—dynamic, smart, passionate.

Their teacher was handed a challenge. All that reading for over a decade, yet I had never taught women writers. My reading list, including Tillie Olsen, Virginia Woolf and Adrienne Rich, reflected the baby steps stage of what would become an entirely new field. This course was more personal than the composition courses I was used to teaching. We saw our lives reflected in the words of these women writers. I loved many of the male writers I had read but now I realized that I had often felt at a remove from their experience. There is nothing wrong with that; after all, one of the reasons we read is to understand lives different from our own. In contrast, we felt close to women writers. Sometimes it was shared experience and sometimes it was just that they had done it, written it down and gotten into print these words against great odds. They inspired us.

The personal nature of Comp. Lit. 40 was both its draw and its drawback. I mimeographed a few sheets with biographical notes from each member, along with address and telephone number. I wrote that "my marriage and divorce was one of my most important female experiences" and that I regarded "the new solidarity with women a real breakthrough." We often met in my living room on Virginia Street. I wanted to admit some "personal" into class but not too much. This was a university class, not a therapy session. Nor was I equipped—professionally trained—to handle large spillovers of emotion. And I wanted to teach my students something about reading, how you bring a combination of your own emotions, a knowledge of historical moment, literary style, and the writer's other works and biography to a work of art. Reading well is a complex process. Comp. Lit. 40 was my introduction to "feminist pedagogy," as we would come to call it in the ensuing years.

In 1972, I got upgraded from a teaching assistant to an instructor. I had a TA now and was put in charge of registration for the composition courses. I was appointed by our new "chairman," Janette Richardson. She told me her first act was to dust thoroughly under the file cabinets in the chairman's office. The only other woman we knew as "professor" was Louise Clubb. I could understand why she projected such a cold, even male, image in a male domain. But I could also not identify with her or with Janette.

In the summer of 1972, I got to work on my dissertation, a perfect Comp. Lit. topic, as my director, Andrew Jaszi put it, a comparative study of the imagery of decadence in Stefan Mallarmé and Stefan George. At night, I read clandestinely. My fare was American women poets.

Soon I decided to bring women's poetry into the light of day and to change my dissertation topic. After years of reading European languages, I found myself transported, learning the cadences of American anew. I had barely heard of these poets—Teasdale, Millay, Rukeyser. Their verses entered my head, my heart. As I read women poets for the first time, it was clear I was confronting new subject matter. Later on we would debate whether there were also links between gender and style. My reading made me feel less lonely. I wrote in my journal, "I am a feminist because I need a philosophy outside myself for doing things that are considered strange anyhow but *especially* for a woman who is living alone and trying to create." These writers ratified my devotion to work, my drive toward solitude. All through graduate school, I had agonized about my desire not to "do" lists of writers but to write myself. But I had to earn a living. Now I was hearing from Tillie Olsen about all the reasons women do not write. Rilke had spoken of a need for "unconfined solitude." But he had all those women to take care of him.

After wide-ranging reading, including a whole quarter spent on Muriel Rukeyser's vast *oeuvre,* I settled upon Louise Bogan, Denise Levertov and Adrienne Rich.[2] I liked the historical perspective these women would bring, writing from the twenties to the present. I was also interested in how Bogan identified with modernist male poets as she disassociated herself from the "lachrymose" lady poets, as she called them. Levertov's poems about women showed a split self, a woman attracted to the traditionally feminine but one who also longed for imagination's wild freedom. Rich's early books were influenced by formal poetry; in the seventies, she would become a major innovator and theorist in the creation of feminist poetry.

I stayed in touch with some of the students from my Comp. Lit. class. And then we hatched a plot. There were only a handful of classes on women at Berkeley in 1973 and hundreds of students trying to get into them. There were also a few undergraduates trying to do independent majors in Women's Studies. Ellen Carleton was one of them, making her way on her own through the Berkeley bureaucracy. Why shouldn't we help Ellen and others like her? So the undergraduates and I formed "the Women's Studies Committee."

We started a newsletter, *Woman*, in which we listed women's courses and students doing independent majors. We started to notice how few women faculty taught at Berkeley. In 1971, the proportion of tenured women had sunk to 2.9 percent compared to 4.8 percent in 1933. In 1973, of a faculty of 1,480, there were 86 women, 41 of them untenured. Of the 45 tenured women, none did research on women.

In 1974, we wrote our first proposal for a Women's Studies major at Berkeley. By now we knew something about organizing in other parts of the country; there were seventy-eight colleges and universities offering programs in Women's Studies. An administrator, Betty Jones, had suggested we pursue a group major, which gathered together existing courses and thus cost the university no money. The proposal was signed by me and three undergraduates, Susan Andre, Lynn Witt and Marti Dickes. It began:

> Over the years, there has been a gradual recognition of the ways in which sex roles have defined and limited us. The culture has suffered as a result of its expectations that Woman should be passive, submissive, and find complete fulfillment in the home. The present century, however, has seen a movement of women into the factory, the office, the university. This migration has to a certain extent been acknowledged by society; for example, laws have been passed which insist that women receive equal pay for equal work, and attempts are being made to give women the right to pursue studies in fields which have been male-dominated. A certain amount of progress has been made but equality is still a long way off. And we need not talk in such general terms for inequality exists in our own backyard. The May 1970 report of the Subcommittee on the Status of Academic Women eloquently presented the facts of discrimination against women on the Berkeley campus. Yet four years later, the university is barely beginning to devise an acceptable Affirmative Action plan.

After this general introduction, we went on to outline the role of the academy in the fledgling movement for women's equality in the United States, setting out the intellectual goals for a new field called Women's Studies: "to critically examine assumptions about women held by each academic discipline, to test these assumptions in the perspective of current research and individual experiences, to examine traditional and changing sex roles in various cultures, to explore new alternatives for women and men in our society."

Anne Kilmer, then a dean, helped us to route the proposal to the Executive Committee of Letters and Science. I could never figure out what she thought of our ideas but she was teaching us how to work the system. It was turned down. We understood we had to get faculty support.

But the fact is: students started Women's Studies at Berkeley.

Most of the undergraduates of our original Women's Studies Committee had graduated. So I enlisted the help of Arlie Hochschild, my next-door neighbor, then an assistant professor in sociology, and Carol T. Christ, an assistant professor in English. Carol had agreed to direct my dissertation, readily admitting she knew nothing about my topic. Moreover, because of her status, she said she couldn't help me get a job. I wanted a director who didn't obstruct, as I had watched so many do. Natalie Z. Davis, tenured in the History Department, gave us a little money from her teaching award and signed on as well. We submitted yet another proposal in April 1975. It was turned down again. The committee's most memorable objection this time was the lack of a biology requirement. Our students really should hear "the other side," they said. But, lucky for us, Carol now sat on the executive committee. In the summertime we gathered more faculty support. And I wrote another version of our request for a group major.

My new immersion in women's poetry meant that "writer" was no longer the far-off man in classic editions from the nineteenth century. I had met Diane Wakoski and was now writing about her poetry. After meeting Wendy Martin, editor of *Women's Studies*, one of the first feminist journals, I proposed an issue on women's poetry. At meetings of the Modern Language Association in New York in 1974, I met young scholars from around the country working on establishing a tradition of American women's poetry. Soon we were a group of colleagues sharing papers and perceptions. In the spring of 1975, I gave my first professional paper at Philological Association of the Pacific Coast, the regional division of the MLA. It was inspired by the work of Susan Griffin and other feminist poets. I said that "the feminist view of the world, which sees traditional sex roles as no longer viable, is so radical and far-reaching as to demand new poetic forms. The feminist poet feels that she has to start all over again, to begin at the beginning, to find structures expressive of feminist content."

My network was growing. I was gaining a sense of professional identity.

In fall 1975, at its first meeting, the Executive Committee of Letters and Science, with Carol at the table, approved our proposal for a group major in Women's Studies. The major would not go into effect until fall 1976. But we had prevailed.

We now had a major—but no money. I decided to apply for funds to the Council on Educational Development (CED), which gave seed money to new programs. Carol was pessimistic: "Maybe you should go elsewhere if you want to do Women's Studies." But a visit to Vice Chancellor Ira Heyman, a law professor of liberal reputation, was fruitful. I argued that the major would fail without coordination. He agreed to shepherd a request for funding for a coordinator, core courses and administrative support through CED.

Through all this organizing, and its attendant anxiety, women's poetry nurtured me. I finished "Suppression and Expression in American Women's Poetry" in May 1976. Three women graduated with Ph.D.s in Comp. Lit. that year. Libby Eielson, who had written about aestheticism in Pater and Nietzsche, and Judy Wells and I agreed we wouldn't show up at graduation; we were all too broke to pay for cap and gown. Janette got wind of our reluctance. The department seldom had three doctorates in a single year. She offered to pay for our regalia.

Graduation with other literature departments was held in a grim academic hall. A mustachioed professor emeritus of Spanish grimaced as he heard the title of my dissertation and yet again with the announcement of Judy Wells' work: "Madness and Women: A Study of the Themes of Anger and Insanity in Modern Literature by Women."

I thought of the black athletes at the 1968 Olympics in Mexico City. In my mind's eye, our fists were raised.

One day in June I heard a knock on the door. It was Arlie, with a letter in her hand and a big grin. I was perched on the edge of my couch. "We got it," she said. "We got the money for Women's Studies."

Our office opened in July. I became the first coordinator and would remain so for seven years, shepherding the program through curriculum development and numerous reviews, including a favorable one in our fifth year which recommended ladder faculty. I would edit a well-received text called *Theories of Women's Studies*, which argued that our field was a discipline in its own right. And out of my dissertation came a book on Louise Bogan's "aesthetic of limitation." I have completed a memoir of my Women's Studies years at Berkeley from 1973 to 1985 called *Living Ideas*.[3]

Living ideas, which started in the living-room gatherings of the Women's Caucus and of my Comp. Lit. 40 class. That's where it all began.[4]

10

Yours, in Sisterhood

Lisa Gerrard

In my memory, the early feminists I study in school are caricatures: strident and histrionic, bustling about in prim hats and flounces of skirts, they fuss about women's rights until they eventually get the vote and stop complaining. The image, planted by history textbooks of the 1950s and early 1960s, is rife with stereotyping. Dainty bodies, tiny waists and feet, shrill voices, high-pitched emotions. Identified with the Prohibition movement (which was likewise oversimplified and dismissed), the suffragists are shown as overreacting to trivial problems and, by undertaking political activism, venturing beyond their rightful domestic sphere. Something never seemed quite right with this image—despite their patronizing depiction of these women, the textbooks never questioned their right to vote—but as a child, I had neither the vocabulary nor understanding to challenge it. That was before I heard about the personal being political and vice versa.

In my photo album is a picture our neighbor Bernie took of my father circa 1945, hanging diapers on a clothesline. Bernie, a strict believer in segregated gender roles, found the sight of a man doing laundry outrageous, hilarious—so much so that he commemorated it with his camera. When it came to defining male and female work, my family was traditional in some ways, less so in others. It was understood that my father, an accomplished violinist, was to be the primary support for the family, but my mother worked, too; given the instability of the theater-recording world, we needed her income. More than that, my mother sought jobs that offered intellectual stimulation; though not trained for a career (her formal education stopped at high school), she found work where she could develop her interests, in an art museum, a medical research laboratory, a social work agency, a hospital. And though on one level we accepted the

1950s dictum that primary responsibility for housework and cooking resided with women, we resisted it in other ways. My mother was a meticulous housekeeper who worried about what visitors might think if they found dirt in her home, but she also resented the ethic of the time, particularly as it played out in middle-class suburbia, that a woman's value could be measured in the cleanliness of her home. She also promoted what must have been a revolutionary idea in our neighborhood: that a household should be run like a kibbutz, with each member contributing to its upkeep. And for the most part, it was. Though I understood that my mother, sister, and I were responsible for the housework, in reality, my father did quite a lot of it; when he was home he unquestioningly cooked, vacuumed, ironed, and got groceries. Hard-working and responsible, he never played king of the castle.

Discovering Feminism

When I went to college in 1964, discrimination against women was all around me, but I didn't perceive it as such. They were personal difficulties rather than political injustices. Abortion was illegal, so women I knew would scrounge for money for a trip to the back streets of Mexico. In my sophomore year at Berkeley, my roommate got pregnant, went to Tijuana, and returned from her abortion with a serious infection. A doctor at the Student Health Service saved her life, but treated her with undisguised hostility. The whole experience was cloaked in fear and secrecy. It wasn't just that she had committed an illegal act. Many of the doctors saw unmarried sexually active women as sluts and made sure we knew it. One, in particular, gave notoriously painful pelvic exams and was rumored to be especially rough on women with sexually transmitted diseases.

But nothing developed my feminism quite like dating. It was my male peers, not my women friends, who opened my mind. Berkeley seemed to have attracted a large share of the world's sexual predators. The ones who fancied themselves hippies or radicals (or a bit of both) also cast themselves as foes of capitalism. As such, they felt philosophically and politically proscribed not only from paying for their date's movie, but also from keeping cash on hand, thus ensuring that their date would pay for both of them. The joke making the rounds of Berkeley at that time did not exaggerate: a date is when he comes for dinner and stays for the weekend. But the saying omits the coercion that dominated much of this experience. For while it was possible to go on dates that cost little or nothing, there was no avoiding the battle over sex. If you didn't sleep with the guy, more often than not, he'd deliver a harangue, always on the same theme: you were "uptight," one of the most deprecating things you could call a person in that supposedly freewheeling, self-expressive time and place.

This language enforced a form of sexual tyranny. Ironically, these free-spirited flower children (hippies) or warriors for the downtrodden (radicals) were autocrats, in love with their self-entitlement. Today much of their behavior would be labeled sexual harassment or date rape. At the very least, it contradicted their ideology. These radical men, so self-righteous about the moral superiority of their politics, their opposition to an undeclared war in Southeast Asia, to the oppression of people of color at home and abroad, so quick to label a conservative professor or senator a fascist, thought nothing of forcing their will, not to mention their muscle, on the women they wanted to bed. The pressure ranged from hectoring to outright rape. Some men would refuse to leave my apartment. Others issued threats. A few were violent. Calling the police was not an option in those days; the prevailing attitude was that if you invited a man into your life, you invited what ensued. Few women reported rapes committed by strangers and if they did, the legal system was more likely to treat them as criminals than as victims. As for acquaintance or date rape— legally, it didn't exist.

Berkeley dating in the sixties showed me how unprepared I was for deflecting sexism, or just for standing up for myself. I'd get mad at myself for caving in to the pressure when I felt afraid—or, I'm sorry to say, merely worn down—and mad at myself again for feeling uncomfortable when, overcoming my training to "please everyone," kicked the guy out. In either case, this was not dating as my childhood mentor—*Seventeen* magazine— had described it. The disrespect was so personal, raw, and persistent, it put all the more subtle—and far more damaging—habits of a sexist society into focus. Though many of the men I met in those years were gentle souls and many quite sincere in their politics, it is the boorish ones—and my own difficulty fending them off—that unexpectedly taught me about feminism.

The Women's Caucus

In 1968, I graduated college, and after a stint in Paris, hoping to improve my French (which I did) and eventually become a French-English interpreter (which I didn't), I returned to Berkeley. In need of an immediate income, I worked as a teller for the Bank of America. On my lunch breaks, I walked up to the Berkeley campus and, in my incongruous little dress and Mary Quant shoes, joined the picket lines campaigning for Third World Studies. On one of these lunch breaks, I read a handwritten notecard on a bulletin board inviting women to participate in a women and literature discussion group. I felt an immediate affinity for the idea and wrote down the phone number, but never called.

Six months later, in the fall of 1969, I entered graduate school— Berkeley's Comparative Literature program. In my Proust seminar, I met Marsha Hudson, the author of the note on the bulletin board, and she invited me to join her as she formed another feminist group, this one a consciousness-raising group made up of female graduate students in the Comparative Literature Department. Marsha was outgoing, forceful, and passionate, and we shared the same political views; both of us had participated in the Civil Rights and Anti-War movements of the 1960s; both of us saw that extending basic human rights to women was a logical extension of that activity. As in similar groups forming in other parts of the country, we discussed our personal experiences as women, generalized them, and resituated them in a political context. It wasn't long before we began to look to our immediate political situation—our graduate program—for redress of sexist practices, and the consciousness-raising group evolved into the Graduate Women's Caucus in Comparative Literature.

The caucus created a much-needed community within a graduate department which had a large number of students and faculty—and because Comparative Literature was interdisciplinary and all faculty members held joint appointments in two departments—dispersed. The graduate students were dispersed, too. Each student in the doctoral program specialized in a major and two minor literatures, and because we studied all literatures in their original languages, took courses outside the Comparative Literature Department, in Japanese, Danish, or whatever our specialization was. As a result, the Graduate Women's Caucus in Comparative Literature served both a social and political function: it created a community among a group of graduate students who might not otherwise have met, and it agitated for feminist goals.

The Women and Literature Courses

We were all white, middle-class women, privileged in many ways— particularly in our education and ambitions for an interesting career. We were the first generation of women to attend college in substantial numbers, and, in the spirit of political change that dominated the period, we challenged the male-centered curriculum in our field. The department was receptive to our initial request, to institute two courses (one upper- and one lower-division course) on women and literature, which it allowed us to develop and teach. In keeping with the consciousness-raising focus of early 1970s feminism, the early versions of these courses were informal and student-centered rather than governed by lecture; often we sat on the floor in a circle, using a carpeted conference room rather than traditional classroom. We encouraged our students to weave their personal experiences into class discussion and writing assignments and were eager to give them charge of their education; we often assigned students to lead class discussion, and even to teach the class on specified days. Students might be asked to write autobiographical, expressive, or self-discovery pieces in addition to literary exposition. While much of this pedagogy is now standard in many kinds of college courses, at the time, it represented a significant departure from the educational practices we were familiar with.

The lower-division course was taught each quarter of the academic year, including summer; the upper division course, once a year. Melanie Kaye Persoff taught the first lower-division course in the spring quarter 1972. Anyone could submit a course proposal to the caucus, which would then vote on whether to accept it. (Well, probably not anyone; I doubt the caucus would have been receptive to a male teacher; in any case, only women chose to participate.) The themes of each course ranged widely: among them, "Fairy Tales, Chinese and European," "Tragedies of Women's Individualism," "Third World Women," "The Devil's Handmaiden: Demonic Women in Literature," and "Self-Image and Alternatives." Some courses emphasized self-discovery through the study of women in literature; "Centering and Coping: Short Prose by Women about Women" described its goals this way: intellectual objective—self-knowledge; experiential objective—self-discovery; personal objective—self-introspection;

In this version of the course, each class meeting began with an "experiential-personal phase" in which students learned different "centering" techniques and then spent "some moments of self-contemplation in which we might record our insights in our diaries or share our reactions with each other." The rest of the class time was the "academic phase" in which students made presentations about the "centering or coping" devices used by the characters in the works studied or by the authors of these works in their own lives.

Other versions of the course were more traditional, devoted to literary themes ("The Myth of Romantic Love"), literary tradition ("Women in Enlightenment versus *Sturm und Drang* Theater"), or genre (my own course, "The Female *Bildungsroman*"). "Twentieth-Century Women's Poetry: Themes and Images" explored the way female poets spoke "for humane values in poems of wide stylistic and thematic range." Though clearly drawing on the department's traditional literary training in its emphasis on the theme and structure of the works, it departed from convention by focusing exclusively on female poets, by giving equal attention to lesser-known poets "who deserve a wider public" (e.g., Ruth Pitter, Charlotte Mew, Leonora Speyer) as to celebrated ones (e.g., Elizabeth Bishop, Sylvia Plath, Denise Levertov), and by incorporating the local poetry scene into the curriculum (trips to women's presses and bookstores, readings by local poets, such as Alta, Susan Griffin, and Mary Norbert Körte).

The tension we felt between providing consciousness-raising and teaching literature is articulated in an unsigned document, written by a caucus member and modestly titled "Random thoughts on ... Assumptions governing the CL Women and Lit classes up to now ... (subject to change)":

> The Great Problem in teaching the course is Consciousness-Raising vs. Teaching Literature. Those who have taught the course have finally accepted their expertise in the latter, and the importance of [teaching literature], and encouraged small groups outside of class for [the] former.

The document goes on to point out, however, that one of the goals of the course is to cut down "the usual dichotomy between The Academic and The Personal ... in its own subtle, intelligent way."

The most controversial issue concerned whether to admit male students into the course, a problem that persists in Women's Studies courses today. We wanted to provide a forum where women's opinions, usually silenced in the presence of more vocal and assertive male voices, could be heard and valued, but legally, we could not exclude men. As it played out in our classrooms, this was less a philosophical or legal conflict than a pedagogical one. How could we effect consciousness-raising unless our students felt safe to speak openly? Our female students felt this problem acutely: eager to connect their personal and academic lives, they argued passionately that they could not talk about their personal lives in a coed classroom. While men rarely ventured into our courses, in a few classes, verbal warfare broke out between the men (or more often, man) and women, and I do remember hearing about one sensitive male student driven in tears from the room, while in other courses, a lone man, hostile and defensive, fired off a few rounds of sexist hate speech. Fortunately these eruptions were rare. Most of our courses attracted enthusiastic students, thrilled by the subject matter and the new approach to teaching. I was a fairly inexperienced teacher when I taught my women and literature course, and often awkward and nervous, but my students acted as if I could do no wrong. Bless their hearts.

As the courses gradually became institutionalized, the caucus evolved a set of principles that reflected our democratic, woman-centered, and collaborative objectives—as articulated in the "Random Thoughts" document:

> ...that no woman should teach the course more than once
> ...that the general orientation should be toward a reading of literature by women (rather than a discussion of the stereotypes of women in male literature)
> ...[that] women who teach the course should continue the notebook [describing previous courses]; some women have also written lengthier summaries and analyses of their classes. The latter is to be encouraged.

The Political Context

Though I was not privy to the faculty's deliberations as they approved these courses and shepherded them through university committees and into the catalog, the lack of resistance probably had to do with the increased awareness of women's issues on campus and the pressure being placed on the university, a research institution that relied heavily on government grants, to comply with federal anti-discrimination legislation. In May 1969, Berkeley's Academic Senate (the faculty's governing body, made up of tenured and tenure-track faculty members) found it "surprising that so few women—only 15 at the present time—achieve the rank of full professor at Berkeley,"[1] and appointed a committee to investigate the status of women on its campus. The committee polled department chairs, faculty members, researchers, graduate students, and former graduate students who had dropped out of school, checking their personal testimonies against university records and statistical information collected by other agencies. It concluded, in May 1970, that women faced "a large number of obstacles in obtaining recognition as members of the academic community in their own right."[2] The committee's 78-page report catalogued a broad range of discriminatory practices, among them anti-nepotism rules—which prevented wives with Ph.D.s from being hired at the same campus where their husbands worked; reluctance to tenure qualified women or promote them through academic ranks; preference awarded to men in graduate admissions, and after admission, in financial and intellectual support; crediting male colleagues for research and research reports

written by women and rewarding both of them accordingly; and substantial psychological abuse at all levels of the academic hierarchy:

> There are departments in which women students are told in seminars
> that women are unable to think objectively or analytically. There are
> departments where suggestions that women might be dissatisfied are
> met with wit and jibes or with scornful comments about aggressive
> women.... [T]he woman who tries to pursue an academic career at
> Berkeley ... is less likely to be judged on her own merits than as a
> member of a category for which there is a highly developed stereotype
> endowed with characteristics which run counter to academic
> demands. In some instances [women] are told not only that they may
> marry and drop out, but that they ought to marry and drop out; not
> only that they may follow a husband to another part of the country,
> but that custom demands that they do so; not only that they may be
> unable to pursue more than a part-time career if they have children,
> but that they must give first priority to family obligations.... Many
> women also come to accept the stereotypes about their worth and tai-
> lor their goals accordingly, or they find the barriers to professional
> success too great for the minimal rewards offered to them.[3]

The university was feeling pressure from other sources as well. Less
than two weeks after the Academic Senate published its report on the status of women, a national organization, the Women's Equity Action
League, filed a complaint against the University of California, Berkeley,
for violating federal law, Executive Orders 11246 and 11375, which forbid discrimination on the basis of sex. In December 1970, the Political
Science Department's Women's Caucus filed a complaint against the university with the U.S. Department of Health, Education, and Welfare for
violating those executive orders. In April 1971, the university's League of
Academic Women and the National Organization of Women filed a class-
action complaint against the university for the same reason. In June 1971,
the federal Office of Civil Rights initiated a review of university practice
and policies, and the following month, the Department of Health, Education, and Welfare began a "contract compliance" review. This latter
review led to considerable tension between the university and HEW; a
few weeks after beginning its work, HEW cut off new funding to the university for 24 hours for denying them access to personnel records.
Throughout the investigation, the university used delaying tactics and
HEW repeatedly threatened to suspend funding of new federal contracts
and grants. In February 1972, Berkeley's League of Academic Women
and a dozen female academic and non-academic employees filed a class-
action suit in San Francisco Federal Court, charging the University of California, Berkeley, and the president of the university system with

widespread discrimination in employment and promotion. In March, the judge who heard the case gave the university 120 days to propose a plan to remedy discrimination in employment.[4]

While the university resisted HEW's investigation, throughout the early 1970s it also made efforts to support affirmative action. In 1970, university President Charles Hitch announced a policy to initiate affirmative action programs, and a few months later, an affirmative action coordinator was named. At the same time, the university required departments to show that they were considering qualified women before making faculty appointments, and several departments undertook reports on the status of women. This was the climate in which our caucus activity took place.

Our work in the Comparative Literature Department was thus part of a larger political and consciousness-raising context in which women at all levels of the university were reconsidering their status and making demands on the institution. In 1970, the Comparative Literature Caucus helped form a Women's Caucus in Language and Literature departments, and in other fields and departments, similar groups emerged. In December 1971, female library employees filed a report with the university, making recommendations for affirmative action. In April 1972, female union members throughout campus formed the Interunion Women's Caucus (coordinated by the American Federation of State, County, and Municipal Employees) to represent their common interests. In the same month, women in the School of Education organized their caucus. A winter quarter 1973 list of Women's Studies courses shows, too, that academic departments besides ours—Anthropology, Asian Studies, Criminology, English, and Sociology—had begun to bring women's issues into the curriculum.

Activity of this sort was taking place all over the country. In 1969, the Modern Language Association, the national organization for academics studying modern languages and literatures, established a Commission on the Status of Women in the Profession. This commission reported on widespread inequity in the profession, including these findings:

> —Women constituted 55 percent of the graduate students in the modern languages, but only 8 percent of the faculty teaching them: "Though more than half of our graduate students are women, about nine out of every ten professors who teach them are likely to be men ... many of whom have internalized our culture's prejudices about women."
>
> —Men were present at all ranks of the academic hierarchy, whereas women were massed at the bottom, in the lowest-paying, least-stable positions: "The number of women at each rank declines steadily and significantly as the ranks rise."

—Women were paid substantially less than men of equivalent rank in the same department, about $1,000 less at the assistant and associate professor level, about $3,000 less for full professors.

—Female Ph.D.s were clustered in two-year colleges, and B.A.–granting institutions rather than at institutions offering graduate degrees.[5]

The commission summed up its findings this way:

> Basically, the profession has said: you may study here in our department; in fact, we want you to study with us; indeed we need you to fill our classes and sustain our department and justify our numbers. But you may not work here.[6]

Political Efforts

Shortly after the MLA Commission published its report, the Comparative Literature Women's Caucus wrote a letter to our department chairman (as he was called) and to its vice chairman (as she was called) for graduate studies, reminding them of the committee's recommendations, and—"since we have already devoted considerable energy and thought to the situation of women in the university"—offering "our services and expertise" in helping the department prepare its affirmative action plan.[7] Not surprisingly, the faculty did not embrace this offer. Nor did they respond to a letter we wrote in December 1973, to which we appended an article from the *MLA Newsletter*, written by Nancy Jo Hoffman for the Commission on the Status of Women, on sexism in letters of recommendation. The *Newsletter* had catalogued the kinds of damaging comments professors included in letters intended to recommend their students for academic jobs: praising the candidate's husband's achievements, thus implying that the candidate is merely an adornment to her husband's career; focusing on the candidate's physical appearance ("her mousiness belies a sharp mind"); overt prejudice against feminists ("[she] is no fem. lib. type, but a real gentlewoman"); and language such as "sweet," "warm," "charming," and "shy," that suggested that:

> Though the letter writer himself may clearly admire the personal, private virtues, the gentleness and the modesty he considers appropriately womanly, he himself would never designate these qualifies as befitting the public dignified role of college professor.[8]

Despite these supportive documents from the MLA, which was surely the most credible authority (from the faculty's viewpoint) in the profession, and despite all the affirmative action work taking place on campus, as graduate students in a traditional department (the graduate program had been based on a longstanding European model), we felt vulnerable. And we were frustrated, aware that, for the most part, the faculty in charge of our education and positioned to affect our careers did not take us seriously as scholars. While they had given us freedom to design and teach women and literature courses, sexist attitudes in the department were far harder to address. In fact, as students, we had little power.

In 1976, however, we were invited to speak out—by Berkeley's vice chancellor Ira Michael Heyman. Federal law—specifically, Title IX of the Education Amendments of 1972—required the university to undertake a self-evaluation in order to uncover and correct possible sexist practices. For the first time that we were aware of, the principal concern of affirmative action was not faculty and staff, but students. As each academic department conducted its own self-evaluation, it was advised by the vice chancellor to include "student input": "It is essential that students participate, since the treatment of students is the specific focus of this self-evaluation."[9]

So it was that the Comparative Literature Women's Caucus met, discussed its concerns, and presented them in a letter addressed to the vice chancellor (see Appendix). We noted that while most of the undergraduate (73 percent) and graduate (67 percent) students were women, an equal number (three men, three women) received doctorates in the year under review, a shift in proportion that suggested subtle and not-so-subtle sex discrimination:

> —A lack of female faculty mentors. In 1976, only two of the twenty-four tenured faculty members were women. The ratio of male to female faculty members overall was three to one, and the department was continuing to hire more men than women.
> —A failure to take Women's Studies and Literature seriously as a discipline. Students working in this area reported that their professors did not regard Women's Studies as a legitimate academic field. Nor did the department attempt to recruit faculty members specializing in this area.

In addition to recommending that the department correct these problems (and that it offer the required graduate introductory course during the day rather than at night, so that female students could get to it safely), the letter faulted the department for tolerating "ritualized ... undermining of the female student's self confidence ... through sexist jokes and comments," several of which we itemized:

[1] One woman was told on her Ph.D. exams that she "thought like a woman," while another faculty member on the same exam told the woman she "thought like a man." Both comments were intended as criticisms, the first meaning that the woman was insufficiently logical and rational, the second meaning just the opposite, but adding the implication that she was not "womanly" enough.

[2] Another woman was greeted by the chairman of her master of arts oral exam with the comment, "Would you like to sit in that empty chair there or in Mr. _____'s lap?"

[3] One woman reports that before her M.A. oral exam a male professor said to her: "My dear young lady, you overestimate your abilities. You are overambitious." She was so demoralized that she temporarily withdrew from the university. She is now a Ph.D. and a literature professor.

[4] Several female graduate students commented that faculty joke about women's appearance and clothing.

[5] Several women reported that faculty used words with sexist bias to evaluate their exams or dissertation research ... such statements as "she's a charming girl, but...."

[6] A female graduate student, consulting her male advisor, reported the following interchange. When she went to his office, he greeted her with "I'd kiss you, but I have a cold." He then saw a male colleague passing his door, and called out to him loudly, "I'd kiss her, but I have a cold."

While we recognized that most of these comments were meant to be innocuously funny, we also saw what few of us would have noticed before the feminist movement: that underneath the stance of counseling ("You are overambitious") or banter ("I'd kiss you, but I have a cold") was a belittling message for someone devoting eight to ten years of her life to graduate study: as a woman, she would never be a scholar.

If the letter made a difference in professors' relationships to their female students, I couldn't tell. In fact, I'm not sure we accomplished more than irritating the department chair. As chair of the Women's Caucus that year, it was my job to deliver the Caucus' letter to the department chair, and though I no longer remember the conversation we had, I clearly remember my chilly reception. Not surprisingly, the department chair did not appreciate seeing her department maligned, and though the letter made its way to the vice chancellor, it's hard to know if it had an impact. The Women's Caucus continued to meet, but the letter was the last political effort I know of. In the department, we functioned better as students and scholars than as political agitators. After that, we existed largely for the women and literature course, and as a social group, offering the support and mentoring that the department doled out so sparingly.

Reading and Learning

If our political efforts were limited, our intellectual ones were expansive. Together we discovered the feminist texts just being published: the inaugural issue of *Ms.* magazine, Phyllis Chesler's *Women and Madness*, Eva Figes' *Patriarchal Attitudes*, Robin Morgan's *Sisterhood is Powerful*, Vivian Gornick and Barbara K. Moran's *Woman in Sexist Society*, and a few dozen others, which are still on my bookshelf. We were also reading literature in a new way. We were a generation of literary critics trained in the 1930s "new" criticism, which had downplayed social context in favor of the structure and language of literary works. I had learned to explore a text as an artifact, but the historical background had always interested me, and now I could indulge that interest, analyzing male and female characters as products of patriarchal societies, both those described and those lived by their authors. And we were discovering that the literary canon we had devoted so much of our lives to exploring was not just male. As dutiful students, most of us had simply accepted the assumption underlying years of academic study in literature: every course syllabus, reading list, anthology of literature, by ignoring women's work, sent the message that all the great thinkers and writers in the world were men. It was a revelation to read wonderful female authors we had never even heard of before—Sylvia Plath, Gwendolyn Brooks, Muriel Rukeyser, Doris Lessing, Zora Neale Hurston, Tillie Olsen—and to learn to value the uniquely female experiences they often wrote about.

What made this enterprise so engaging is that it was not only intellectually rich, but it also touched us personally. As women, we identified powerfully with much of what we discovered in these works, literary and nonliterary: they spoke to our lives. Many of us were inspired to write feminist dissertations, exploring female writers or characters. Mine, "The Romantic Woman in Nineteenth-Century Fiction: A Comparative Study of *Madame Bovary, La Regenta, The Mill on the Floss,* and *The Awakening*," argued that the constricted social position of the heroines of these novels encouraged them to find joy in a fantasy world and then prevented them from realizing their fantasies; and that the limitations in real nineteenth century women's lives created problems like those of romantic individuals of both sexes, struggling with an unromantic world. My understanding of these works was very much a product of 1960s and early 1970s feminism, with its emphasis on female identity and social roles, especially those of middle-class white women.

In Sisterhood

The Women's Caucus provided emotional and intellectual support as we wrote these dissertations and, in fact, throughout the entire graduate program. If the professorate was remote and unhelpful (it was for me), my peers cheered each other along, reading drafts of one another's dissertations, and sharing reading lists, department lore, and advice on the sequences of exams. The written exams, at both the master's and doctoral levels, went on all day for a week; the oral exams at various stages (there were four), an hour and a half to three hours. It didn't take much for panic and despair to set in—in my case, when all the nineteenth century Spanish plays I had read so meticulously and often began to smudge together in my mind along with their female protagonists, all of whom seemed to be named Emilia. Melanie Kaye Persoff coached me on my master's exams. We sat on the pine needles in her backyard, and her calm words carried me through that and all subsequent exams: "You won't remember everything," she said of the hundreds of works of literature I was responsible for knowing in critical detail, "but you'll remember all you need to know." She was right. I quoted her for several years afterwards, to colleagues who entered the program after I did.

Marsha Hudson organized us, stirred us up, and gave us confidence, urging us to trust our abilities as writers, literary critics, and department gadflies. As a group, we shared knowledge, exhorted one another to finish what seemed to be an endless program, and commiserated with one another's frustrations. We weren't a perfect sisterhood, if there is such a thing; sometimes confidences meant to stay within the group spilled outside it—one woman's abortion, another's fling with a professor—but for the most part, we provided sisterly support in our enclave of the world. In doing so, we built a little piece of the feminist movement that was developing rapidly across the country and helped extend the work the women's rights activists began a century and a half ago. Far from fussy ladies in fussy clothes, these were our powerful, courageous foremothers. And they were our sisters, too.

11

"Uppity Women": At the Heart of Contradiction

Deirdre Lashgari

As I listen for voices from almost thirty years ago, the image that emerges—felt as much as seen—is of a group of women crowded together on someone's living-room floor, sitting on pillows. There is a keen energy in the air, a sense of urgency, an awareness that—as Marsha's "Uppity Woman!" button proclaims—we are not here to take in, passively, someone else's formulations. What we're setting out to do is more ambitious: to construct together a new understanding of issues and definition of goals that will make a difference in our lives and the world. We've each brought something for the potluck of food and drink in the kitchen that will sustain us for as long as the discussion takes.

The Women's Caucus itself came together as a kind of potluck—an unlikely assortment of different, often clashing, ingredients that when brought together somehow produced extraordinary nourishment. We shared the fact that we were students—graduate students mostly—in a complex and relatively new department. We came not only from a wide array of academic fields, but also from diverse socio-economic contexts and individual backgrounds. We differed in our personalities, expectations, and snapping points. We often disagreed, sometimes bitterly but most often in that spirit of creative conflict that, as Audre Lorde reminds us, produces the spark of transformation. These differences were the strength of the caucus, as of the women's movement as a whole.

Here, as I retrace my own experience, what I most want to look at is the way the women's movement, funneled for me largely through the Comp. Lit. Women's Caucus, both derailed my life and profoundly empowered it. Contradiction's at the heart of it. Contradiction marking a crossroads, an intersecting of contraries. A fructifying reminder of other directions, other possibilities. As Walt Whitman said (and one of you sisters quoted to me when I needed it), "I contradict myself? Well—so I contradict myself."

There were conflicts and contradictions aplenty within the women's movement, each of us contributing some. The clashing selves I carried with me into the ferment of the caucus included political activist as well as translator of Iranian literature; a self-identified nonconformist who strove to mold myself into the "good Iranian woman"; would-be medical doctor who chose literature because it was—for me—the "harder path"; the "good" student, shackled by the praise I got for doing well in school; the daughter of a dedicated world-lit professor father and a mother forced by the gender ideology of the early '40s to quit her loved graduate work in English when she was pregnant with me.

I was already a feminist of sorts as a child, drawn to mud and bikes and playing "intrepid explorer" in the woods by our house. From the beginning, my parents provided a fairly gender-neutral environment for my two younger brothers and me, insisting on shared household chores, whether dishes and dusting or mowing and weeding. We each got presents of dolls and weaving sets as well as hammers and saws and softballs. But all this was no defense against the invisible gender socialization I got in school. I remember well the vivacious young, just-married woman who taught 7th grade social adjustment class warning us girls (the boys had required shop instead): "If you want the boys to like you, never let on that you're smart; just get them to talk about themselves." Later, in college, after years of programs in English, French, and Farsi, studying literature written almost entirely by men, under male professors who taught us all to read *as if* we were men, it never occurred to me that there was anything seriously amiss. The first overtly feminist (and, I felt then, "unprofessional") rumblings among women classmates in the Comp. Lit. grad program embarrassed me. I had to be prodded, feet dragging, to join their efforts to undo the department's patriarchal stranglehold.

Some of them may have attributed my hesitation to my long marriage to an Iranian husband. On the contrary, it was Parviz—writer, activist, restaurant worker—who got me into the university in the first place. While I was counting beans at an insurance company in Los Angeles, he discovered that UC Berkeley was a good place for pursuing my interest in Iranian literature, investigated admissions policies and financial aid, and dug up an obscure scholarship to get me started. He also gave me the continuing sustenance and courage to stick with it. At the same time, he was pulled between his conscious commitment to equality and an ingrained gender socialization to take the lead. As a result, the marriage created a triple bind in which I tried to be not only the "perfect Iranian woman," but also a writer-philosopher-teacher Iranian Simone de Beauvoir to his Jean-Paul Sartre.

And then there's the influence of my mother, with whom I fought furiously through much of my growing up and whom I later, as new feminist convert, tried to see as the "mere housewife" victim of a patriarchal world. The fact was, she had given me much of my feminist backbone from childhood on—along with an entrenched and contradictory self-doubt. When I made a brief visit back home in summer of 1972, I discovered—to my surprise—a feisty closet feminist with a breathtaking range of reading that made me eager to learn at her feet.

In addition, there were contradictions between my political activism of the '60s and early '70s, focused on large-scale structural problems like war and racism, and the more "self-centered" personal and interpersonal focus of feminism's early consciousness-raising and support groups. And yet even then, of course, the global and the local were inseparable, the personal was—as we said—political. The sense of voiceless and marginalization with which we struggled was profoundly connected to the persistent dysfunctionality of society, from the Pentagon to our Comp. Lit. doctoral exams.

All these contradictions played a part in my involvement with the caucus and its many spinoffs. They also had a lot to do with the decade and a half it took me to finish my dissertation, which—wouldn't you know it—was the literary reflection of social forces that undermine or empower female subjectivity.

But I'm getting ahead of myself. As I said, I might never have been in the Comp. Lit. grad program in 1970, much less teaching now, without the influence of my "Iranian connection." The love of Iranian literature, classical and modern, that I got from Parviz fed my desire to learn the language. My progress led me from the Iranian equivalent of the Dick and Jane books to conversation immersion (when Parviz's younger brother and sister lived with us for three years in our tiny Berkeley apartment), then to a master's degree in Near Eastern Studies and a research Fulbright in Iran. There I turned the tables, living with Parviz's large family in tight quarters in a working-class district of Tehran.

Through much of the sixties, dreaming of bridging what we saw as the dangerous cultural gulf between Iran and the U.S., Parviz and I translated volumes of poetry, short stories, a novel. After our day job or classes, we stayed up translating late into the night, he doing the rough Farsi to English, and I working to make the English more solid. One major problem: my lack of confidence in both Farsi and English blocked my ability to make the leap out of academic prose into a lively literary language adequate to the original. Though our production was massive, the work we accomplished seemed to me never "quite there," never strong enough for me to dare to subject it to a critical public gaze. Until, that is, those exhilarating translation workshops the caucus spawned ... but more on that in a bit.

It's significant that my reluctant entry into what became the Women's Caucus followed close on my return to the U.S. from a Fulbright year in Iran, theoretically immersed in pre-dissertation research on "Western and Folk Influences on Modern Iranian Poetry," but primarily just immersed in "being Iranian." Living there with Parviz's family, I was surrounded by strong women. As we sat drinking afternoon tea around the samovar, Maman would tell stories of her life—her precious two years of school-ing, her defiant rejection at age 12 of an arranged marriage to an older man, the daily heroisms of a village woman's world. My sisters-in-law taught me tough feminist self-protection on the crowded, at times macho, streets of Tehran. They bought me a stiff, sharp-angled purse and showed me how to wield it, how to identify likely harassers by reading their faces, and how to make serious "I've got your number" eye contact as I shifted the purse in my hand.

I learned the paradoxes of gendered dress codes from the young girls and women in our neighborhood. In the wealthier districts, women dressed Western style, whatever that happened to be at the moment. In the most traditional bazaar district in the south of Tehran, women covered them-selves in public with black full-length veils, or chadors. But where we lived—poor but only semi-traditional—a hybrid code prevailed. Houses here didn't have the Western innovation of chairs and tables. Since meals and conversation took place sitting cross-legged on the carpet, girls and women wore the traditional home-wear of slacks and blouses. If, dressed in slacks, they ran out to the corner store for yoghurt or onions, tradition demanded a chador. On the other hand, professionals on their way to the office, or school-girls wearing their required Western-style uniforms, were judged by 1969 Western standards: "mini-skirts above the knee okay." My ironic, self-taught sociologist of a father-in-law found the contradiction both delicious and disturbing.

My other close influences were in Shemiran, on the opposite side of town, where Jalal (Parviz's high-school teacher and mentor) and his wife, Simin, took me under their wing, including me in their weekly gather-ings of writers and teachers. Some months later, one of their friends offered me a teaching job at the University of Tehran—freshman English (with sketchily prepared, but eager and dedicated, young students from the boondocks) and a senior-level European drama class (filled mostly with blasé government employees climbing the pay scale). The experience was invaluable, giving me a chance to know students and colleagues from a broad range of class, ethnic, and cultural backgrounds. It also, three years later in Berkeley, helped me get a position as instructor in Comparative Literature.

The Berkeley home I returned to in early 1970 was in many ways Iranian as well. Several years before, Parviz and I had opened a small Iranian import store we called The Persian Caravan. In addition to supplementing my meager income (scholarships plus typing and child-care jobs, and later, part-time grad student teaching), it provided furnishings for our small apartment, one of three carved out of what had, a hundred years before, been a farmhouse. The living room and bedroom were decked with handmade fabrics—huge, modern block-print bedspreads hanging from the ceilings, classical paintings and antique block-prints in deep reds and blues on the walls, and inexpensive carpets on the floors where we ate or read or talked. And, most important, the always-present bowls of fruit and nuts were waiting, Iranian-style, on the front coffee table to welcome unexpected guests. When we cooked—Parviz taking the role of head chef, as Woody does now—it was huge pots of rice and Iranian stews, enough to feed any impromptu gathering of friends.

This was where I met with Women's Caucus cohorts, and later, groups of students from my first Comp. Lit. classes. Women I worked with in the poetry translation workshops hung out with me here, as well as co-editors on the two poetry anthology projects, the Fairy Tale Group, and various incarnations of the eight-year-long dream group. It was also a meeting place for colleagues in the anti-war movement and early dissertation groups in the '70s. Later, my anti-nuclear affinity group, the Quantum Mechanics, met there to prepare for our part in blockading the UC-managed Livermore Nuclear Weapons Lab; and, after our two weeks in county "jail" (it took a converted warehouse and two huge tents to hold the 500 of us), the Women's Jailbook Collective met there to document the anxieties, exhilaration, conflict-solving, humor, and mutual learning that took place in the innovative women's peace camp we had created there.

If the living room was the main place for communal gatherings, the huge 12-foot-square kitchen was my study—books and papers and typewriter spread out over the table and floors. For the most part, I loved studying (a few over-my-head general ed classes like "Intro to Astronomy" notwithstanding). By the time I had gotten my master's in English, though, I felt fairly alienated from the department. My most inspiring professor had been denied tenure—as I heard it, for treating his students, grads and first-year comp students alike, as colleagues in learning and research. Other English grad students complained that professors wouldn't share their work in progress, even with colleagues, for fear someone might "steal" it, and then they adopted the same mistrustful, self-isolating attitude themselves.

I had left English for the doctoral program in Comparative Literature partly so I could do a second M.A. in Iranian Studies, but also because I had had it with hard-edged competitiveness and lack of community. It didn't occur to me that being a woman in a male-centered program might have had anything to do with it. At the time, there was only one woman professor among several dozen men in English, the poet Jo Miles. (She had for some time been badly crippled with rheumatoid arthritis. Years later, when a friend asked her what it had felt like being the only woman in the department, she said, "Oh, they regarded me as a neuter, not a woman.")

I was first introduced to a feminist approach to literature by women more alert than I was to what had been shut out of our education. When women in Comparative Literature pointed out that none of our seminars dealt with women writers, my initial reaction was puzzlement and discomfort. While I was away in Iran, Marsha, Doris, and several other women in the department had organized unofficial off-campus classes focusing on women writers. After my return to Berkeley and the horror of Nixon's bombing of Cambodia that spring, my time and attention were consumed working with thousands of other students to "reconstitute" the university—turning regular classes into mini teach-ins on the war. By the next fall, the regular curriculum had resumed. When Doris protested the exclusive focus on male poets in a translation class she was taking in the English Department, the visiting poet-translator summarily closed the discussion with "Women don't write poetry; women make babies." Her outraged response: to organize collaborative translation workshops on women poets, eventually including dozens of translators on and off campus. These exhilarating gatherings finally got my own translations out of the closet into a supportive environment where they could begin to breathe.

By spring, I had gone underground again. My main contacts with campus now were two study groups designed to help us prepare each other for the daunting Ph.D. qualifying exams. Both groups crossed disciplines, including members from English and French as well as Comp. Lit. The requirements for Comp. Lit. were clearly the harshest. The founding professor had been determined to justify our new program by proving that our grads could out-perform grads in any of the other literature departments. As a result, what we were asked to do was patently impossible. In my case, with English as my major subject area and French and Farsi as my minor areas, I was required to know (1) "everything that had been written from the beginning to the present" (i.e., from *Beowulf* on), plus "everything written about everything that was written"; and (2) "everything written and all criticism in the 150 years of each secondary literature" (i.e., from 1820 to 1970 in Farsi and in French). I survived, as did most of the others. But among those of us in Comp. Lit., anger was building. After our exams in the fall, energized in part by the massive anti-war organizing of the spring, a number of us formed a Graduate Student Association that eventually succeeded in pushing reforms that made the requirements saner and more precise.

Meanwhile, Doris had for some time been trying to persuade other women in the translation workshops to take the next step and publish an anthology of the women poets we had translated. At a large reading by workshop members and friends, she put out a call for a first editors meeting, to take place at her house on January 2, 1972. I went, feeling both excitement and trepidation at what I might be getting into — on top of my first year of teaching as a graduate student instructor in the department (supposedly part-time, but actually more than full-time), plus my (supposed) preparation for choosing a thesis topic. Had I but known — it would be four more years before our first, 20th century, volume appeared, and another five before we saw the fruition of our original project, poetry by women from 2300 BCE to the present with accompanying historical essays.

I don't recall when the Women's Caucus formally organized. My first meeting, I think, was some time that spring of 1972. Concerns had moved from Ph.D. exams to the courses we were being offered, limited almost exclusively — once again — to writing by male authors. The women who had been meeting off campus to study women writers were outraged at the implication that "if there were important women writers, they'd be taught," and were ready to push for courses specifically on women writers. The chair at the time, Blake Spahr, was reputed to be starchily traditional, and we didn't expect much sympathy. We were determined, though, not to water down what we wanted. In May 1972, we went to him with a full package of demands:

(a) the addition to the permanent curriculum of a 4-quarter (non-sequential) lower-division series of courses entitled "Women and Literature"; students to be allowed to take any or all in the series; one course to be taught each quarter of the year;

(b) the instructor to be a woman graduate student in the department, who would be chosen, based on her course proposal, by a vote of the Comp. Lit. Women's Caucus;

(c) the focus to vary depending on the course proposal chosen; plus

(d) one upper division course on a specific woman author or specialized topic, to be taught once a year either by a grad student or by a qualified, to-be-hired woman professor; and

(e) hiring of additional women faculty in the department, with input and veto power by the Women's Caucus. (At that time, there were only two women in a department of around 14, neither of them specialists in literature by women.)

To our surprise, the chair accepted the core of our proposal. (He did insist that the caucus could only "recommend" instructors; but he gave us oral assurance that our recommendations would probably be accepted by the department. As far as the hiring of women professors went, he "welcomed" our help in reading candidates' publications, but said any other involvement on our part would violate campus rules.) His closing bombshell was, "Can you start teaching the lower-division course this summer?"

We left, breathless and exhilarated. The first course was to be added to the department schedule of classes for summer, a month away. We called an initial meeting of the caucus, and asked for volunteers to teach the lower-division Women and Lit. course in its crucial first year. Melanie Persoff (now Melanie Kaye/Kantrowitz) was selected for the summer class, Marsha Hudson agreed to do fall, I was asked to do winter, and Diane Levitin had spring.

There was a continuing pedagogical genealogy involved here, a matrilineage for the most part, as women students and teachers passed on significant texts and strategies for learning. In planning my class, I had a number of influences to draw on. When I had begun teaching the required freshman comp course the year before, my first teaching assistant had been Diane Levitin, who had previously been Melanie Kaye Persoff's teaching assistant, who had in turn been J.J. Wilson's. Much of what I learned about the sense of community and shared discovery that best nurture learning came from this lineage. I had also just discovered the work of educators like Postman and Weingartner and Peter Elbow, with their emphasis on student-directed and collaborative learning, discussion rather than lectures, and the use of small peer groups. In summer of 1972, new to feminism and in a quandary as to where to start in preparing to teach the new course, I found unexpected support from my "housewife" mother, who gave me lists of women authors she urged me to read, from Olive Schreiner and Southern slave narratives to the novels of Willa Cather.

Most important, between fall and winter quarters, women students from the first two classes met with me to contribute ideas for both content and structure. This continuity (which we had built into the program from the beginning by assuring that students could take any or all of the courses in the sequence) was crucial to the success of the courses. It served as a catalyst for community in each new class, provided a core understanding of issues and collective process, and transmitted developing traditions (potlucks, small research groups separate from the large-group meetings, end-of-course anthologies).

The focus of the winter course was women's experience of being silenced and finding voice. We worked from diverse genres, from autobiography, essay, and "dream" to fiction and poetry. Tillie Olsen read "Tell Me a Riddle" aloud to the class, and infused students with her sense of the urgency in women's task of setting their experiences to paper. Poets Mary Mackey and Joanna Griffin read from their work, providing inspiration for an outpouring of strong poetry by the students, some of it in direct response to the readings. We dealt with issues of poverty, race, and literacy in Brazilian writer Carolina de Jesus's autobiographical *Child of the Dark* and the Indian novel *Nectar in a Sieve* by Kamala Markandaya. And we read contemporary poetry that came to epitomize our shared task in the course of self-naming: Marge Piercy, Adrienne Rich, Mari Evans, Nikki Giovanni, Sexton, Levertov, and Plath.

One of the things students in the class helped me learn was to trust our ability to identify and solve problems together—in fact, to trust that it was in the shared solving of problems that we all learned the most. One problem was a class and racial imbalance among the students, who were predominately white, young, and middle-class. The one black woman in the class resented having to be the one to point out issues of race and class, and insisted that others share that responsibility. Following her critique, she and four other women formed a group that did reading and research culminating in a class presentation on contemporary black women poets. Lesbian women, also concerned that their experiences were not reflected in the class readings, formed their own focus group and did a presentation including autobiography and poetry.

I recall vividly an experience early in the class that had strong impact on me, and set the tone for the rest of the quarter. Thirty-five students and I were sitting in a circle on the carpeted floor of the campus ecumenical center, our assigned "classroom," discussing Chopin's *The Awakening*. We had had a lively discussion the meeting before, but this one was dragging. A handful of articulate and outspoken women, all strong feminists, were doing most of the talking. I tried to get others involved, to no avail. Then one woman said, hesitantly, "I have the feeling that there's an orthodox line in here that we're all supposed to be following, but I'm not sure what it is—and I don't think I'd fit it anyway." When she finished, an audible sigh of relief spread through the group. Others spoke up, saying they had each thought they were the only ones who didn't know something everyone else knew. Now that they knew they weren't alone, they felt free to speak. Out of that discussion came a renewed commitment to affirm the diversity of views and experiences among us, to value our differences and disagreements. Students also agreed to speak out when they were most afraid their questions might be "stupid" or their ideas "off the wall," knowing now that it was difference, not uniformity, that made for the most powerful learning. And when they sensed an incipient orthodoxy in the air again, they would make a point of seeking out the "other voice," even if it meant taking a devil's advocate position themselves.

Other problems arose, were defined (often by the students), and solved collectively. I learned to value rather than feel dismayed at student rebellions, to see them as the surest sign of real learning. Together we negotiated the delicate dance between text and personal context, and between the twin "tyrannies" of rigid structure and loose structurelessness. At the beginning of the course, we had conducted a meta-analysis of the role of grading in the learning process, with students pointing out the way the sense of powerlessness involved in being graded worked against trust and community and shared discovery. I agreed, with initial reluctance, to let students contract for grades: a certain number of acceptable projects (written, visual, or oral) for a given grade. Increasingly, we built into class meetings an ongoing discussion of process—how we felt about what we were doing, and how we could make it work better.

The students taught me a lot—reinforcing my commitment to non-hierarchical learning, questioning assumptions and "unspoken orthodoxies," and showing me the extraordinary energy and commitment that could be unleashed when the class was genuinely open to student shaping (as in the student-selected research groups that met outside the classroom). The groups developed such closeness and mutual commitment in the process of discussion and shared research that most of them were unwilling to disband at the end of the course. The "Dreams and Madness" group, which I took part in, continued for the next year and a half as a dream group, sharing, interpreting together, and riffing from dreams to gendered experience in the world. The group eventually outlived its original membership—losing some, taking on new people, but retaining its energy until the early '80s.

Much of what we did then has become a widely accepted part of contemporary teaching, no longer "innovative": collaborative learning, use of small peer groups, discussion rather than lecturing, anthologies of student writing. However, much has changed in less congenial ways since the early '70s, on campus and off. Not long before our first CL40 courses, Reagan as governor boasted of the brilliant solution he had found to the problem of student protests and activism: to hike the cost of education, so students would either have to have rich parents or spend all their nonstudy time working to pay for school. I think of his strategy now, as I teach students who struggle with multiple jobs, family, and an impossibly heavy course load.

Since the '70s, support for education has continued to diminish as a national priority, along with student financial aid. Despite a recent period of economic boom for those at the top, the national economy is generally much more precarious today. On the state university campus where I teach, student priorities tend toward "doing the right thing" professionally, rather than "finding themselves" or making a difference in the world. Students seem less willing to take risks, more anxious about grades and "getting it right." This anxiety plays itself out for many working-class students, paradoxically, as a reenactment of the Horatio Alger myth, a desperate conviction that there is no real discrimination against women or people of color, that anyone can make it to the top—by themselves—if they just try hard enough, keep their noses clean, and don't let themselves be distracted by "irrelevant" issues.

The student-centered approach that was so exhilarating in our early courses requires a level of risk and personal responsibility that's hard for many students now. That hunger for self-definition, that collective urgency about "diving into the wreck" to discover what can be salvaged, seems overlaid now with a cautious, and isolating, self-preservation. It's hard to imagine women students today confronting entrenched sexism with the outrageous gutsiness of the three Berkeley women in 1971 who turned tables on the catcalling men outside The Forum Café on Telegraph Avenue. Tired of running the men's macho gauntlet on their way home from campus, the women decided to provide some guerrilla theater consciousness-raising. One afternoon, they arrived at the Forum before the harassing men got there. Whenever a lone man walked by, they called out "Ooo baby, swing those balls!" The men invariably looked around in terror, then broke into a run. Awareness clicked, in victims and audience alike. Word must have gotten out, because the catcalling men called off their act. Today, though, my women students are more likely to excuse, or just put up with, individual or institutional sexism. It's not simply that they lack courage. Society has changed—economic survival now seems more uncertain; and the tightly corporatized media mocks the possibility of rebellion, or dissent.

In today's more constricting context, I've found it hard to balance what I know about the liberating effect of community and the realities of a working-class commuter campus, which make potlucks, out-of-class meetings, and extra projects hard to manage. Especially with today's administrative demand that we quantify faculty labor and student learning, it's harder for teachers to balance assigned academic writing with personal and creative writing, or transmission of information and skills with a focus on experiential learning and student involvement. Now, when I ask students to evaluate the class in mid-course, envisioning ways it could work better for them, they often call for a return to the old, comfortable top-down mode, where the teacher tells the students what's what, and their job is to digest it. Or perhaps I too have changed and become cautious, so that I fail to model the risk-taking essential to the kind of collaborative discovery we experienced in those early courses designed by the Comp. Lit. Women's Caucus.

This project, this collecting of experiences in and from the caucus, holds particular significance for me now. It forces me to look for patterns, meanings, in what we did and didn't do, giving me a chance to recapture the voice and power I've lost and to celebrate what I've managed to keep. My best work in the years since the caucus has continued to come from the margins—feminist, anti-racist, postcolonial. My old problems with confidence and daring remain—in teaching, writing, speaking, dancing, the whole thing. The boogey-woman of "I'm not/it's not/it won't be good enough." A key seems to lie in that central feminist crux, the pull between community and the necessary lone journey through fear—the conflict that lay at the heart of my long-gestating dissertation. Communal support provides the necessary inspiration and occasional slap upside the head that make the individual journey possible. In the past, I had a connection with clusters of uppity women who kept calling me back to my strength. Now that's largely missing, a casualty of constant fatigue and more "to do's" than I can ever get done. Or maybe it's that I've been seduced into privileging institutional demands on my time and spirit over the call of potential comrades and sisters.

The re-gathering of the Women's Caucus at Bridget's house in January of 1999 carved out crucial space in which I can begin to trace patterns in the threads of my own experience. Recalling what we were and did back then calls me to invent new ways of seeing, being, acting now. Paradoxically, seeing that time also allows me to let it go. I want to be able to welcome today's students and issues, today's entrenched problems and potentially transformative conflicts, on their own terms—ready to learn from them, with them, anew, carrying with me the vision and daring and power of the past.

In the broader arena, new social movements emerging over the past seemingly quiescent decade have finally come into public view, from Seattle to Washington, D.C., Philadelphia to Los Angeles. Students throughout the world have joined in organizing on a plethora of interconnected issues, including human rights, sweatshops, environmental degradation, racism in the justice system, and corporate control of media and politics. This time, women's rights and feminist process seem to be an integral part of the struggle.

In Los Angeles, I had the chance to take part, actively and as witness, in the demonstrations and marches and creative street theater surrounding the 2000 Democratic Convention. These actions, led collectively with such wisdom and egalitarian commitment and humor and courage by today's generation of young women and men, undo my easy pessimism about self-centered conformism and passivity. They aren't simply redoing what we invented, as we weren't inventing out of thin air in the first place. They and allies across the globe, across generations and cultures and classes, are using the "sparks of creative conflict" to create something beyond what any of us can yet see. I wish them well. I wish us well. To share the journey, I'll need to shoulder my own contradictions and reclaim the spirit of the caucus, the collective Uppity Woman.

From Student to Teacher, from Teacher to Student: A Pedagogical Matrilineage

Lauren Coodley

As an undergraduate student at Berkeley, I participated in each of the first four courses established by members of the Comparative Literature Women's Caucus, initially as a student in Melanie's class, then as a co-creator and collaborator with Deirdre Lashgari, and finally with J.J. Wilson as an official undergraduate teaching assistant, or tutor. The early Comp. Lit. 40 teachers envisioned and taught the course in a kind of "matrilineage of creation as women students and teachers passed on significant texts and strategies for learning." We created course materials, structures, and methods in a process by which students and teachers participated in each others' learning. Although I had always loved reading books on my own, that first section of "Women in Literature" in summer of 1972 gave me my first experience discussing literature with other students. And from the sheer exhilaration of its discoveries, I went on to make a career as a community college teacher of Women's Studies (as well as psychology and later history).

I had been alienated from education before I went to the University of California at Berkeley in 1968. In high school, I suffered the stigma of being intelligent and letting it show. Like so many women at that time, I came to college for social rather than professional reasons. I found the courses I was offered stultifying and irrelevant. In one psychology class, the professor lectured from a book he had written years before. I took a course in the sociology of women in 1969, expecting more and getting the same: standard fare, taught by a woman professor in the standard way, with the teacher as expert and students as passive receptacles. There were no positive female role models in my field, and I had no chance to make connections with other women students. That same year, when I was given a multiple choice final in an lower-division English class on Shakespeare, I dropped out of school and drifted into low-paid and marginal employment.

I might never have returned to college, had it not been for two crucial influences. First, an exceptional woman, J.J. Wilson, had been my teacher for freshman composition during my year at Berkeley; she introduced me to Virginia Woolf, and showed me that literature could have meaning in my life. Second, some of the women I came to know (through the men in our lives) began meeting as a women's group, discussing relationships, self-image, and what we really wanted from our lives. With their encouragement, I decided to return to school to become a naturalist in the new program in Conservation and Natural Resources in 1972.

Soon after my return to campus, I looked up Melanie Kaye, the woman who had been J.J.'s teaching assistant, and learned from her about the new comparative literature course on women in literature. Immediately, I became involved.

In that first Comp. Lit. 40 class, the one Melanie taught in the summer of 1972, some other women and I made a film which brought together what the course texts had taught us about how we saw ourselves as women—the disabling patriarchal images we had swallowed, as well as images we were only beginning to create. The film represented our 1972 student attempt to throw off male images of women and find our own. That first class was predominately white and middle-class; in making the film, we generalized naively from our own experiences to "all women."

None of the women in these classes were mothers; all of us were daughters seeking—in the works we read, in the example of women writers, and in our teachers—models who seemed to us more honest than many of our own mothers had been. In our discussions, examining the texts for multiple levels of meaning, we found inspiration and guidance that we needed in living our lives. In our teachers, we found role models, proof that one could live as an intellectual creative woman, contrary to all we had been taught. We saw women, only ten years older than ourselves, who were challenging the assumptions of their discipline. They opened up their houses to students, meeting outside the institutional setting. And they shared with us the intellectual excitement, the detective thrill, of unearthing and examining new texts and ideas.

The second class, taught by Deirdre Lashgari in winter 1973, produced an anthology of writings; for it, I described the film and what was involved in the process of embodying our group visions in the film we gave the title "Reflections." And I showed it in subsequent sections of the course. In 1999, at a meeting of the Women's Association of Western Historians, Deirdre Lashgari and I showed the film and reflected seventeen years later on its successes and failures.

Reflecting today on *Reflections*, I see a film that could only have been made possible by the imagination and vigor of the graduate student women in Comparative Literature at Berkeley, who were my teachers in the early seventies; I find an untouched photograph of who we—students and teachers—once were. It takes me back: It is 1972 and I can recall screening our student-made film for the first time in our Women in Literature class. After weeks of sleeping and eating to the songs we'd chosen, days of arguing, culling out images and choosing quotes—finally, the thing was done: 16 minutes of words and images, spliced to a sound track of Joni Mitchel, Buffy St. Marie, Janis Joplin. We had no book of art by women available, so we selected images of women made by male artists to accompany the words we chose from women poets, writers, and feminist thinkers like Robin Morgan in *Sisterhood is Powerful* and Vivian Gornick in *Women in a Sexist Society*. When the credits flickered, the room exploded into applause. We were all stunned by what we accomplished. We had hardly ever seen a film made by women.

Now it is 1999. And I am concluding my class on twentieth century history of women, the class I first developed in 1976 and have been teaching at the same California community college ever since. I am trying to help my students imagine what it was like to be part of the rebirth of feminism some thirty years ago. As the video production of *Reflections* rolls across the large screen of the lecture room, the room is silent. The students hear the voices of young women their own age. The realization shakes them: *they were just like us.* Our student voices reach them across the decades and the words we speak are very similar to the ones these students expressed this semester at Napa College in 1999. The parallel is inescapable: *feminism was recreated 30 years ago by women like me; and it could be about my most secret griefs and fears.*

The questions posed in the 1972 film are eerily resonant for my students. As working class young women, they have no expectations of careers in medicine or law or engineering. They hope, simply, for four years of college before pregnancy or the need for family income sweeps them away from their education. Overwhelmingly, when these young women picture feminists, they imagine women like me: white and middle-aged. In their construction, feminists are invariably divorced (they notice I wear no wedding ring); feminists grouch about being called "Mrs."; they dress haphazardly and are careless of style. My students may picture us as bitter, too demanding to be with men; as indifferent to the needs of family, seeking and achieving power only in our "careers."

So, it is the young voices of *Reflections*, then, that draw my students in, let them hear the girl voices of my generation talking: "Why are we either a Jealous Wife threatened by other women, or The Other Woman? Nothing succeeds in male society so well as divide and conquer. Why don't we think of the other woman? We fool ourselves when we ignore her. Must we always compete with each other? Must we dwell on looks? on men? Must we always think about the personal?" For the most part, the story of second wave feminism has not been recorded: there were no video cameras then. But here, for 16 minutes, the girls themselves speak, softly yet with growing confidence, and the film *Reflections* becomes at once a record of who some of these largely invisible girls and young women of 1972 were; and hauntingly, the film becomes a bridge to another generation, one which has never known the explosion of feminist bookstores, of anti-sexist children's books and records, of consciousness raising groups, of marches and speeches; nor our feelings of solidarity and optimism as we strode over the world like Athenas.

My community college classes in women's history are popular, as are similar classes around the country. Young women seek in them the knowledge they were deprived of beginning in first grade. They want to know more than Madonna and Princess Di—the role models they begin with. They are dazzled and then furious at what has not been taught them. They are not hungry for more Ally McBeal catfights or news of conflict and strife between women; rather they seek visions of themselves as stronger, more self-sufficient. They want families and meaningful partnerships, and they learn that feminists have always struggled with these desires as well. In response to the course readings, these young women of today write to advertisers to protest the images of women. They seek to link up with the movement against sweatshop labor, even though they are intimidated by the counter-cultural style of its university student organizers. They learn that a torch has been passed to them, and they accept it, seriously and with trepidation. *Reflections* has told them, finally, that we who were once young tried to remake the world, we succeeded perhaps primarily in creating classes like the one they are taking with me, and that the rest is up to them.

Through the almost thirty years I have taught courses *about* women *to* women, my classes have worked best when students and teacher have all felt our work to be on the cutting edge of what we know, when I have cast off my role as expert. This has happened when I have had to learn new skills along with the students (writing, journal work, math, drawing), or when I was sharing information which was so empowering and so exciting that we felt we were on a journey together, creating a body of knowledge together. This is the model of teaching I first learned when I was a student at Berkeley helping my graduate-student Comp. Lit. teachers create a new course on women. There are so many aspects of those first "Women in Literature" courses which are no longer possible in my community college load: meeting off-campus, in my home or the homes of students; requiring and reading journals from all students; staying up late at night uncovering exciting new materials to copy and share with the students. I no longer let students participate in curricular decision making, or help develop classroom rules and grading policies. It is too bad. Much of the exhilaration and power of those courses derived from this sort of direct student involvement.

As my colleague and former teacher Deirdre Lashgari commented in a joint presentation we gave at the Western Association of Women Historians, "Much of what we did then has become a widely accepted part of contemporary teaching, no longer even particularly 'innovative' [collaborative learning, use of small peer groups, discussion rather than lecturing, gathering of student writing into end-of-class anthologies].... The student-centered approach which was so exhilarating in our early courses requires a level of risk and personal responsibility that is hard for many students [and teachers] now. That hunger for self-definition, that collective urgency about 'diving into the wreck' to discover what could be salvaged, seems overlaid now with a cautious, and isolating, self-preservation."[1]

Today it is hard to balance what we know about the liberating effect of community and communal learning with the realities of the commuter, working-class campuses where we each teach. Belenky and the other editors of *Women's Ways of Knowing*[2] maintain that traditional modes of education ignore women's experiences and needs—in fact, ignore the needs of most students, male as well as female. Those of us who have been forced to teach in a conventional structure after experiencing a Women's Studies context know how much our students are now missing. I hope that there are lessons here for newly hatching feminists and for a generation that is now retiring. I pray that today's young women may experience a piece of the excitement we felt in a new movement, that they develop a deeper and more socially committed understanding of democratic feminism, and that our work, and our words, are not forgotten too completely. The future, I reflect, is now in their hands.

Outwitting Our Captors

Elizabeth A. Wheeler

When I was a graduate student in Comparative Literature at UC Berkeley in the 1990s, I did not realize the continuity of my work with the women scholars who came twenty years before me. Feminist history easily gets lost. I didn't know that the women of Comparative Literature had edited *The Other Voice* and *The Penguin Book of Women Poets*, two of my favorite books, or that the women of my department had played a major role in the general development of Women's Studies. I also didn't know that Bridget Connelly, one of my favorite professors, was one of those founders. I did know, however, that our foremothers had bequeathed a specific legacy to the women of my department and generation: the Women's Caucus and the Comparative Literature 40 course.

For the Berkeley graduate students who comprised the Comparative Literature Women's Caucus, the Comparative Literature 40 course was an outcropping of independence in what often seemed like a rocksolid wall of required courses and professors' judgments. It was the first chance, and for many the only chance, to design a course from scratch while still in graduate school. It was certainly the only spot in the curriculum where graduate students got the final say. Comp. Lit. 40 was the Women in Literature course, our legacy from the successful politicking of women who came before us. Amazingly, the department's women graduate students retained sole control over the staffing and content of the 40 course. Each year, students submitted their own course ideas and the rest of the women graduate students voted in their favorite choices. The course still remains the bailiwick of graduate students, although recently and appropriately, men have joined the competition as well.

In the spring of 1991 I was the lucky one who got to teach the class, and the course became my introduction to Women's Studies. I am now

an associate professor of English at the University of Oregon and a mother
of two. My wonderful husband is a homemaker who holds a Ph.D. in gender theory. Bridget Connelly and I have kept in touch, and have had many
good conversations about being mothers, scholars, and "serious girls."
Along with me at Oregon are two other professors from my generation
of the Berkeley caucus, Lisa Freinkel and Leah Middlebrook; today we
will go hear a talk by a job candidate who is a current caucus member
applying for a job here in our department. The lineage continues. And I
am still drawing on the lessons in teaching, listening, and community-
building I learned from the 40 course so long ago.

That spring of 1991 was a watershed semester. My teaching coincided
with a new intertwining of the personal and the political in my life. I blos-
somed in the Bay Area, a hotbed of personal growth. I went through a
necessary phase of belated mourning and anger. In the context of 1980s
identity politics, I reevaluated my family history of white privilege, alco-
holism, and male aggression. Continuing a fine old Berkeley tradition,
my friend Elizabeth and I had a political epiphany on the steps of Sproul
Hall. We suddenly identified ourselves as adult children of the military-
industrial complex. At Berkeley I learned how to translate closely guarded
family secrets into collective action and understanding. I joined in
anti–Gulf War protests and abortion clinic defense. I saw how my history tangled together with the histories of Japan, South Africa, Vietnam,
the West Bank, and East Oakland. I came to admire scholars like Edward
Said, who transformed personal anger into useful analysis. My own anger
went through a refiner's fire, translating itself into the strongest writing
I had ever produced.

With the 40 course my teaching joined these acts of translation. I
had just found names for nameless experiences. I wanted to share my joy
at learning to speak up. My course plan, Verbal Combat Between Men
and Women, focused on the polemical voice in women's writing. The syllabus featured sassy, witty, enraged, combative, elegant, responsible and
irresponsible women's voices, a smorgasbord of verbal assertion from Harriet Jacobs's ironic and ladylike negotiating of impossible situations, to
Virginia Woolf's elegant argumentation, Valerie Solanas's fun and disturbing paranoia, Rita Mae Brown's sassiness, Hattie Gossett's poetic
jokes, Gloria Anzaldua's marvelous rage, and M.C. Lyte's quickdraw
rhymes.

However, my agenda going into that class is not as important to me
as the things I got out of it. It was the first time I saw a class cohere into
a new creature which did not previously exist. Throughout the term, the
students and I increased our willingness to listen to the books and to each

other. In our excited speech and respectful silences, we created a collective body. Transformed by its students, my 40 course moved from verbal combat to verbal collaboration.

One key question became: how can different generations of women learn from one another? There were significant age differences among the students and between me and the students. Also, we studied authors of various generations from the Victorian era through the present. The course itself was a gift from a previous generation of women. How could we make the best use of this gift?

Watching women of 35 and 19 interact with each other, I noticed how much difference personal knowledge makes in our intellectual comprehension. With their greater life experience, the older students gave a practical edge to the younger students' theoretical feminism. One woman had just returned to college at age 35, after a divorce and a career in retail. Her goal was to become a psychologist working with inner-city kids. She told me it was difficult for her to sit and listen to young women declaring they would never let a man get the better of them. She said, "At moments like that I think about my husband telling me he was leaving me for another woman while I was up on the ladder decorating the Christmas tree."

The 40 course made me speculate on the split between theory and practice, thought and emotion, and on possible ways to reunite them. Although I welcomed the personal into the classroom, it complicated our intellectual life. I had to negotiate conflicts on the spot, not just on paper or in retrospect. Women's histories of hurt from men enriched our classroom climate but also vexed it. Sometimes the more a woman knows, the less assertively she can speak. Yet, understanding the ways we've been hurt and have hurt others is a precondition to understanding anything else.

Our first reading was Valerie Solanas's *The SCUM Manifesto*. SCUM stands for Society for Cutting Up Men. One after another, the nineteen and twenty-year-olds stated that they did not believe in cutting up men. As young adults just defining their own moral principles, they felt a strong need to distance themselves from Solanas's homicidal streak. The SCUM Manifesto is a paranoid rant, a parody of a paranoid rant, and a foundational text of second wave feminism. A 28-year-old senior, a devotee of Inanna and other pagan goddesses, already had a strong grip on her own principles and beliefs. She reminded the class how much we owe to the women who came before us—even the crazy ones.

At first, the younger students sometimes weren't willing to acknowledge how past hurts could make you angry, could make you shy, could even make you crazy. They had to suspend their disbelief in order to hear other people's remote and unfamiliar stories. I spent a session playing women's rap music and discussing its particular mode of verbal combat. At the end of class, a white student launched a diatribe against rap musicians and African Americans in general. Why are they so angry? she asked. I was stunned. I didn't know what to say. Should I give a quick rundown of five hundred years of black history? Or point out that she herself spoke angrily? I had presumed a feminist course did not have to justify the graphic expression of rage. Learning belatedly how to express anger, I offered M.C. Lyte and Virginia Woolf as gifts to the students. I hoped these wide varieties of verbal combat would help them speak out sooner than I did.

I let the student's diatribe go unchallenged until the next session because I needed more time to cobble up a response. In some ways this was a good strategy, and in some ways a bad one. Another student wrote in her course evaluation that my silence in the face of racism made the classroom climate feel unsafe to her. Now that I am a more experienced teacher, I would probably respond briefly to the student's diatribe at the end of class, then reply in more detail later. I could have said something like, "If you are referring to African Americans in general, I think they have very good reasons to be angry. Let's talk more about this next time." Or something like, "I don't see anything wrong with expressing anger. Next time, let's talk about what kinds of expression we believe are OK and not OK."

For the next class session I did what came naturally to me: I used analysis to cool things down and bring the discussion back to specifics. I prepared a brief lecture with the thesis that everyone of every race expresses anger—we all just do it differently. I showed them a clip from *Eyes on the Prize II* showing Governor Nelson Rockefeller explaining his decision to put down the Attica prison revolt with bloody force. The genteel understatement of the white patrician governor was so much more violent in its results than the angry rhetoric of the African American inmates. This lecture was my first critique of my own class and racial background and my first foray into white studies, now an important part of my scholarship and life. The strategy seemed to work. As I concluded, I felt the class breathe a sigh of relief. A useful discussion ensued.

The only male student in the class also taught me how to create safety in the midst of controversy. Jason knew how to remain a safe presence, even when women were telling stories about sexual assault or uncontrollable anger against men. He had a way of going very still at tense moments. This stillness prevented him from becoming a target, and thus could be seen as an act of self-interest. However, his manner also said, "I'm willing to hear this. I'm willing for your gothic moments to be important, true, and real." I have often taken Jason's manner as my guide in other life situations, for instance at certain times when I have been the only white person in the room.

In the course of the term, the students became more willing to hear one another across differences. This willingness came from their commitment to the class, an entity larger than themselves. We transformed individual feelings into something big, fun, and beautiful, the class itself. After many years, the faces, names, and stories of these students stand out in my mind with crystalline distinction. I knew so much more about them than one does in the average class, because they brought so much of themselves to bear on every essay and every discussion. They expected this class to answer real questions from their lives. I was surprised to learn that one student took the class to help her decide whether or not to join a sorority. I'm not sure Harriet Jacobs or Gloria Anzaldua or I aided her with that decision, but I hope we did.

My proudest accomplishment from that class is our good talk and our good silence. By the end of the term, a warm blanket of listening gave shy persons the strength to speak and gave good talkers the strength to say tough things. The class included one extremely shy, extremely smart young woman, one of the few students to whom I have said, "You ought to be a literary critic." Fortunately she ignored my advice and went to medical school. At semester's end, students did class presentations. Few of us had heard this young woman's voice before. It took her a while to get her talk started. As soon as she began, however, we were in awe. There was something so delicate, surprising, yet accurate about her handling of *Rubyfruit Jungle*, the brash and brazen novel she chose to discuss. She linked the novel's lesbian sexuality to imagery of fairyland and wonderment. Way back in 1991, this college senior was doing complex work in queer theory. With her deft touch, she must be a wonderful doctor.

As we negotiated our conflicts with each other, we were also negotiating our freedom from old captivities. I first knew we were getting somewhere special by the utterly involved and respectful silence greeting one particular talk. Telling her own story, this student also had important things to say about girls' and women's stories in general. From *The Yellow Wallpaper* to *Boys Don't Cry*, so many feminist classics are tales of victimhood, shocking stories which reveal how badly the world treats women after all. We need these stories; we need to know the worst of it. And we are not to blame when we cannot prevent others' hurting us.

But we also need something more heartening, more encouraging, from the tales we tell each other. This student wrote about something that happened to her when she was a little girl—or rather, something that didn't happen to her because she was smart enough to prevent it. She was ice skating on a pond when a man started trying to get her to leave with him. She sensed the danger, but pretended to go along with his game. She managed to scramble behind some bushes, take her skates off, and run away. Her essay concluded, "We need more stories about little girls in blue snowsuits who outwit their captors. When we convert personal terrors into action and language, when we share a place to tell and listen, we outwit our captors."

14

From Women's Caucus to Coalition of Women in German

Jennifer Ruth Hosek

If I bear the message of a sea change from the halcyon first wave of the Comparative Literature Caucus, what does this mean?

When I began my graduate school career at Berkeley in the mid-nineties, the caucus was well past this first wave. What remained was the bi-annual potluck. Unlike the association's early days, intellectual exchange was fomented primarily at these potlucks and was then continued informally, rather than under the auspices of the caucus. Seemingly this shift in organization reflected shifts in the needs of the caucus members.

Rather than being explicitly interested in the caucus's agenda, I was drawn to these gatherings because they offered the occasion to meet advanced graduate students. Such opportunities are rather far between due to Comparative Literature's diffuse character, which is a function of the diverse interests and knowledge bases of its members. At the dissertation writing stage in particular, students tend to scatter to all corners of the university, the Bay Area, and indeed the globe. The potlucks fulfilled my goal of meeting some of these colleagues, but I could not have anticipated a much more important impact. For, in that environment in which everyone was "out" together, I realized the prevalence of feminist and gender issues in the work of so many of my very own colleagues and the presence of a working solidarity between women that I had never previously experienced in action. This revelation was quite an inspiration, even though at this period the caucus itself was not the primary motor for critical feminist inquiry and activity.

In retrospect, my experiences at the potlucks, much as they were formative, were probably anachronistic. Unlike many of my colleagues, I had had little formal or personal exposure to feminism by the time I arrived in graduate school. My undergraduate training in feminist theory had consisted in having coffee with the wife of my undergraduate mentor and thesis advisor. This talented novelist gave generously of her time to discuss *The Cinderella Myth* with me, a text she considered useful for helping me think through Anne Sexton and Grimm's fairy tales. I did not experience her meetings with me as feminist acts, but as kind gestures that gave me a taste of a discourse that seemed anomalous and certainly not scholarly. At the potluck, I discovered to my surprise that these discourses were a vibrant part of the academic world.

More normative for those of my own and later cohorts, in my experience, is a decreasing focus on praxis-oriented feminism and on the praxis of feminism. Many graduate students are moving away from working on explicitly feminist topics; fewer of them self-identify as feminists. Some in my cohort have suggested that studying or teaching feminist topics might pigeonhole them as feminists, which may hurt their job marketability. In this, they are responding to perceived shifts in academic trends, which notoriously and even blindly privilege the new without regard for the continued relevance of the current. This shift may indeed also enable hiring committees to unceremoniously weed out the more rambunctious embodiments of feminism.

The academic climate of recent years, moreover, has often furthered adherence to a "new" mythology of the non-situated intellectual stance over the critical application of these notions of the radical instability of knowledge. Where the former academic *modus operandi* has garnered more cultural capital, ambitious graduate students have heeded the interpolation. For given that intellect is our hardest currency, the straightest path to center stage in today's job market seems to be a dance across standpoints, signifying everything—and nothing. From this perspective, good old feminism, having both been around the block and out in the streets for its beliefs, just ain't the wagon-hitchin' star she used to be. Seen in this context, feminist studies reveal themselves as sometimes more about academic trends than critical practices; meanwhile, professionalization is about the politics of timeliness.

This shift in theoretical, professional and political goals is reflected in the function and activity level of the caucus. Over my years at Berkeley, the Women's Caucus has increasingly fallen into a slumber, currently waking each year only to kiss the Comparative Literature 40 course, Women and Literature, into action.

Comparative Literature 40 remains vibrant. Any interested Comparative Literature graduate student may now teach this course, whose existence we owe to the departmental struggles of our earlier generations. Several men have taught it in recent years, as well as students who have little prior knowledge of feminist topics. Thus the drive to professionalization functions in some cases to shore up feminist practice; in the process of developing their scholarly breadth, graduate students gain experience with feminist concerns. The course topics continue to be selected by the students. Every year, the current caucus—a self-defined, loosely organized group whose core consists of those students who are teaching the 40 that year—vets the course proposals. The best syllabi, sometimes all of the syllabi, are voted on by all of the students in the department and the top three are selected to be course offerings during the next school year and summer session. This inclusive and democratic system ensures graduate student—rather than faculty—governance over the course themes. The entire department benefits from this situation; all students gain exposure to the most current issues in feminist topics, and graduate students have the opportunity to have more influence on undergraduate education. This is a case in which past feminist efforts have translated into more voice for all of the graduate students of the department.

The courses selected over the last years have treated women and literature in conjunction with topics as diverse as war, travel, colonialism, stage performance and cross-dressing, sex work, criminality, law, reproductive technologies, and religion. My own experiences teaching the 40 have been intensely rewarding. Both courses that I have taught under this rubric have been overenrolled with enthusiastic, demanding participants. Each course dealt with contemporary issues of interest both to my students and myself and took an accessible but theoretically sophisticated cultural studies approach.

My semester course, "Getting Ahead?: (Post) Feminism, Individualism and Literature," used primarily literature and film to explore contemporary concerns surrounding the history and future of feminisms, particularly as these intersect with ways of thinking about the self in various societal, political and economic paradigms. My summer course analyzed the construction of women's bodies in literature and film, as well as in autobiographical and medical writing. Its eye-catching title, "The Breast Exposed: A Search for the Body in Identity," drew several male students, who may have been surprised to leave the class with a much more solid understanding of and support for the feminist project. The course description reads:

Everybody wants a body to call Self. For women in particular, the struggle over body ownership has been long and hard. One of its offshoots is the current debate in feminist circles over the status of the [female] body's materiality. Some contemporary feminists like to think it as constructed in order to avoid an essentialist "straight" jacket. They hope this strategy will offer new freedoms for individual identity construction. Others theorize a viscerality that can't be subsumed into language. For them, the body is a place of oppression and so must remain as a weighty place of resistance and agency. This course is a way into this complex discussion of the body and identity via that quintessentially female attribute—the breast. We will explore how these appendages are portrayed and what they represent in four literary works. In *Beloved*, Sethe's maternal breasts make her both vulnerable and invulnerable. Initially the unrelenting impetus of her drive for freedom, they also become the starting point for claiming her free Self. Hong Kingston's Woman Warrior attempts to eliminate the significance of her breasts to attain her (masculinely gendered) ends. Kleist's Penthesilea, one in a long line of literary Amazons, has also chosen to buy her independence at the price of this symbol of womanhood. How do breasts in each of these contexts figure in the identity formations of the female protagonists? Is it possible to distinguish between their subjective and societal meanings? We will also look at Audre Lorde's *The Cancer Journals*. How does her narrative of disease and treatment take up or refuse the assumptions of the other texts? What does the breast and its loss mean in the context of medical discourses about the female body? This course will include a talk by Barbara Brenner, Executive Director of Breast Cancer Action.

When facilitating such courses, I employ a particularly overt feminist pedagogy. The course structure works to unsettle hierarchies of knowledge and power, for instance by offering my overwhelmingly femininely gendered students opportunities to facilitate class discussion. The form and the content of the courses complement each other, for instance, we explore the gendered issues that contribute to these students' trepidation at performing authority. My experiences in these sessions and the feedback that I receive from my students are convincing evidence of the continued importance of such courses and the projects of feminism. Indeed, in its various thematic permutations, the 40 remains popular with undergraduates, which speaks to the continued interest in and felt need for knowledge about her story, despite the trend among students not to identify as feminists.

"Women and Literature" has to-date escaped being subsumed into the rubric Gender and Literature; the two continue to co-exist. Thus, in the institutional structure of the department, gender studies remains a field of inquiry that complements and is imbricated with the feminist project rather than a theoretical development that calls the latter into question. It is perhaps not surprising that the maintenance of this institutional structure is significantly indebted to the female administrative assistants, whose own personal histories contribute to their perception of the value of distinguishing between and retaining both courses. Indeed, the efforts of these assistants have contributed stability to the 40 courses time and time again. Most recently, the faculty expressed concerns regarding the course after graduate students failed to organize the voting for the upcoming year. This concern was mitigated after the current graduate assistant took on the task of administration, while leaving the process of selecting the particular course to be taught in the hands of the caucus and the graduate students. In this way too, a slightly older generation of feminists supports its younger sisters.

I view the shifting importance of the Comparative Literature Women's Caucus with optimism and skepticism. I am optimistic because seemingly, in the Berkeley Comparative Literature Department at least, women feel enough support for themselves and their scholarly endeavors that they do not require a forum such as the caucus. Many female graduate students today seem not to need a sisterhood in their scholarly endeavors. Perhaps they are receiving the type of institutional support that earlier generations did not. This speaks to the inroads that feminism and the feminist project have made in at least this part of the academy. Indeed, male and female students alike now often incorporate feminist issues and perspectives into their work somewhat as a matter of course. At the minimum, a female author will grace every course. There is now some room in the academy for thinking about the imbrications of feminism with gender, class, sexuality, ethnicity and nationality. This all seems quite positive.

I also have a more skeptical view: Many younger, privileged women in academia today have succumbed to a competitive individualism against which interventions such as the caucus struggled and perhaps still struggle. This may be related to the fact that the glass ceiling has become increasingly transparent due to increased, although still inadequate, supports for minorities and women, and attention to political correctness. For these reasons, the ceiling has also been raised, so that the more egregious impasses commonly manifest not in high school, undergraduate, or graduate school, but at the level of junior faculty and beyond. Without being confronted with significant, blatant discrimination in their formative years and having been raised with the confidence and entitlement born of the bourgeois women's movement, many female graduate students very logically tend to believe that their successes are their own, as well as their failures. It is up to them to ace the job interview between breastfeeding sessions, to beat the gendered odds at the tenure game, to assert their intellect while their interlocutor eyes their chest at the cash bar. Perhaps it is all this hard work that causes amnesia about their mothers' gardens and their sister outsiders—in academe and across the globe.

I believe the benefits of these attitudes to be short-lived and the costs high. Such belief structures serve to legitimate a playing field that has never been leveled. The extra effort needed to succeed in this game is effort not used to attend to change. How sustainable is this attitude? Students and colleagues seek us out because we are "nice," because our social-psychological training requires we help out in pinch after pinch. Confronted with their demands and our needs, we successfully manage it all. And we hear story after story of the successful female academic becoming ill. And the story of my brilliant colleague, who, overloaded with an unfinished dissertation, family pressures, and the demands of a new job at a prestigious institution, chose to literally blow her brains out.—This is for you, S.L., may there be no others.—A recent *New York Times* article points to a new trend of highly educated women choosing to leave the paid labor force to become full-time wives and mothers. No doubt in contrast to the difficult life of the '80s "super mom," they see this as a feminist choice. I am certainly pro women's right to choose, but privileged choices such as these do nothing to change the structures in which they can be seen as rational.

My observations have been underscored by my work with the Coalition of Women in German (WiG), the feminist Germanist organization that has grown from concerns similar to those of the Women's Caucus to become a powerful, national scholarly organization. Finding the Women in German organization was crucial to my academic career. Until then, I had not been part of a political or scholarly community in academia. It was via the institutionalized feminism of WiG and Wiggies' personal and professional commitment to feminist aims in the largest senses that I saw what was possible. Here were women—and men—who had done and continued to do backbreaking work for my generation and generations to come. We see the continued relevance of our project today; our academia strives to be about more than personal egos and paltry aims; it seeks to foster community in order to engender change.

The coalition fulfilled and fulfills a distinct and pressing demand for an institutional linkage of German studies and women's studies. Started in the '70s primarily by graduate students and untenured assistant professors at the University of Wisconsin at Madison and Washington

University, St. Louis, WiG sought to develop alliances among feminist scholars across the nation. This coalition building gained momentum at academic conventions such as those of the Modern Language Association (MLA) and the American Association of Teachers of German, and via a newsletter that distributed information about the German woman's movement and feminist projects in Germany and the U.S. Within a couple of years, this newly formed community of scholars and educators organized its own annual conference. Applying feminist theory in praxis, it was organized as a workshop in order to emphasize communication and process over presentation and product.[1] The coalition has consistently sought to develop links to other communities, as well as to strengthen its own. Thus WiG now has strong ties to professional organizations such as the German Studies Association and the Modern Language Association, as well as relationships with academic women's organizations outside of the U.S. In the '90s, Wiggies embraced electronic communication with the WiG website—www.womeningerman.org/—and the women in german listserv. And what goes around comes around: the WiG listserv was created and is owned and maintained by the UC Berkeley German Gender (formerly Women's) Caucus, which was founded in the same feminist uprising that birthed the Comparative Literature Women's Caucus.

It seems important to ask: Why has WiG been so successful, while similar groups born of the '70s grassroots political movements have lost momentum? Several Wiggies suggested the following top 14 list, a blueprint for success that I relate here in their own terms:

> 1. Strong organizational base in the 1970s in the Big 10, with lots of contact among those graduate students in the early years.
> 2. Political connectedness through shared radical experiences in Germany as students in the '60s, '70s and '80s.
> 3. Personal friendships with German & Austrian women writers & filmmakers, also in the GDR [German Democratic Republic—socialist East Germany], which led to the conference format of invited artists. The successful conference format is vital to the thriving of WiG.
> 4. Other venues through which we maintained connections in the early years: work on the New German Critique collective; the GDR scholars network (& GDR Bulletin). These activities built confidence & skills to make us leaders in the profession over time.
> 5. A strong relationship with DAAD [German Academic Exchange Service—an important funding source for academic work] from the early years on, which gave validity to the enterprise.
> 6. Early WiG leadership in the German Studies Association, as well as in the MLA, which built ties and developed more leadership potential.

7. German as a field has been small enough to develop strong friendships among women as well as professional relationships. Also, this personal connection meant that sympathetic men could also feel a part of the organization and its successes [for themselves or for feminist friends, students and colleagues]. Good backup.

8. Wiggies are activist organizers: they invite Germanist feminists to their own events [Washington University Symposia; various events at Universities such as Massachusetts, Wisconsin, Berkeley, and Oklahoma State; the Kentucky Foreign Languages Conference; the 18th and 19th Century Women's Literature Group, and many others]. These conferences and symposia reinforce WiG's importance to the field and solidify careers.

9. Engaged membership at all levels and from all types of institutions [liberal arts colleges, regional universities, etc, as well as research institutions].

10. A deep commitment to the WiG project that manifests in hours of unpaid labor that is vital to the WiG's continued vigor.

11. Active and multi-faceted mentorship across the membership.

12. WiG's academic publication, the highly regarded *Women in German Yearbook*, boosts the prestige of the organization and provides a venue for the distribution of top caliber feminist scholarship.

13. WiG has tolerance for a wide range of feminisms.

14. We don't take ourselves so utterly seriously all the time—the cabaret as a touchstone. [Every WiG conference includes a cabaret created and performed by the conference participants that parodies the themes and events of the conference itself. This very unusual embrace of good-hearted and insightful humor in a scholarly setting functions to decrease hierarchies and build self-reflexivity and community.]

What else has the WiG got that the caucus might want? The WiG continues to fulfill needs, but it also continues to spawn desires, desires for continued change in the structures of power and knowledge. This seems to me to be the conceptual key to the energy behind the coalition's actions. In bearing the message of the shifting structures of the Comparative Literature Women's Caucus and its national sister, the Coalition of Women in German, I seek not to weave a disapproving fable. I seek instead to bear witness to a contemporary, successful forum where the personal strives to be political and the self is understood as intersubjectively constituted. As comparatists, we are in particularly good positions to look beyond the individual and focus on making a change in the bigger picture. The tenor of transnational politics suggests that a return to these ways of thinking will not be far in the offing. The precise shape of the next wave of the caucus remains to be seen; that it will draw on the history of the caucus and its sisters seems clear.[2]

Liberation Studies Now

Melanie Kaye/Kantrowitz

Reprinted from The Women's Review of Books *16, no. 5 (February 1999): 15–16.*

In two days I will attend a reunion of the Women's Caucus of the Comparative Literature Department of the University of California at Berkeley. As graduate students during campus mobilization against the war in Vietnam, we joined together to raise consciousness about sexism in the world, the movement and the department, and to mentor each other through orals and dissertation prospectuses. Our lasting legacy was a successful demand for a departmental course on women and literature, which I, as the ranking ABD (All But Dissertation), was blessed to teach. On the first day of class—this was 1972—we pooled the names of every woman writer we could think of. The list fit on one page.

That class (and I suspect many of the early, ecstatic, openly politicized Women's Studies classes) was distinguished by a near-leveling of power between students and teacher because of our mutual vast ignorance, an ignorance matched by passion to learn: students and teacher, at least at this elite state university, put so many hours into extra meetings, projects, and readings that the concept of grades and credit seemed bizarre. The class was of necessity interdisciplinary—the texts were literary, but our discussions of them demanded forays into territories nothing in graduate school had prepared me for—and it emphasized the commonality of women's experience.

Second-wave feminism is often ridiculed for this glib notion of monolithic sisterhood. In that intensely political moment, we knew that all women were not middle-class housewives longing to work outside the home; we read the work of black and white women, as wide a range as I could find in that time of almost no texts. But differences in experience were muted, and the complicating issues of location and privilege likewise.

If that first phase of Women's Studies might be characterized as "add women and stir"—women and politics, women and literature, women and whatever, huge topics because there was so little written—the next phase, initiated by the challenge of identity politics, asked: Add *which* women and stir? Who does the stirring? Yet the era of identity politics generated its own distortions, an ever-lengthening list of seemingly equated identities ("I am a white Norwegian thirty-something able-bodied s/m lesbian vegetarian Virgo from the suburbs"), while the "politics" aspect shriveled in the Reagan-Bush years. From mass movement to small groups to self-help: not an inspiring trajectory.

The current phase of Women's Studies emerges as we dislodge the U.S. (or "the West," or "the North") from its imaginary position at center stage and in the vanguard of feminist progress; as we disrupt the assumption that "we" are advanced and women in other nations must pass through identical stages, if they're lucky. This phase advances a transnational perspective essential in the light of globalization. Look at the movements of peoples—refugees and workers—across national borders, driven by economic and political changes as well as by forces set in motion by colonization; the reformulation of identity and community in diaspora. Look at the migration of capital across national borders, the power of the U.S. dollar and of the International Monetary Fund. As we in the U.S. witness essentials like shelter, food, health care and education transformed from a hard-won category of human rights to a private store of goodies for those who can afford them, we can investigate how human rights are imagined in other parts of the world. This means a shift from conceiving of women's studies as an annex or ladies' room to envisioning it as a site of at least a little insurrection—a perspective that unsettles traditional disciplines and academic frameworks and examines the ways in which structures of oppression and privilege inflect one another.

Why, then, "women's" studies? A good question. I am not for discarding the name—even the new fashion of "gender studies" makes me nervous, dangling as it does the possibility that men will wind up at the center once again. Still, I resonate to the suggestion offered recently by Vivien Ng, of SUNY-Albany, that we should be yoking together women's studies, ethnic studies, Jewish studies and queer studies under the rubric of liberation studies—which reminds us of the point. And in this time of capitalist triumphalism and worldwide resurgent fundamentalisms, we need to remember the point.

What might a course from this juncture of postcolonial and feminist perspectives look like? In 1995 I joined the Hamilton College faculty as the Jane Watson Irwin Visiting Professor of Women's Studies, a position that has been occupied by such shaping influences as M. Jacqui Alexander, Chandra Talpade Mohanty, Ama Ata Aidoo and Papusa Molina. I was handed the course title "Gender/Race/Class/Nation" with some general goals which I interpreted thus: to teach students to see through a multiple lens, and to understand that gender is inherently a multiple lens; to destabilize whiteness; to refocus so that where we are, in this case in the U.S. at a small elite liberal arts college, is not construed as the epicenter of the universe; to heighten awareness of economic class and the shift of resources from public to private that typifies contemporary social policy.

Remember the first day of that class in Berkeley in 1972, the one-page list? With "Gender/Race/Class/Nation," in the mid-nineties, on the first day I divide the students into small groups, hand each group a different *New York Times* article, and give them twenty minutes to read and discuss the relationship of the constructs in the course title to the events in the article. On any given day, the *Times* will have at least five or six highly appropriate articles, treating, for example, childcare for workfare mothers; ethnic Chinese, "the Jews of Asia"; growing support for English-only legislation; sweatshops in Manila and in New York's Chinatown; statistics on AIDS among heterosexuals; high incidence of domestic violence reported by police wives; gay adoption tearing a town apart.... Students are encouraged to tease out the various threads: What has workfare to do with organized labor? How does scapegoating serve the status quo? Why are sweatshops always perceived as located "out there?" What has happened to the public discourse on AIDS as the epidemic's perceived center shifts? Is there a relationship between racist police brutality and domestic violence? Why is homosexuality threatening?

Now instead of excavating basic texts, our task is to make sense of—at least, to make questions of—complex and seemingly infinite information. I use a range of materials and disciplines, but the daily news remains central. I want my students to see gender, race, class and nation in practice.

Also on the first day I discuss objectivity and bias; centrality and margins; and state very clearly (though I will have to repeat this many times throughout the semester), "I am not saying it's not OK to be who you are, white, middle-class, Christian, male, straight, whatever; I am saying, you have to notice it and where it places you." Because my own perspective and biases are sharp and explicit, I need to stress again and again (and model, through behavior in class) that students need not agree with me. Even so, I expect each semester at least one virulent accusation of favoritism or bias; I have learned the best defense will emerge from all the students who feel respected despite differences in values and opinions.

But it is worth mentioning that I, an itinerant academic, was not constrained by hopes of tenure, and, as a white woman in middle age, I no longer have to fight to establish my authority (as I did when I was young). My colleagues of color, on the other hand, face privileged white students whose main contact with women of color has been as domestic workers; women professors of color are often perceived by such students as inherently unauthoritative, unkind (if at all critical) and vulnerable to attack. All of which argues for white women tackling these hard questions in our classes.

For our opening readings I establish a postcolonial feminist perspective with Chandra Mohanty's "Under Western Eyes" and Edward Said's "Reflections on Exile," and challenge the myth of objectivity with Maia Ettinger's witty "The Pocahontas Paradigm, or Will the Subaltern Please Shut Up?" I also establish a format: we begin each series of new readings with written questions (my own, or drawn from their questions about the readings), to be answered in small groups of three or four.

Questions might include: (1) Ettinger describes a Person Lacking an Agenda—a PLA. What does she mean? Is there such a thing as a PLA? What might another name be? (2) Drawing on Said's essay, what relationship do you see between exile and national identity? Between nation and nationalism? (3) What connections do you see among the three articles? (4) What is Mohanty's criticism of Western feminist scholarship? Is she saying Third World women aren't oppressed as women? What is the "Third World difference?" Dividing into small groups with focused questions gets quieter students talking and makes each student responsible to the others for completing course readings on time.

Such a course demands some tricky footwork. This one has no prerequisites, but is required for the Women's Studies major, which means that students with very sophisticated gender and race politics are learning alongside of those whose understanding is rudimentary. For traditional-age students, often most interested in the self, the course's emphasis on situating the self in the context which makes said self possible can feel like a guilt trip. Adept and complex as the instructor and materials may be, some students will nevertheless freeze in the stance of victim, therefore shunning responsibility. Others will jump on the attack bandwagon.[1] If there are only one or two students in any of the minority categories, there's a danger of voyeurism, or of one or two people pressed into service, or appointing themselves, as spokespeople.

This is a class in which students get angry, be it about sexism, racism, class, or other experiences of oppression summoned in classroom discussions as some students reveal attitudes that others find offensive. A white woman, eyes brimming with tears, tells the class that Elsie, the African American housekeeper who raised her, was really family, and a *Puertorriqueña* counters, "Who was raising Elsie's children?" A white man blurts out, "Why do we need pigeonholes, why can't you see me as a person?" "You make us feel guilty for being straight," two sorority sisters accuse the in-your-face class queers. For the instructor, finding the delicate balance between supporting the anger while keeping the classroom a safe place takes skill, tact, time and attention to group process, including figuring out when students need to meet in small groups and divided according to what logic.

This is more complicated than it sounds. When we focus on gender, groups divide into women and men. On sexuality, I ask them to self-identify; given the paucity of out queer students, I group them together, and the straight students likewise—though I think next time I would create a group for exploring students unwilling or unable to pin themselves down. On race, again, the small number of students of color at Hamilton means I place all the students of color into a single group, the Jewish students into a group, and the white Christian students into several small groups. I ask them to answer the following questions: (1) Describe your growing up family, race/ethnic/ class/cultural/religious background. (2) What other peoples were around in your growing up neighborhood(s)? What were your/your family's relationships to them? (3) What are your earliest memories of color other than your own? What information were you given to deal with these differences? (4) What are your relationships with people across lines of color now?

When we focus on class, I ask each student to complete a form which elicits very concrete data about class status. Students are often angry about what they perceive as prying, which makes for fascinating discussion. Using these forms, I divide them into groups according to similar class background. The mix-and-match format works well to create multiple bonds, though a small "why can't we just be people?" contingent is never quite convinced that discreet silence about difference is not a solution.

Students at Hamilton were most detached from the "nation" unit, and I found films and guest speakers invaluable for embodying abstractions like "occupation" or "sweatshops," and for teasing out the relationship between the U.S. and these concepts (foreign aid, sweatshops at home as well as abroad, union busting, etc.). Speakers during past semesters have included Saraswati Sunindyo on feminism and militarism in Indonesia and JoAnn Lum on organizing women sweatshop workers in New York's Chinatown. Films on Nike plants and on the School of the Americas were also useful.

Two topics proved most compelling. First was violence against women—no surprise, as young women on this campus were raped at fraternity parties on an average of one a weekend. Connections between hate of all varieties were easy to draw, and when a lesbian student received an obscene threatening letter, I was proud that it was students from this class who leapt into action, covering the campus with graffiti and hundreds of copies of the hate letter, transformed by their comments.

The second topic of great power was economic class. There is always electricity in the room when I explain—an obvious point which rarely gets made—that while differences in gender, race, etc., do not inherently dictate inequality, class structure cannot exist without inequality because class is inequality. The related issue of surplus value was also useful, to interrogate the notion of property and wealth, and as a lens trained on reproductive labor ("wages for housework"; the gap between what a professional woman might earn and what she pays another woman to care for the children and the house).

Some of the most provocative and engaging student projects focused on class. One analyzed how students perceived and treated housekeeping and janitorial staff at the college. (This project also included an analysis of work dynamics between the student co-authors, an Asian-Pacific woman whose mother is a housekeeper, and an upper-class European man.) Another project organized a cost-sharing experiment: drawing on the work of Felice Yeskel, "Coming Out About Money: Cost Sharing Across Class Lines," this student elicited class identity from a group of friends at the college and through open discussion of this information facilitated the group's allocation of the cost of eating dinner at a restaurant in a way that "felt fair" to all of them, breaking through the silence around money that often pervades even close friendships, and modeling an approach not strictly based on private property.

I will be teaching a similar class this summer at SUNY-New Paltz. Aside from updating the syllabus and adapting it to a very different student body (appreciating the greater diversity, bemoaning the reduced resources), I plan to add a unit on Christian hegemony. This seems critical: to counter media hyper-emphasis on Muslim fundamentalism; to investigate possibilities of alliance—in the U.S., among religious and sexual minorities confronting a rising and virulent Christianity, and around the world, among women in struggle against fundamentalisms of all kinds.

One final point: women's studies, especially at public institutions, is under attack by the same forces which savage affirmative action and public assistance, trash immigrants, defend courses that depict happy slaves, cheerfully bomb Iraq and relentlessly pump out misinformation to keep all of us at each other's throats. (Witness a recent report that "many educators are beginning to think boys should get more attention," pitting the educational needs of girls against boys, and, more insidiously, against students of color—as if such concerns are mutually exclusive.)[2] The intersections of gender, race, class and nation are not abstract. What's needed is a post-post-modernism to move beyond fragmented identities, not merely to name the dots but to connect them, and to rebuild the bridges between theoretical and practical work that characterized the best of early women's studies.

16

An Interview with Joanna Bankier

Sheryl St. Germain

Reprinted from Translation Review *17 (1985): 17–20.*

Joanna Bankier is co-editor of two ground-breaking anthologies of women's poetry in translation: *The Other Voice* (et al., Norton, 1976) and *Women Poets of the World* (with Deirdre Lashgari, Macmillan, 1983). This conversation took place at the American Literary Translators' Association conference in Boston, November 1984.

You were involved with two anthologies of women's poetry in translation: The Other Voice, *and* Women Poets of the World. *Could you tell us a little about how you became interested in these projects?*

At the time, when we—a group of graduate students at UC Berkeley—began collecting poetry of women in translation there was practically nothing available. We spent weeks, months, years, traveling, digging in libraries and talking to people in order to bring the poems together. It took us from 1972 to 1975 to collect, polish and bring out *The Other Voice*, which is a contemporary collection as well as a thematic one, and an additional five years for *Women Poets of the World*. We felt we were really breaking into virgin territory.

You had originally intended to do an historical book, I believe. It's interesting that you started with the twentieth century, although I suppose those texts were the ones most readily available.

Yes, we were not able to publish an historical anthology until six years after *The Other Voice*.

The history of how we got started is worth mentioning because it was rather unusual, yet at the same time typical, for the period. We started off as a Women's Caucus in Comparative Literature at Berkeley. This was the first Women's Caucus within the field, and we met outside of classes in people's homes. From 1969 to 1971 it functioned as a consciousness-raising group: We were reading and talking about literature from a feminist perspective. We were in various fields—Greek, French, Russian. There was this tremendous surge of energy. It turned out that all of us had been reading women poets we were very fond of, in our respective languages, whom nobody else knew about. For example, one of my languages is Swedish, and there were two major Swedish women poets very rarely translated into English, whom the American audience didn't have a chance to read.

Over a period of time we set up meetings every other Sunday; we had some wine and cheese, and we opened the meetings up to the non-academic community so that anyone who was doing translations could come and read their work. There was just an explosion of interest. People who had been working for ten years, doing the most exquisite translations that they had never published, showed up.

I remember one session in particular. A woman came with translations of Hungarian women poets in a sort of surrealist, very, very rich language, a style that sounded very unusual to us, and very striking. At that same session someone read Welsh translations—polished, beautiful pieces, very exciting. Somebody else brought Icelandic translations, somebody brought Byzantine Greek, and somebody brought Sappho translations. This activity continued over a period of a year or so—these bi-monthly meetings. In this way we collected altogether maybe thirty percent of what is in *The Other Voice*.

At that point were you consciously organizing it for a book publication?
Yes. We were hoping to have enough material for an historical anthology. It turned out that many of the translations needed some doctoring. They were good, one could see the possibilities, but they were not finished.

How did you check them? Did you have specialists for those languages you weren't familiar with? Or was the concern at the time more to see that the translation worked as a poem in English?
We looked at them as poems in English. That has been our focus throughout. In *The Other Voice* and *Women Poets of the World* we primarily focused on having a poem in English because we felt that what we were doing was introducing unknown authors to an English audience. We thought—and this was a deliberate policy—that when you are introducing

something entirely new, you have to make sure that it is accessible and that it is a poem that works in English.

Very rapidly these meetings turned into translation workshops; somebody would translate a poem and we would say, it's good but it needs some revision, so we would work on it. Nobody was in charge of these workshops, there was no hierarchy; we were helping each other. Sometimes I would help the person who had brought a poem, and sometimes I would be helped with my work. That created a sense of trust and also a sense of perfectibility. But even with the workshops, even with these meetings, we did not have enough material for a book.

So what did you do, did you go out and commission translations after that?

Yes, but we also did months of research in libraries. We discovered that anthologies of poetry usually contained only male poets, with maybe one token woman—most of them, not all. We found many excellent translations of poems by women in journals, however. *Modern Poetry in Translation* was tremendously helpful, *Mundus Artium* was a great source for us, and also the Canadian journal *Contemporary Poetry in Translation*. At the time it was very difficult to find women's poetry in book form.

This was, I guess, the first international anthology of women's poetry to be published in book form.

Yes, and we felt very strongly that there was a need for an international anthology of women poets. American women who were writing at that time had a rich distinctive voice, but so few people seemed to know that this other material existed. We felt we had a mission to bring the work of women poets from non–English cultures to the attention of the poetry-reading public. One thing that happened to us that was very satisfying was the change in the anthologies that came after *The Other Voice.*

I wanted to ask you in particular about the Barnstone anthology.

Yes, but I wasn't thinking about that one, I was thinking of anthologies like Hamburger's *German Poetry 1910–1975*, which came out after the appearance of *The Other Voice.* It included thirteen women poets instead of the usual token women. Of course, the women were there before but they went unnoticed. *The Other Voice* helped focus attention on them.

Let's get past The Other Voice *and go on to* Women Poets of the World. *How did it come about?*

There were six of us working on *The Other Voice;* then we divided into two groups. Six people is just too much for a long time. It's hard for six people to work together for ten years. Three of the women who had worked on *The Other Voice*, Kathleen Weaver, Carol Cosman, and Joan Keefe, went on and did the *Penguin Book of Women Poets*, and Deirdre Lashgari and I did the Macmillan book, *Women Poets of the World*. We contracted separately and went in separate directions. My participation in the Penguin book project did not continue beyond the early stages, where we collected some of the basic material. The final shape of that book, I had nothing to do with.

The Other Voice was organized according to theme; Women Poets of the World *was not. Why the different approach?*
It was a practical reason. We didn't have enough material to organize the first one culturally. We tried to. At the time of *The Other Voice*, even after four years of collecting translations, we just didn't have enough poems to divide it up historically or culturally. But I think it was a fortunate necessity. It was a necessity that allowed us to be creative.

It works very well, and the other approach is well-suited to Women Poets.
The Other Voice is a lighter and more accessible book. *Women Poets of the World* is more substantial and it has all that historical information.

How did you decide which poems to include?
There had to be a consensus. If there weren't, we wouldn't include the poem. If one of the editors—there were six of us for *The Other Voice*, and Deirdre and I for the Macmillan—each one of us always had veto power. Only the poems we could all agree on, then, were included.

How did you personally choose whether or not you wanted to include a poem? What were the criteria?
Quality, or as Emily Dickinson said at one point, when a poem makes your hair stand on end, then it's a good poem. Of course, there were other restrictions as well. As a rule we did not include very long poems. The nature of the anthology requires that the poems included be rather short. They also have to be representative. The poet has many various interesting poems and several voices, but there are only a few poems that are representative of the poet.

What about when you had various translations available, for example, in the case of Sappho? Did you commission translations, or use ones already available?
It was hard to decide between the translations of Sappho. We started off with the Mary Barnard, but I was never really very happy with her

versions, although for a long time I went along with them. Ultimately after long discussions, we reached an agreement to use the Lattimore translation.

Did you ever edit any of the translations that came to you that had already been published, or ask for changes?

Yes. Usually with the translators, if we approached them and explained that we'd like to make some changes and wouldn't impose, we would reach an agreement. You mentioned the Barnstone anthology earlier. I wish we had Willis here so that we could ask him how *he* worked with the translators, because it seemed as if there were a different process there.

I wondered about that because both The Other Voice *as well as the Penguin book came out before the Barnstone one, and it seemed that such a tremendous amount of research had to be done to get those books out—I wondered if that research was being done simultaneously on his side and your side.*

I don't know, I suppose so. We were working differently, I think, than they were, on a grassroots level, in teams, training our translators as we went along. We had no money, no research assistants; and we were operating on feminist principles of equality and non-hierarchy. It was a slow, cumbersome process but well worth it.

You did some translating yourself: French and Swedish?

Yes, but far less, simply because the editing was such an overwhelming job. And the worst part about it was the permissions, which we, unlike the Barnstones, did ourselves.

It must have been a very tedious process.

It was tedious, but it was also very interesting. There are so many different kinds of publishing houses. Some would want $265 for one poem, or others wouldn't answer at all, and we'd have to call them long distance. In other cases the publisher would write back, "I'm delighted, go ahead, good luck with the project, we'd like to see the book."

In some of these original meetings, when you were discussing translation problems, were there any problems that occurred with a certain regularity that were related to the fact that these poets were women?

We were searching for a common thread, or a woman's voice, and I don't know if we found one, but some poems seem to me to use imagery that you wouldn't find in poetry by men. Praxilla is a good example:

> Loveliest of what I leave behind is the sunlight,
> and loveliest after that the shining stars, and the moon's face,
> but also cucumbers that are ripe, pears and apples.
>   (Translated by Richard Lattimore)

The reason these lines have survived is because they have been quoted as an example of terrible poetry. How could you possibly put cucumbers, pears and apples together with the moon and shining stars? According to Greek standards you could not mix high and low language that way.

We would think of that kind of juxtaposition as very modern.

Women's writing has often flourished in the margins of the literary tradition. One of the advantages of being "marginal" is that you do not have to obey the rules very rigorously. You can mix high style and low style, the public and the private. We happen to like that kind of break in stylistic decorum in the twentieth century. And that is one of the reasons why I think that the modern period is a good one for women.

A favorite genre among modern women poets is the sensuous poem about food, as in this poem by Novella Matveyeva, translated from the Russian by Daniel Weissbort:

> The eggplants have pins and needles.
> Long dreams have plagued their sleep.
> By the redbrick garden wall
> Cucumbers droop like whips.
> The Poppylamps blow out in the wind....

Or "First Things," by a French poet, Lucienne Desnoues, translated by Miller Williams:

> We come to uncrate the newness of this world,
> First fruits of the season, the crates of flowers,
> Orchard morning, burst and lying open,
> Markets, raise your colors....

Women played an important role in making fit for poetry an area of experience and a world of images that had seemed unacceptable before modernism. Modernism was congenial to female experience and women have made a great contribution in the modern period.

They certainly have. The poems of Louise Labé are modern in tone, as well as those of Sappho and Praxilla. I've always thought that the modern spirit was very feminine in that sense. One could almost call modernity feminine.

French feminist theorists are getting close to that.

Which translations have you personally most enjoyed publishing?

Wislawa Szymborska. Szymborska is a poet I read now and again with pleasure. And I'm so glad I discovered her. We published her poem "The Women of Rubens" in *Women Poets of the World:*

> Female giants, fauna of women
> naked like the rolling of barrels.
> They nest in trampled-down beds
> sleep with mouths open for crowing.
> Their eyes have escaped into depth
> and penetrate to the centre of glands
> from which yeast seeps into their blood.
>
> Daughters of the Baroque:
> Dough rises in mixing bowls,
> baths emit steam, wines slowly redden,
> piglets of cloud trot across the sky,
> trumpets neigh an alert of the senses.
>
> Oh you creatures pumpkined to excess
> doubled by the stripping of shifts
> trebled by the violence of posture
> you succulent dishes of love!
>
> Your slim sisters had got up earlier
> long before dawn brightened the picture.
> They made their progress, in single file,
> to the unpainted side of the canvas.
>
> Exiles of style, with all ribs showing,
> with birdlike feet and hands like claws.
> Trying to flap their angular shoulder-blades.
>
> The thirteenth century gave them a golden backcloth,
> the twentieth—a silver screen;
> the seventeenth had nothing to spare
> for flat-chested women.
>
> For even the skies are convex:
> convex the angles and convex god—
> a bewhiskered Phoebus on a sweaty mount
> heading straight
> into the alcove of bubbling flesh.
> (Translated from the Polish by Jan Darowski)

I also was happy to publish Gloria Fuertes, who has her own book now.

It's a great field for a translator now. Each woman in your book should have her own book.

That's what we were hoping for, and it is already happening. Forugh Farrokhzad, Anna Akhmahtova, Edith Sodergran, and Gloria Fuertes all have their own books.

How do you see Women Poets of the World *as being different from the Penguin and the Barnstone books?*

It seems to me that *The Other Voice* is the kind of book that you keep at home and you read from time to time while the Penguin book you would go to for reference, because it's handy, and it has biographical notes. If you're doing an anthology, teaching a course, it's a wonderful reference to have. Between *The Women Poets of the World* and the Barnstone book, I think the main difference is that Barnstone is a poet, so there is a kind of contemporary poetry stamp on everything. You can hear 1970s, 1960s American rhythm and diction in it; it rarely misses, it is sustained throughout the book, which is a drawback, in that the poems often sound alike, but it also has the quality that nothing seems really alien. In *Women Poets of the World* we have more variety of styles, and that might turn some people off, but other people might like it because it is more faithful to the variety of cultures we're dealing with.

Barnstone also has long biographies. For me, what is most interesting in *The Women Poets of the World* are the cultural introductions. There we feel we are breaking new ground, and we would like to continue—have the people who wrote these essays do a more in-depth study. There have been periods in the literary history of certain cultures when women were so prominent that they were the ones who defined the forms. Then they would vanish for five or six hundred years and reappear only in the modern period. That's true of the Arabic—there were some important pre–Islamic, pre–Mohammed Arab women poets, and then practically nothing until the modern period. Women probably wrote, but they did not get anthologized. They were excluded from the tradition. It's also true for Japanese. From 700 to 1200 in the Heian period, the novel and the tanka were primarily written by women. When that period ended women practically stopped writing and there were no important women writers until the modern period. But women were the ones who defined the forms of the Japanese tradition, which was later carried on by men. We started asking ourselves: when is it that women are able to enter into the world of literature? When is it that their work is taken seriously, their experience, their perceptions, their way of formulating? When are they included into literary circles, journals, published in anthologies?

If we look at translation in the larger sense of communication, this book communicates or translates a certain perspective of women.

For me, it was a passion. I started out with the feeling that poetry was a male prerogative, that female experience was considered trivial, or inadequate for poetry, and I wanted to see if that was so.

The passion does come through, and while I was researching for this interview, I thought that it must have been such an exciting time to have all those women working together. But I think the perspective that comes out is that in one sense there is no perspective, that there is a multiplicity of concerns, which is important to say because so many people lump women into calcifying categories. We hear many voices in your anthology, and not necessarily those traditional women's voices that fit into such neat categories. We had not taken into consideration women of color, Chinese women, we were talking about American women as if their experience and art represented that of the women of the world.

We did not have an opinion about what we wanted to find. We wanted to see what was there, and it turned out that this variety existed, so we just had to reflect it in the book.

What are your future plans?

I'm working on a male poet, and have been for the last three or four years, because I thought I needed to get away from this. Ten years is a long time. Then I would like to get back to the essays of *The Women Poets of the World*. I am fascinated by the historical, sociological dimension of women's experience: why it is that in decentralized cultures, where poetry is a marginal entity, women flourish, and where there is a strong centralized power, poetry becomes a prestigious activity, and, by the same token, women vanish from the literary scene. I am more than ever fascinated by these kinds of questions.

The Way We Were

Joanna Bankier

Story One

Our meetings at Marsha's must have been indistinguishable from many such gatherings of women in the late 1960s and early 1970s. Although most of us, being doctoral students in Comparative Literature at UC Berkeley, had a special literary angle on things, we were part of a grassroots movement which swept across America between 1968 and 1975. According to a footnote in the *Norton Anthology of Theory and Criticism*, such group meetings were at the origin of a revival, "the second wave of feminism," which acquired its name in relation to the first wave, whose founding document, "The Declaration of Sentiments," was adopted at the Women's Convention in Seneca Falls in 1848.[1] It is nice to have the history of the American feminist movement thus officially acknowledged, although it would be nicer still if the acknowledgment had not been confined to a footnote.[2]

How to tell the story of the way we were without claiming too much but somehow get out of the footnotes? Obviously, words lose and change their value. Does that mean the words we used can no longer convey the memory of the way we were? Does that mean it is impossible to translate into today's language the paradigmatic shift we felt we helped give birth to? We thought we were being subversive when, in the face of the prevailing mind set of the English and foreign language departments, we advertised that we intended to "place the poets and the poems in the context of the culture that shaped them" and that "the kinds of poetry that women wrote reflected the social, economic, and literary conditions that shaped their lives." (From the preface to *Women Poets of the World*, our second anthology of women's poetry in translation.) The hardest thing to

185

convey is perhaps the freshness of that feeling. Hard to believe that such talk about literature, which today sounds so sedate and ordinary, could have shocked anyone. Yet when New Criticism ruled in the humanities and literary scholarship did not concern itself with matters external to the text, only the structure, the texture, the ironies in the text were within the purview of scholarship. Social and economic conditions were irrelevant. Literary conditions, what later was to be called "the institution of literature," was beyond the pale of professional discourse. Merely to mention the word "experience" in an oral exam was to introduce something dirty into the "pure aesthetics" of the modernist poem. It was enough to give the graduate student the reputation of not being serious.[3]

Well, so be it. We had tested the waters and we knew there was no going back. And when, in writing the introductions to one of our anthologies, we wrote "there is much in the experience of women throughout time and across cultures that is universal," we in the same breath told our readers that the concept "universal" is a distorting prism, nothing but a "twentieth century perception," which makes us see the past through "the blinders of our own generalized cultural assumptions." At that point the cards are on the table. And the epistemological shift is right there; the attack on Eurocentrism, on Enlightenment self-assurance, on the neutral, objective, unbiased perception and on all the other accoutrements of the ideology of modernity. We, the women who had been gathering at Marsha's place on McGee Street, trembled at the thought of the danger of crossing the line, but took a bet on the support we had in each other and went ahead. It was exhilarating to be thus deliberately and happily subversive. Free women at last.

The wide-eyed freshness of thrashing through conventional categories! The cheek of putting "Native American" on the map from Canada in the North all the way down to Argentina, saying it "obviously" and "clearly" belongs there—because this section spans a longer history than either the Latin American or North American, and because it represents a synthesis, an integration and a renewal—and it is appropriate to put it last in the book ending with the words "My name is I Am Living. I am here." How does this read today? As foolishness? As the patently obvious? Maybe. Or maybe, as a new consciousness and a new epistemology which come crashing through the ceiling, yet another Angel—and not only in America—breaking through.

That is very much what it sounds like when Stuart Hall, director of the Center for Contemporary Cultural Studies in Britain, tells about how he encountered the women's movement of the very early 1970s. With the growing importance of early feminist work, many people in the Center—

or the men there—thought they needed feminists to come into cultural studies. And they "tried to buy it in, to import it, to attract good feminist scholars." They were trying to be, as Stuart Hall puts it, "good, transformed men. And yet, when [feminism] broke in through the window, every single unsuspected resistance rose to the surface—fully installed patriarchal power, which believed it had disavowed itself. There are no leaders here, we used to say; we are all graduate students learning how to practice cultural studies. You can decide whatever you want to decide, etc. And yet, when it came to the question of the reading list ... that's where I really discovered about the gendered nature of power.... Talking about giving up power is a radically different experience from being silenced. That is another way of thinking and another metaphor for theory: the way feminism broke, and broke into cultural studies."[4]

In Stuart Hall's narrative of the meeting of cultural studies and feminism, violence and insight are tightly intertwined. All the stuff about "influence" written *post factum* tends to obscure that you rarely can have one without the other. Often violent conflict was part of what we called "consciousness raising." Remembering that it rarely was a polite and socially acceptable event helps bring it to life.[5]

But so does, of course, the many ways of telling the story of the early feminist movement. There is the sneering version of "women's lib." The bra burnings. The not shaving one's legs and armpits. The marches and demonstrations of aggressive women. Angry women. And, yes, of course, the movement had its silly moments. But then again, silliness shows up in most human endeavors, while the women's movement, already in its earliest stages, may, just may, have ushered in a new paradigm and a new *zeitgeist*. It's tempting to get intoxicated by an exaggerated sense of our own importance, but maybe we found ourselves in one of those moments in history when ordinary people were able to have their say, something quite unusual under modernity. De Certeau tells in *La prise de la parole* (*The Capture of Speech*) the story of the elevator boy at the Paris department store, La Samaritaine. Being asked by a TV team during the *événements* of May 1968 what he thought about what was going on, he answered diffidently, in that characteristic pre–1968 and pre-women's movement fashion, "Je ne sais pas, Monsieur, je n'ai pas d'èducation" (I don't know, sir. I am not educated.)

Ordinary people used to feel they did not have the right to interpret what was happening to them or what they could see with their own eyes. Somebody else, a professional or an expert, had to tell them what to think. The prevailing ideology of scientism and positivism prevented women and non-experts from trusting their own perceptions and from believing in the authority of their own voices. Within a few decades, it all changed. Men and especially women, ordinary women, felt they had the right to speak without authorization or education.

That was perhaps the major thrust of the cultural revolution: to abandon the modernist notion that there was an Archimedean point from which the world could be scientifically, objectively and truthfully observed; to empower women, but also to empower people in other, non–European, parts of the world to start looking at things from their own perspective. This insight would have been formulated in pre–Derridean terms at Marsha's on McGee Street in Berkeley thus: "He says he is objective and you merely subjective and emotional? Can't you see that that way of using language is a power play? Can't you see that you own the relationship as much as he does? Can't you believe us when we are telling you that you have the right to define it and make your interpretation stick?"

If we were part of any larger movement, it was that of critical theory or cultural studies etc. According to Lynn Hunt, the women's movement of the 1970s was "the motor that drove the theoretical revolution in the United States while Thompson, Williams, et al. probably did so in England." It is a curious fact, rarely noted in scholarly circles, and probably yet another instance of the perpetual process of re-forgetting women's history, that in Lynn Hunt's words, "In the United States, in particular, (and perhaps uniquely) women's history and gender studies have been at the forefront of the new Cultural History."[6]

The shift brought to the surface the awareness that the writing of history and the teaching of languages and literatures has always been intensely ideological. It challenged the ideology of modernity. It put to the test the convictions of male scholars in our field that binary oppositions of objective vs. subjective, reasoned vs. intuitive, scientific vs. emotional were somehow essential, generic, biological and that they corresponded to an underlying opposition between male and female. We thought we saw, in a flash of insight, what we later discovered in other places articulated as the theory of the knowledge-power nexus: an attempt of people to hijack the meaning of language in order to maintain privilege and entitlements. The empowerment of women, of outsiders, of marginalized people and those not particularly distinguished by education or money or social class was in the air. Yet because it had come to us as part of an ongoing dialogue with other women in a supportive and generous environment—and not in a course on logic—we knew that it was fear or ignorance that made people raise the twin spectres of relativism and nihilism in the face of "theory" or "cultural studies." There was no dangerous relativism in there being two perspectives on a relationship, two stories, his or hers. Because it had all come to us as intimate experience in dialogue with other women, we had difficulty understanding all the talk about the "nihilism and despair" that "post-modernism" was supposed to bring about.

And as Eurocentrism was crumbling under the weight of all these "other peoples" speaking up—Japanese, Korean, Indian, Persian, African, Arab, not to mention Vietnamese and Chinese—there were also different interpretations of events which were geographically and culturally situated. There was no moral danger in that. It was simply the way things were. "Truth" was partial, contextual, and contingent. We who gathered at Marsha's surely were full of joy and hope and excitement, which is hard to convey to a skeptical post–9/11 world. But there have been other periods of enthusiasm in history. We thought of women's rights as an extension of human rights, as a self-evident, albeit belated, extension of these rights to the other half of the human race. If we broke new ground, these ways of knowing have now passed into the mainstream and into sociology, anthropology, literature, and other fields of the humanities. Power, we said at Marsha's place, is maintained through the control of discourse, by creating meaning and making our interpretations stick. Power, we said to each other, is passed on through discourse and stabilized through the creation of institutions. Consequently, what we had to do was to seize power by creating our own institutions. And to some degree, we did. The women's course in Comparative Literature was a way of seizing the right to speak in our own voice and making it last by institutionalizing it. *Women Poets of the World* and the essays inscribing women in the context of their history was another. Yet, the one that is perhaps closest to my heart was *The Other Voice*, the Norton book which was edited by a whole collective of six women, most of whom had been part of the group from the start. It became quite widely known and was recommended reading by the New York Public Library in 1975. It happened that I met women who would recommend the book to me.

Once, I was invited to come and talk about it at a poetry conference organized by the Department of Comparative Literature and the Writers Workshop at the University of Iowa. It was our old friend Daniel Weissbort from the London-based *Modern Poetry in Translation* who was running the show and had invited me. Apparently, he had been looking for a woman to put on an all-male panel and his woman, or significant other, had handed him *The Other Voice*, which I had sent to him and which had landed, business card and all, on her bedside table. Those were the days of the token woman. I remember walking up to Mark Strand and introducing myself to him as someone who was going to be on the panel with him. Mark Strand, who must have been twice as tall as I am, replied, "Oh, yeah, you wanna sit on my lap?" I guess it was meant to be funny and seductive, but I, being a foreigner, did not even understand it was meant that way. To his credit, at the end of the conference, Strand came up to me and apologized: he had read the book and liked the poetry. There were many similar culture clashes. People got their feelings hurt. It was a culture war—as Lynne Cheney a few years later insisted, a war that is still going on.

It bothers me to tell the story in such, as it were, heroic terms. Yes, it is true that our generosity was sometimes not reciprocated and that in some respects we were very naïve. No, we did not end the fashion of high-heeled shoes, plucked eyebrows and slim waistlines. We did not end all power struggles once and for all. God knows we did not put an end to female competition. Poetry did perhaps belong to all women in some sense, but when it was a matter of whose name was to be on the cover of a book, the reality of name recognition and professional acumen came to the fore and there was intense competition. There was an individual price to be paid. Maybe the price that I, for one, had to pay was becoming addicted to the rush and excitement of breaking taboos and conventions, of political struggle, of common goals and common hopes; in short, I developed an impatience with ordinary life and ordinary people, life of the common routine. Then again, that happened to a lot of people, and not only in the women's movement. But I have never understood the rush toward the so-called realism and the slight embarrassment which seems to attach to its opposite. To adhere to the "real": is it not to be on the level of the lowest common denominator? The sort of things that any large number of people can agree on? Workers unionizing for the first time in the 19th century must have felt something of the exhilaration we felt when we decided to put competition aside and support each other in tak-ing exams and writing the dissertation. Actually, the women's movement in the 1970s was close to being a socialist utopia realized in some small way wherever women met and interacted. Utopias usually don't last, but the memory of them may survive in the telling.

Perhaps it should also be said that sometimes the so-called "realism" can be a mindset which produces envy, narrow-mindedness, self-serving-ness, the looking-out-for-number-one mentality. As such it needs no spe-cial promotion. Left to its own devices, the world produces and reproduces "realism" and "pragmatism" relentlessly. It is the stories of the rare vision-ary moments in history that need to be told and passed on. These moments are as vital to our historical memory as they are diffiicult to remember in all their force and fervor. Writing about the French Revolution, Robert

Darnton notes that while we may readily accept the abstract idea of sweeping, revolutionary change to everyday life and social conventions, "few of us really assimilate" its full meaning.

> We take the world as it comes, and cannot imagine it organized differently.... We define ourselves as employers or employees, as teachers or students, as someone located somewhere in a web of intersecting roles. The Revolution at its most revolutionary tried to wipe out such distinctions.... How can we grasp those moments of madness, of suspended disbelief, when anything looked possible and the world appeared as a *tabula rasa*, wiped clean by a surge of popular emotion and ready to be redesigned?[7]

If we had not had visions, ideals, plans, utopias, we would still be stirring the soup with a stick and doing back-breaking physical work. Is it naïveté to take a stand on the side of the innovators, the utopians and the visionaries? But then again, there is a built-in naïveté in what we consider realistic: the notion that the future is identical with the present, only more so. And is that not a problem of the imagination? So the memory stubbornly brings us back to the power of solidarity, of mutual support, of the self-confidence that comes from following one's desire, and the coming face-to-face with one's identity.

Here we go again. I can feel the intoxication that comes from devising new projects, of constructing new discourses and dreaming up new institutions. We, the women in the graduate program in Comparative Literature, who started meeting at Marsha Hudson's in 1969 and went on to teach women's studies, to write poetry, to do the translations and compile the anthologies and made women's courses a regular offering at Berkeley, were we really responsible for the paradigmatic shift in the *zeitgeist*? We were carried along by a much wider popular movement which swept like wildfire through our generation of women. Who knows where it came from? Having had a germinating effect on our minds, it went on to contribute to the epistemological and institutional revolution in the humanities which we call cultural studies or critical theory: Stephen Greenblatt's search for cultural context which spearheaded New Historicism. Clifford Geertz and James Clifford turn the anthropological gaze inward, toward the ethnographer's writing style. And of course the work in gender studies and queer studies.

Early feminism of the 1970s integrated a variety of conflicting voices and the metastory I have tried to tell here is just one among many possible narratives. It is perhaps even more difficult to move forward in time, to reach toward a new position for feminism in a post–9/11 world. Questions like: Is the development of feminism toward cultural studies, ethnic studies and global feminism focused on the subaltern in the manner of, say, Gayatari Chakravorty Spivak, the way we wanted things to go? Were the changes from feminism to gender study to queer study radical? Were they necessary? And, above all, has the movement been changed in the last few years by the emergence of totalitarian terrorism? Or, the other way round, can we remain loyal to our positions and insights from the early feminism of 1968–1975? Because of the multiplicity of perspectives and interpretations, maybe it would be better to abandon the ambition to write a coherent narrative and opt for the stylistic figure of parataxis. Here, then, is a way of looking at the women's movement today from another angle.

Story Two

As I write, Sweden is marking the second anniversary of the death of Fadime Sahindal, a young Kurdish woman who was murdered by her own father. He had objected to her non–Kurdish boyfriend and had been raging about her free western lifestyle. She went underground and was given a secret identity. But the dad caught up with her and killed her when she stole a visit with her sister in the quiet university town of Uppsala. People woke up to the news on a cold January morning and tried to make sense of the cruel and unnatural act. Yet in the eyes of Fadime's father and in the eyes of his community, a murder for the sake of "family honor" was neither senseless nor criminal. It was the sort of thing a man had to do when the woman was breaking the norms of this intensely patriarchal culture. But in the eyes of modern Swedish women and the Swedish culture in which Fadime had grown up, the idea that Fadime's lifestyle could be seen as polluting the purity of male honor seemed very strange indeed. It was a culture clash if ever there was one, and by no means the first of its kind in Europe, but the first that caught the Swedish public's attention.

Sweden's population of eight million was relatively homogeneous until three decades ago. Since then there has been an influx of about one million immigrants from a variety of countries. The immigrants are geographically and socially isolated while at the same time expected to integrate into the mainstream culture. The inner conflict or double bind, which tends to be the result of this ambivalent treatment, is unfortunately not only the fate of immigrants to Sweden but happens elsewhere in Europe as well. Not surprisingly, problems abound. In Holland, an openly gay politician is murdered for bringing these conflicts into the public sphere. In France, the issue of Muslim girls wearing headscarves in public schools is shaking the very foundations of French collective identity. *L'esprit laïque*, the firmly secular culture of modernity in which French public education for the last two hundred years has passionately been inscribed is suddenly undermined. The girls and their families are demanding the right to express their religious identity to which they ought to be entitled in a democracy; yet this right runs headlong into the enlightenment values on which the French Republic was founded, the separation of church and state. If Europeans are unable to deal with their internal divisions and the anti-modernist trends in their immigrant populations, the whole continent seems to heading for a catastrophe of one form or another.

Yet, strangely enough, the story of Fadime—or rather of Fadime's death—seems to have the ability to bring people together and to build bridges across the cultural divide. In the news and on the streets, everybody is on first name basis with Fadime. She has become something of an icon, signifying both sadness and hope, a symbol around which indigenous Swedes and immigrants, various cultures and communities, meet and find common ground. And what are we to call this common ground? Swedish women and women from Middle Eastern cultures, old women and young women, feminists and those who say they are not feminists, but.... They all seem to find a common cause in the solidarity with a young Muslim woman crossing over to a Western lifestyle or choosing modernity over tradition. Standing there in the freezing cold listening to the speeches and to the singing, watching the flowers, the banners, the signs, I start thinking that maybe these young rebellious women are doing the work of history in these post–9/11 days. They are perhaps keeping the channels of communication open and finding ways for non–Western people—at least some of the young women among them—to negotiate a truce with the culture of modernity. Academics and intellectuals are clamoring for Muslim moderates to rein in the anti-modernist rage, to be a counterweight to their brothers and cousins, followers of the violently anti-modernist ideology of the Muslim Brotherhood and Osama bin Laden. And yet, all the while the women's movement—which no longer wants to be known by that name yet so clearly and obviously is an offshoot of it—is doing the work of moderation, of cultural translation, of absorbing and integrating aspects of Western culture into their collective identity.

I pick up the documentation distributed at the rally and the Swedish discourse is all about setting up networks and safe houses for young immigrant women who want to escape from the patriarchal control of their families. It tries to raise consciousness by telling people that the police are currently investigating five to ten potential cases of this new kind of crime: "honor related murder"; and that four to five hundred young girls are currently on the run from the males in their families and have protected identities. It is all new and a little confusing, as the males are not getting a hearing here. There seems to be no two sides to this issue. The discourse is all about the women's rights over their own lives. And after having consulted my multicultural self, I decide that I am all with Fadime and the Swedish women on the podium. I am even on the side of the figure of authority, the minister of integration, Mona Sahlin. For however much I treasure tolerance and the rights of cultures to self-determination, it cannot be pushed to the point where the achievements of the French and American revolutions and the enlightenment principles of human rights are undermined. If it has taken us two hundred years to discover what we have to do to enforce the granting of human rights to women, our civil liberties cannot be taken for granted. Imagine the women's movement—which we participated in from 1969 and into the 1980s—somehow thirty years later morphs into defense for self-determination for Kurdish and other immigrant women in Sweden. How did it happen and why is nobody saying so? The young women growing up in Sweden in Muslim families are often tempted by the choices open to them: go to university, study, get a job, have fun, get control over their own lives and choose their mates.

A young Kurdish woman is interviewed (anonymously) in a paper distributed free among the demonstrators. She says that people in Sweden still do not understand how serious the problem is. It took too long for Fadime to get help. She would have needed to get into protected housing right away. Now "the culture of honor" has become a well known concept in Sweden. Everybody knows what happened to Fadime, but who will do something about us? Who will help us who were left to live this conflict after her? She is right. More needs to be done. But there is hope because this is the sort of thing for which Sweden has the resources and the ability to mobilize. Freedom for a woman to choose her own lifestyle is self-evident to the very modern western Swedish culture and generates the kind of consensus that Sweden feels comfortable with. Swedish women are no strangers to violence and oppression in their own lives.

Please note that nobody at this meeting begins her speech with "I am not a feminist, but...." Please note also that this movement of solidarity and this bridging the culture gap between Swedes and "immigrants," feminist and young Muslim women, is coming about spontaneously, as a consequence of women identifying with women. Make no mistake, this is not a Muslim issue solely. But of course, the impact of the murder in Swedish political life also owed something to Fadime's engaging persona, her private and public struggle for the right of young Muslim women to have a life of their own choosing, and perhaps also to her beauty and to her free flowing mane of curly black hair. But never mind, she has become an embodiment of a new wave of feminism with a potentially intercultural reach. Swedish feminists of the 1970s fought for access to jobs and top positions, equal pay and day care centers. And as one of them reminded me the other day, much of what the women's movement in Sweden, "Group Eight" as they were called, fought for was won and needs no apologies. By contrast, some of their male colleagues must now apologize for their support of weird causes like the Cultural Revolution in China and Pol Pot. The struggle for women's rights in the home and in the work place is nothing to be ashamed of; these rights have, since the 1970s, become institutionalized and accepted as basic rights in any country that wants to call itself a democracy. And although I just heard a young woman talk about the "trend" of feminism which "had existed five years ago" but was no longer, I chalk that up to the limited range of her vision and experience. It does not matter that some young women talk about "trends of feminism." History happens behind their back, as it were. Swedish women in the new millennium speak with authority from prestigious positions on every level in Swedish economic, social and political life. Pretty blonde women occupy posts in the social democratic government and some of them are very smart and competent to boot. Yet when it comes to violence against women, we discover to our amazement that there is an undertow of a less edifying story.

We need only to think of the late Anna Lindh, who was Sweden's foreign minister until September 10, 2003, when she, not unlike Fadime and for perhaps not so unlike reasons, was assaulted by a violent male who caught up with her on a shopping tour in a department store in Stockholm and slashed her in the abdomen seven times, saying, according to witnesses, "You got what you deserved!" and "You had it coming!" At this point, I hope no one starts thinking in terms of a vast global conspiracy against women; it is only marginally relevant that Anna Lindh's murderer was a young Serb with a hyphenated Swedish-Serbian identity. What is noteworthy here is the similarity of the two women's fates, in spite of the gap in social status between Anna Lindh and Fadime: Lindh, with her intense cool beauty, moved with ease, charm and self-assurance among the grand power brokers of the new Europe; and Fadime relied on Swedish culture and joining a handful of politically active Swedish and Kurdish women to assure her escape from the traditional subjugation of women. They both had their lives snuffed out by archaic male violence. Is there a connection between, on the one hand, the extension of full human rights to women and, on the other, a certain kind of visceral male rage? And isn't it premature to talk about feminism as slightly passé in the face of this murderous rage and violence directed against women moving in the world as free agents, owned by nobody? So maybe what we are facing today is violence against women and a growing solidarity among women across every conceivable divide. A new solidarity growing, woman to woman, between immigrant women and other *femmes engagées* in Europe and across the globe. We have a wild growth of movements and grass root organizations which have the potential of becoming, in many places, a new wave of a women's rights movement focused on the issues of the 21st century; a struggle on a whole range of issues touching on many social conflicts and problems, a cultural war in miniature.

The Swedish Prime Minister is speaking as I write: "References to a religion or a tradition," he is saying, "should never be allowed to get in the way of a woman's human rights. This has to be affirmed in the face of violence not only in our country but also all around the world." And the opposition party attacks him for being too passive and not doing enough and the temperature of the debate goes up several degrees, and the debate will go on because everyone seems to think that somewhere here, maybe, we will find the core of the problem and also the germ of the solution.

Widening our focus, let us look at the role played by feminism in the world today. What I know of it comes from CNN and BBC and an occasional lecture, article or novel written by a woman, most often in India but sometimes in China, Korea or Japan. There are a handful of articulate and authoritative voices of Indian women in the academy. It is not much, but it is a beginning. I have seen programs on the BBC about Muslim women in Jordan organizing for education and for better childbirth preparation, and I have been wondering if that means there is a struggle for Muslim women's rights in other places all across the globe. Reports from Egypt and Jordan tell us about how women struggle for their rights.

Hard to tell without more detailed information. What is not hard is remembering the recent war in Afghanistan. Initially it was supposed to root out the al-Qaeda training camps and deprive Osama bin Laden of territory where he had the means to plan, organize and train people, means which made launching attacks like the one on 9/11 possible. But the end of the war was often described as successful in the Bush administration, not because of the capture of jihadists but by the liberation of Afghan women from their veils and burkas, by the number of schools up and running and the number of girls attending school. It was as if the war for the hearts and minds of people was supposed to be won—globally as far as I can tell—precisely on the issue of the girls in Afghanistan at last being free from the anti-modern Talibans, the girls throwing off their burkas and marching to school in large numbers. It was a victory, worldwide, for the discourse of feminism and modernity. I do think Paul Berman is on to something when he writes: "The Afghan War was, I would think, the first feminist war in all of history—the first war in which women's rights were proclaimed at the start to be a major war aim. No one seemed to notice though. The war was won, more or less, and the scenes of education for women and girls got underway."[8]

Of course, the reality on the ground is much more complicated. A recently released film, *Five in the Afternoon*, by the 23-year-old daughter of the filmmaker of *Kandahar*, Samira Makhmalbaf, shows the heroine intoxicated by the new consciousness, just as we were back in the old days. Her father takes her to school in a donkey cart and she reads the Koran on the way and enters the religious school he has chosen for her. But she exits through the back door and joins a modern school where women are encouraged to want to become teachers, engineers, and presidents of the new Afghan state. Why not? The rest of this wonderful movie, poised between self-intoxication and irony, shows us the heroine trying to figure out what has to be done in the desert of Afghanistan for her to become the future president of her country. Meanwhile, she finds herself together with her father and sister but also with masses of refugees, more and more aimlessly wandering in the desert looking for water, food and some sense of direction, while animals and people are dying from deprivation in the ruins and the sand.

We started something; we happened to find ourselves at the beginning of the second wave of feminism of the twentieth century; we recovered women's history by bits and pieces; we rediscovered women's voices across the centuries and across the geographical and cultural distances; we were part of this large spontaneous movement; we were lucky and in some small way we did our part with our translations, our research and our writings. That women had to have a say in their own lives was something that we had to discover for ourselves; we told it to each other in amazement; and other scholars will come after us and maybe fish us out of the footnotes and say that yes, we were part of the beginning of the cultural revolution. And maybe not. And perhaps it does not really matter because of twenty year old Noqreh, sneaking away to school, pushing away the burka and putting high-heeled shoes on, knowing she would make an excellent president if she just knew how to go about it and, yes, how to find water in the desert.

Appendix: Documents from the Revolution

I. 1971 letter from the Comparative Literature Women's Caucus offering to help the Comparative Literature chair and vice-chair prepare an affirmative action plan

Robert Alter, Chairman
L. Janette Richardson, Vice-Chairman for Graduate Studies
Department of Comparative Literature
University of California Berkeley, California 94720

Dear Mr. Alter and Miss Richardson:

We are sure you are aware of the MLA Report of the Commission on the Status of Women in the Profession reported in the February 1971 Newsletter. As you may recall, the Commission recommended five guidelines for reform in language and literature departments: abolition of anti-nepotism rules, equalization of salaries, part-time tenure-line positions, hiring of women faculty in proportion to the number of Ph.D.'s earned by women in the department, and appropriate course content changes.

The Commission has requested that you submit to them a progress report and explicit affirmative action plans by June, and, as you probably know, preparation for these will require much time, information gathering and discussion. Since we have already devoted considerable energy and thought to the situation of women in the university, we are offering our services and expertise to help you and any committee you establish to prepare a detailed affirmative action plan. We look forward to working with you.

Sincerely yours,

Page du Bois   *Shelley Parlante*
Melanie Kaye Persoff *Lisa Gerrard*
Marsha Hudson   *Judith L. Wells*
Susan Sterling

P.S. Many people in Comparative Literature and in the other language and literature departments have expressed their desire to sign a statement of support for affirmative action along the guidelines of the MLA Commission. We are presently circulating such a statement, and shall forward it to you shortly.

Enclosed: copy of the 1971 MLA Newsletter
cc: Comparative Literature faculty
Elizabeth Scott, Chairwoman of the Academic Senate Subcommittee
    Report on the Status of Women, U.C. Berkeley
Florence Howe, Chairwoman of the MLA Commission on the Status of
    Women in the Profession
Ayesha Andersen, President, A.F.T.1570
Laif Swanson, Chairwoman of the Committee on the Status of the
    Academic Women of the Graduate Assembly

II. 1973 letter from the Comparative Literature Women's Caucus to the Comp. Lit. faculty concerned with placement and hiring, with appended September 1972 MLA newsletter article, "Sexism in Letters of Recommendation: A Case for Consciousness Raising," by Nancy Hoffman

December 4, 1973

The Graduate Women's Caucus of Comparative Literature wishes to call the following article to the attention of all faculty concerned with placement and hiring. This article, which appeared in the September 1972 MLA Newsletter, identifies those groups of women job candidates which have most often been the object of discrimination in hiring, and identifies those practices in the handling of dossiers which contribute to sexual inequality in the profession. We ask that you keep in mind the MLA Commission's suggestions in your writing and reviewing of letters of recommendation for women candidates.

Graduate Women's Caucus
Comparative Literature

SEXISM IN LETTERS OF RECOMMENDATION: A CASE FOR CONSCIOUSNESS RAISING

Over the course of the past year as the jobmarket grew tighter, and the inferior status of women and minorities in colleges and universities came more into public consciousness, members of the MLA Commission on the

Status of Women became increasingly aware of the role played by confidential recommendations in preventing a job seeker from finding a suitable position, or even being interviewed. One young woman, for example, after completing numerous interviews and being offered no jobs was finally told by a frank department chairman that phrases in her dossier like feminine timidity and sweet, retiring nature suggested that she would be unable to survive in the competitive world of the university. Another young woman finally learned that being labeled intellectually assertive, aggressive—qualities appropriate to a male job applicant—had kept her from being granted interviews; male dominated hiring committees are prejudiced against hard-headed women. And still another discovered that a benevolent, protective adviser had simply indicated that this mother's place was in the home, or perhaps a high school, a conclusion that prospective employers readily accepted.

The problem of dossiers is a complex one. Ought dossiers to be confidential? What should we do about a rhetoric of praise that grows more inflated as job openings diminish in number? How can letter writers honestly represent a candidate's virtues when value is measured by a publication record and the dedicated teacher often thought unproductive? What are the serious implications of studies by Lawrence Simpson and Philip Goldberg which show that employers respond more positively to dossiers and articles when they attribute them to a male rather than a female? At a later time, the MLA Commission on the Status of Women would like to examine these larger issues as they pertain to the profile of the new woman academic.

At present, however, in order to point out instances of inadvertent or deliberate sexism, we will examine recommendations as they are written and made in the university world today, and we will propose some practical guidelines for letter writers. We will treat three crucial ways in which letters work to discriminate against women: descriptions of physical attributes and personality; marital status, especially if the spouse is also in academia; participation in women's studies and in contemporary feminism. Some remarks members of the Commission have come upon in their own experience of reading dossiers; others were sent to the Commission by female staff and academic personnel appalled at the remarks of their male colleagues, in the hope that this destructive form of sexism could be acknowledged and then ended. All material in quotation marks comes from dossiers made available to members of the Commission. It is also important to note that the most virulent sexist remarks do not appear in letters written to support a candidate, but rather appear in the written or oral comments of hiring or reviewing committees. Little of this material was available to us in writing, though we could all recall instances of cruelty or humor at the expense of female job candidates.

Physical appearance. Personality. Male dossiers do sometimes include phrases such as dresses well, poised, charming, but such language does not represent a tacit comment that what the male professor lacks in brains, he makes up in beauty. Our experience of women's dossiers confirms that a letter writer, often unselfconsciously, diminishes a female candidate's intellectual power by stereotyping her as too feminine, too pretty. These comments, a composite from a typical candidate's dossier, make a damning package: sweet, but not saccharine, quiet, unaggressive, shy, but very pretty, a decoration to the classroom. Another letter of recommendation from a prestigious graduate school confirms the formula that males see social grace as a substitute for intellectual brilliance: "While _____ probably doesn't have the stamina for independent scholarly work, she loves big parties and mixes well."

Women candidates, to win entire approval, have to be both chic and brilliant, and so the woman who is plain-looking, a spinster-scholar type, evokes a negative response for she is not a complete woman; she lacks sociability, and will not flatter the egos of male department members. Dossier after dossier divulges irrelevant, negative commentary—"large broad-boned somewhat awkward young woman who must be close to six feet in height"; her mousiness belies a sharp mind; "—is tall and proportioned like an Olympic swimmer"; she is a steady woman who will never marry. And within a single paragraph from a male at an elite graduate school, she has a "comfortably upholstered" person and personality, she performed "athletically" in a particular course, she would be the "wheelhorse" of any committee on which she served. And of an older woman, "if she has any faults, they are those that usually accompany the ambitious woman of her age." In other words, the rare comment on a male's appearance is simply a footnote, the frequent comment on a female's, a thesis statement.

Dossiers betray a range of responses to the character of women candidates from the outright misogyny exemplified above to subtle doubt of intellectual equality. The subtle doubts would appear to any good critic of texts. For example, figurative language praising men shows that the writer conceptualizes the candidate's course as active, linear, progressing through time— from lowly instructor to full professor, from fledgling writer to serious scholar, from small reputation to appropriate renown. The young male candidate has "talent," "drive," is "at the start of a long career," "will be on the move," will continue "to surpass himself," to advance; he is "a live wire," "dedicated, industrious, dynamic"; in the classroom his posture is "commanding"; his prose style is "energetic, vigorous." The young woman candidate is praised for being "cooperative, sensitive"; she has "warmth," "good manners," humor, and particularly "rapport with students." She may even be endowed with a "lively intellectual curiosity," and her writing style, if mentioned, is "lucid," "witty," "elegant," or "graceful"[;] "truly readable," one writer said. (Does that mean "light"?) If her future career is under consideration, it is most often to be a "good" one. Letter writers rarely create the expectation of remarkable success so common in recommendations of men. While one would not judge the vocabulary used to praise men as connoting higher moral or ethical value than that praising women, given the values of the university world, the concern for professionalism, the emphasis on publication, the shape of a scholarly career, the qualities ascribed to the woman candidate have a seriously limiting psychological impact. Universities as well as many colleges desire candidates with the traditional commitment to career and profession. Until these values change, the stereotype of the woman candidate that emerges here has the effect of damning her with faint and delicate praise. Though the letter writer himself may clearly admire the personal, private virtues, the gentleness and the modesty he considers appropriately womanly, he himself would never designate these qualities as befitting the public, dignified role of college professor. Men writing recommendations see women as objects of regard, pleasing or otherwise, I mean objects to be regarded, looked at as mistresses and wives, as mothers; women are already tracked in their minds, and they simply track them for employers, reinforcing the vision of woman is helpmeet or playmate, not as intellectual equal and full human being.

Marital Status. Dossiers on women show two distinct patterns—overt discrimination against older women—married, divorced, or single—especially those just entering the job market; second, an almost humorous, but revealing tendency of male letter writers to praise, contrast, describe the work of a female candidate's husband rather than her own, while in men's dossiers wives are rarely mentioned, except as social adornments.

In its affirmative action questionnaire sent to all Ph.D.-granting departments, the MLA Commission on the Status of Women recommended as one guideline flexible institutional policies in graduate study and employment: liberalized rules would remove the penalty many women suffer for marrying or having a family. While strides have been made—some institutions now grant maternity leave which is not counted as time toward a degree, some credit part-time teaching as leading toward tenure—women who would benefit from these changes face deep prejudices in the minds of prospective employers when entering the job market. That is, a woman seeking her first job at age thirty-five, for example, simply does not compete with a twenty-seven-year-old woman or man who has lived continually within university confines; indeed, a university with liberalized rules on degrees may not hire its own graduate because she is too old. Thesis directors and graduate advisers often speak sensitively of their older female students—"Mrs. _____ though a woman and older should be as well received as a younger man," "Mrs. _____ has an adolescent son, knows how to treat teenagers—" virulent prejudice is revealed in the notes hiring and review committees append to dossiers under their scrutiny. Said one reviewer's note on an older woman "Woman named _____ ... should direct mixed choral groups in Pinole." Let her run her household, not our department, said another. By contrast, the dossier of a forty-year-old man asserted that one should hire this man; his distinguished career record (army, public relations) "has been a better preparation for the university than uninterrupted schooling could have been." Of course, more women than men enter the job market in their thirties, and forties, thus all the more reason to be concerned with prejudice against them. Indeed, how many male employers will admit to themselves how frequently these spare statistics—divorced, two children, age thirty-four—represent a woman who interrupted college to support her husband through graduate school, helped to launch his career, then experienced the dissolution of the marriage? Such a woman then completes her degree against great odds, and is now one among the hordes of job seekers. It may be that age, marital status, and number of children should be removed from application forms. Certainly, prejudice against the older woman should be ended, as her varied experience be considered an asset, a valued richness in the often narrow university community.

The invisibility of the female job candidate emerges nowhere more unselfconsciously than in the dossiers of young, married graduate students. The dossiers of undeniably brilliant, serious, promising women, filled with letters of eminent advisers, very frequently compare the woman with her husband, stereotype her as the teacher not the scholar-thinker, and so the less valuable member of the couple. Indeed, one often wonders for whom the letter was written. One woman's letter contains this sentence: "Mrs. _____'s husband ... is an excellent scholar, rather more disciplined and professional in his scholarship. Mrs. _____ complements him with her more imaginative and enthusiastic ... literary rather than historical perspective.... As in the case of her husband, I can recommend ... without reservation...." Or another begins: "and her very able husband _____" and continues, "like her husband, she...." Such letters affect the reader by reinforcing his notion that a woman is an appendage, her career second to her husband's; her talents shine in the light of his. Of course, two people often do desire positions in the same geographical area, and even in the same school, but recommenders do women harm by packaging them in couples.

Antifeminism. Some dossiers provide a commentary on the extent to which the women's liberation movement and its academic component, women's studies, present a threat to the university. One recommender praises his candidate by saying: "If you want a woman who can compete with men on absolutely equal terms—but does not take kindly to letters from the Women's Liberation Front addressed 'Dear Woman'—then I recommend...." Another, enjoying his wit, says she is "feminine indeed, but no feminist...." Another, apologizing for his candidate's decision to write a thesis on nineteenth-century women novelists, claims she is "no fem lib type," but "a real gentlewoman"; that is, her feminism is safely confined to the scholarly. But even with these disclaimers, two prospective employers who read dossiers of women writing dissertations on women were disposed to ask, "Do we need all this feminism that she so militantly carries with her?" and to jeer, "Let's interview her and Ms. _____ [already in the department] can protect the working males." The message, confirmed by this year's reports from the job market, is "we must hire women, but no feminist *activists* need apply."

The need for consciousness raising and for change should by now be apparent. To sum up, the MLA Commission on the Status of Women proposes three guidelines for letter writers:

1. Physical appearance. Personality. Comments on physical appearance are irrelevant to a candidate's ability to succeed in a university career. Comments on personality should individualize a candidate, not stereotype her.

2. Marital status. Marital status, number of children, sexual preference are irrelevant; private facts of a candidate's life are to be divulged as she wishes, and should not be assumed to affect her ability to fulfill career obligations, any more than marriage, children, a lover affect a man's capabilities.

3. Antifeminism. Comments on the relationship of the woman to the women's liberation movement, or women's studies, are appropriate, as any political comments might be, only when they apply to the candidate's field of teaching or scholarship—a teacher of Marxism, a scholar of Virginia Woolf or Jane Austen, an administrator of a women's studies program.

> June 1972
> Nancy Jo Hoffman, MIT
> For the Commission on the Status of Women

III. Letter from Comparative Literature Acting Chair Joseph J. Duggan to Provost Roderick Park requesting funds for continuation of the Comparative Literature women's courses: 40A, B, C and 191D

Berkeley: Department of Comparative Literature
11 September 1974

Provost Roderick Park
Letters and Science
201 Campbell

Dear Provost Park:

The purpose of this letter is to request funds for a series of courses on women in literature and on literature written by women. I believe that the Special State Appropriation for the Improvement of Undergraduate Teaching would be an appropriate source for such funds, but you may know of other resources of which I am not aware.

Over the past three years the Department of Comparative Literature has developed a series of innovative courses treating women and literature. They were offered under two numbers: Comparative Literature 40A-40B-40C, "Women and Literature," and Comparative Literature 191D, "Women Writers in the U.S. and Abroad." Some of the topics presented have been: "Women and Autobiography," "Modern Women's Poetry," "Women in Myth and Fairy Tale," and "The Literature of Androgyny." The lower division course has been taught seven times, the upper division twice. In the upper division course students are required to read literary works written in one foreign language in addition to works written in English, thus upholding the standard employed in all upper division courses in Comparative Literature.

The women's literature courses are innovative in both subject matter and format. Current interest in the roles and contributions of women has led to a re-examination of college and university curricula, where the study of women has often been neglected. One of the aims of this Comparative Literature series is to focus attention on the literary achievements of women who are not yet a part of the critical canon. Such an undertaking is to a great extent a research effort: the discovery of women writers who have remained until now unknown or little known. The courses also include a consideration of sex roles whose importance is increasingly recognized. The form of the courses is innovative as well.

Despite the consistently large number of applicants, the courses have been kept relatively small. Normally around 25 students meet in a seminar situation with guided discussion. The instructor provides a focus, but is also a facilitator and resident expert. This places a great burden upon the student, but despite the difficulties encountered by those who are not accustomed to play an active role in the classroom, the results are impressive, both in terms of the reception of new modes of thought and in the students' ability to articulate complex ideas. Each student is required to undertake an independent project as part of the quarter's work. Proposals for these projects are discussed with the instructor early in the quarter, with advisory sessions as the course progresses. The projects take several forms: films, creative writing (both prose and poetry), television video productions, photo-literary exhibits.

Instructors for the lower division course have been chosen from a ranked list of departmental Associates and Acting Instructors submitted to the Chairman by a departmental screening committee. The proposals reflected a high level of quality. The instructors are able to read in the original language the works which are being taught. Our graduate students must present either two or three literatures for the M.A. and Ph.D. degrees, and must satisfy two foreign language reading requirements for the M.A. and four for the Ph.D. (the latter including either classical Greek or Latin) and are thus well qualified to teach from the original texts. The instructors' enthusiasm has been extraordinary, and resulted in concrete benefits both for themselves and for the reading public. Two groups of students who taught the courses on women and literature have received publishers' contracts for anthologies of poetry. The texts will be printed both in their original language and in translation. *The Other Voice,* an anthology of modern women's poetry, will be published by Norton, and an anthology of women's poetry from all periods of literary history will be published by Penguin Books, Ltd.

During the Spring Quarter, 1974, the women's literature courses were the subject of a discussion in a meeting of the Department's faculty. The virtually unanimous consensus was that the instructors' dedication, the enthusiastic response of students as reflected in the teaching questionnaires which the Department requires in all courses, and the high level of quality in the presentation of subject matter warranted continuation of the women's literature courses. It was felt in particular that a subject of such topical concern easily lends itself to a superficial approach, but that the instructors had firmly shunned such an approach in favor of scholarly concerns and authenticity in the treatment of women's literature as literature.

Two considerations entered at this point. On the one hand, demand for the courses has been high. At first Comparative Literature 40 was the only course on women's literature offered on the Berkeley campus. Despite the introduction of other courses, it has continued to be popular. In the Fall Quarter, 1973, 205 students pre-enrolled for the course. The enrollment figures which follow should be read in the light of our policy of allowing the instructor to limit the enrollment in a particular quarter according to the format to be adopted: lecture (Spring 73, Spring 74), discussion (Spring 72, Winter 73), or seminar (the other quarters):

Enrollment figures for Comparative Literature 40A-40B-40C:

	F	W	Sp
1971–72			31
1972–73	19	30	90
1973–74	23	19	45

Comparative Literature 191-D was approved by the Committee on Courses on a two-year, experimental basis. It was given twice, with marked success:

Enrollment figures for Comparative Literature 191D:

	F	W	Sp
1972–73			38
1973–74	29		

The second consideration is budget.

The Department requested funds to support Comparative Literature 40A-40B-40C for the fiscal year 1974–75, to the extent of two sections per quarter. The budget as approved did not contain sufficient funds to support that course and still maintain the Department's program in the undergraduate and graduate major. At this point, the course does not have funding.

The essence of this proposal is the following. The Department of Comparative Literature requests funds in the amount of $11,133.88 for fiscal year 1974–75, $11,692.67 for 1975–76, and $12,277.31 for 1976–77 (assuming for the last two a 5% per year cost-of-living increase in order to offer Comparative Literature 40A-40B-40C only once each quarter but with an associate acting as a teaching assistant, and Comparative Literature 191D once each year. (It is understood that offering the latter course would be contingent upon approval by the Committee on Courses.) This is equivalent to .67FTE Acting Instructor level plus .50FTE Associate level per year for the lower division course only.

Proposed Budget

	.67FTE *Acting Instructor*	*.50FTE Associate*	*Total*
1974–75	$6,807.88	$4,325.00	$11,133.88
1975–76	$7,150.37	$4,542.30	$11,692.67
1976–77	$7,507.89	$4,769.42	$12,277.31
			$35,103.86

These funds are not available from the normal university budget. The courses are innovative and meet an obvious need which has been neglected in the past. They have the support of the departmental faculty.

Would it be possible to have a prompt reply on this request as it pertains to 1974–75? One of our Associates or Acting Instructors would have to be assigned to the course for Fall, 1974, and another applicant hired as a replacement as soon as possible.

Yours sincerely,

Joseph J. Duggan
Acting Chairman

cc: Dean Anne Kilmer
    Vice-Chancellor Ira Heyman
    Chairman Janette Richardson
    Professor Joyce Kallgren

IV: 1975 fall quarter directory of women in feminist research on the U.C.B. campus, from the Center for Continuing Education of Women

The idea for this Directory grew out of a workshop offered at C.C.E.W. Women's Center in 1974–1975, Women in Feminist Research: *Workshop and Colloquium*. The impetus for such a workshop came from the knowledge that women engaged in research about women were not encouraged or taken seriously enough by their respective departments. In response to this situation, the workshop provided an opportunity for women students and faculty in all disciplines to exchange information, share enthusiasm and support each other's endeavors.

In this spirit, we resolved to find out which other women on the Berkeley campus were engaged in similar research pursuits. Accordingly letters were sent out from C.C.E.W. to all women faculty and graduate secretaries in March 1975. The following list is no doubt incomplete for a variety of reasons; however, it is certainly indicative of a growing interest in feminist research, and representative of the many disciplines through which it may be approached.

You may wish to contact women in your field through the departments indicated, perhaps set up smaller informal workshops in a particular area, or in interdisciplinary areas. We at the Center encourage you to keep us informed of other research efforts and new projects and groups organized around feminist research. We are committed to seeking change in the lives of women, and toward this end, to the creation of a 'community' of feminist scholars on this campus.

In Sisterhood,
Helene V. Wenzel
Associate Director
C.C.E.W. Women's Center

NOTE:
The C.C.E.W. Women's Center is planning a "New Research on Women" conference to be held Spring Quarter 1976 on this campus. We invite all UCB faculty engaged in research on women to contact us in order that the conference best reflect the range of interests being researched.

AGRICULTURAL ECONOMY

Deere, Carmen Diana	"The Division of Labor by Sex Latin American Agriculture: in Peasant Women on Subsistence Farms."	Ph.D. Thesis

ANTHROPOLOGY

Browner, Carole	"Abortion and Family Structure in Cali, Columbia."	Ph.D. Thesis
Katzir, Yael	"The Effects of Migration and Mobility on the Status and Role of Women: The Case of Yemenite-Jews in Israel."	Ph.D. Thesis
Lepowsky, Maria	"A Comparative Analysis of Male and Female Roles: Mishima Island, Louisiade Archipelago, Papua, New Guinea."	Ph.D Thesis
Picard-Mason, Karen	"The Role of Women in a Changing Subsistence Economy: A Tobago Example."	Ph.D. Thesis

ARCHITECTURE

Wright, Gwen	*A Woman's Place Is in the Home: Middle Class Women and Their Housing*	Book

SOUTH AND SOUTHEAST ASIAN STUDIES

Singh, Jane	"Women in the Hindi Novel: The Post-Independence Period."	Ph.D. Thesis

CITY AND REGIONAL PLANNING

Jones, Lynn	"Structural Constraints on Women's Employment: suburbanization, availability of homemaking services, job structures."	Ph.D. Thesis
West, Ann	"Women's Image on the Screen as a Reflection of the American Self-Concept: Implications for Social Change."	Ph.D. Thesis
Grinel, Susan	"Service Institutions for Dependent Children."	Ph.D. Thesis

CLASSICS

Feyerabend, Barbara	"A Study of Maenadism in Graeco-Roman Antiquity."	Ph.D. Thesis

COMPARATIVE LITERATURE

Hudson, Marsha	Poetry of Muriel Rukeyser.	Ph.D. Thesis
Lashgari, Deirdre	"Stasis and Change in the Women Characters in Jane Austen, Charlotte Brontë, and George Eliot."	Ph.D. Thesis
Bowles, Gloria	"Aspects of Poetry by Women: Adrienne Rich, Denise Levertov."	Ph.D. Thesis
Sterling, Sue	"The Change in the 18th Century Heroine in German literature from the Enlightenment to *Sturm und Drang*."	Ph.D. Thesis
Wells, Judy	"Madness in Women's Literature."	Ph.D. Thesis
Persoff, Melanie	"The Sword Philippan: Woman as Hero in Stuart Tragedy."	Ph.D. Thesis

CRIMINOLOGY

Coles, Frances	"Women in Litigation Practice"	Ph.D. Thesis
Schwendinger, Julia	"The Forcible Rape Victim."	Ph.D. Thesis
Grabiner, Virginia	"The Women's Suffrage Movement and Social Control."	Ph.D. Thesis
Truniger, Elizabeth	"Marital Violence: Its Legal Solutions."	Ph.D. Thesis

ECONOMICS

Goldberg, Marilyn	"Housework as a Production Activity."	Ph.D. Thesis
Vickery, C.	Decision-making of Single Adult, Low Income Families.	Article

EDUCATION

Sywak, Marjorie	"Towards Nonsexist Schools Through Inservice Education."	Ph.D. Thesis
Wickstrom, Diane	"Changes in Roles and Relationships of Married Re-entry Women in Community Colleges."	Ph.D.Thesis
Jacobs, Karen	"Moralities: Female and Male."	Ph.D. Thesis

Hurn, Karen	"The Impact of Variation of Parent's Language on the Child's Self Image."	Ph.D.Thesis
Halladay, Karen	"Aggression in Young Women: Correlations and Hypotheses."	Ph.D.Thesis
Brown, Melanie	"A Study of the Effects of the Practice of Transcendental Meditation on Pregnancy and Childbirth."	Ph.D.Thesis
Shelton, Dinah	Curriculum and Education Policy	Ph.D. Thesis
Caffrey, Cathleen	"Stability of Self-Description."	Ph.D. Thesis
Cassidy, Claudia	"Developmental Aspects of Achievement Motivation in College Women."	Ph.D.Thesis
DeGarmo, Elivinia	"Mexican American Women: An Exploratory Study of Social Interactions."	Ph.D.Thesis
Faden, Ruth	"Informed Consent: A Psychosocial Paradigm Applied to Family Planning."	Ph.D.Thesis
Fortin, Michele	"Educational Investment in Women in Canada."	Ph.D.Thesis
Largman, Rita	"The Effects of Length of Time in Day Care on Emotional Health of 4-Year-Old Children."	Ph.D.Thesis
Scherini, Rose	"Occupational Goals of Minority Students."	Ph.D. Thesis
Rhodes, Leanne	"Sex Differences in Mental Test Performance in Medically High-Risk Infants."	Ph.D.Thesis
McClosky, Mildred	"An Exploratory Investigation of the Attitudes, Perceptions, Goals of Mature Women Seeking Re-Entry into Higher Education."	Ph.D. Thesis
Smith, Yvonne	"The Relationship of Skin Color and Teacher Perception of Pupil Behavior in the Classroom."	Ph.D.Thesis
Sund, Alice	"Influence of Achievement, Motivation and Competition	Ph.D.Thesis

with Men on Women's Subjective
Estimates of Success."

| Young, Enid | "An Investigation of the Phen-omena of Body Awareness in Women, Using Yoga as a Thera-peutic Technique in Relation to Body Consciousness." | Ph.D.Thesis |

ENGLISH

O'Neill, Eleanor	George Eliot: Gender Role Identification and the Woman Artist.	Ph.D.Thesis
Brown, Dorothy	"A Study of Feminism in the Life and Writings of Virginia Woolf."	Ph.D.Thesis
Kask, Melanie	"Mrs. Woolf and Mrs. Brown: Form in Pursuit of Process."	Ph.D.Thesis
Katz, Claire	"The Need to Deny Autonomy, and the Impulse Toward Self-Annihilation in the Fiction of Flannery O'Connor."	Ph.D.Thesis
Miller, Miriam	"Henry James's Double Vision: His Ambivalent Stance Towards Woman as a Continuing Source and Determinant of Plot from Earliest to Latest Fiction."	Ph.D.Thesis
Nissman, Judith	"A Study of Schizophrenia in Works by Women Writers."	Ph.D.Thesis
Eggebroten, Anne	"Religious Women in the Middle Ages."	Ph.D. Thesis

ETHNIC STUDIES

Chicano Studies

| Gonzalez, Lila | "The Chicana in Chicano Literature." | Article |

Native American Studies

| Kidwell, Clara | "American Indian Women and Women's Liberation." | Unpublished Paper |

FRENCH

Wenzel, Helene	"Feminist Perspectives on Contemporary French Women Writers."	Ph.D. Thesis
Eisenberg, Helene	"Feminism in the Works of Simone de Beauvoir."	Ph.D. Thesis
Kneeland, Marilyn	"Five Women Novelists at the End of the Ancient Regime: A Literary Study of Mmes. Cottin and Krudener, Mmes. de Duras, de Genlis, and de Sousa."	Ph.D. Thesis

GEOGRAPHY

Marburg, Sandra	"An Examination of Images of Women Reflected in the Professional Literature of Geography."	Ph.D. Thesis

GERMAN

Frederickson, Christiane	"The Role of Woman in the *Sturm und Drang Drama*."	Ph.D. Thesis
Morse, Margaret	"Motifs of Women in the Worlds of Selected Women Writers of the 19th and 20th Centuries."	Ph.D. Thesis
Humel, Gerda	"Motive und Tendenzen in den Prosa schriften der Marie von Ebner-Eschenbach."	Ph.D. Thesis
Wright, Barbara	"Artists, Intellectuals and Politicians: Rosa Luxemburg and the Cultural Milieu of Berlin 1900–15."	Ph.D.Thesis

HISTORY

McLaughlin, Cynthia	Women in France, 1789–1870.	Seminar Paper
Accampo, Elinor	"The Family and Industrialization in France."	Ph.D. Thesis
Davis, Natalie	"Women's History in Transition: European Case."	Article appearing in *Feminist Studies*

Easton, Barbara	"The Family: Revivalism as an Indication of Social Change in Early New England."	Ph.D. Thesis
Reed, Mary	"The Political Woman, A Case Study of Women as Factors of Social Change in Croatia, Yugoslavia, 1929 to 1945."	Ph.D. Thesis
Rosen, Ruth	"The Lost Sisterhood: Prostitution in the American Past."	Ph.D. Thesis
Scholten, Catherine	"Maternity: Childbearing and Femininity in America, 1630–1920."	Ph.D. Thesis
Fass, Paula	*Modern Youth Culture.*	Book

HISTORY OF SCIENCE (Collegiate Seminar Program)

| Iltis, Carolyn | "Women and the Order of Nature: Views of Nature and the Female During the Scientific Revolution." | Article (Part of book in progress) |

INSTITUTE OF HUMAN DEVELOPMENT

Block, Jeanne	Research on ego and sex-role development.	Articles and book chapters
Stroud, Janice	"Women's Employment, Life Patterns and Personality in Middle Age."	Ph.D. Thesis
Peskin, Tsipora	"Divorce and the Adult Life Span: A Longitudinal Study."	Ph.D. Thesis

INSTITUTE OF PERSONALITY ASSESSMENT AND RESEARCH

| Cartwright, Lillian | "Women Physicians." | Monograph |
| Helson, Ravenna | "Creativity in Women." | Article |

ITALIAN

| D'Orazy, Elizabeth | Research on the novelist, Anna Radius Zuccari (1846–1918), who wrote under the name Neera. | Ph.D. Thesis |

LATIN AMERICAN STUDIES

| Knaster, Meri | *Women in Latin America: An Annotated Bibliography.* | Book in progress |

MUSIC

| Susskind, Pamela | "The Works of Clara Schumann." | Ph.D. Thesis |

NUTRITION

Carter, Doreen	"Response of Protein and Selected Minerals to Oral Contraceptive Administration in Healthy Women."	Ph.D. Thesis
Chall, Malca	"Women in Politics: The Suffragists."	Oral history memoirs of 12 suffragists
Chall, Malca	"California Women Political Leaders, memoirs 1920–1970."	Oral history of women political leaders, pre–Women's Movement

POLITICAL SCIENCE

| van Allen, Judy | Research on African women, women and politics, and the "Invisibility" of women to male researchers. | Ph.D. Thesis |
| Greenwood, Lois | "Research on 'masculine' and 'feminine' Authority Patterns, Patriarchalism." | Ph.D. Thesis |

PSYCHOLOGY

Stapp, Joy	Research on Sex-Role Development and Attitudes Toward Women.	
Weston, Amy	Research on Mother and Daughter Relationships.	M.A. Thesis
Solomon, Trudy	"Sex Discrimination in Psychiatry."	M.A. Thesis
Butler, Pam	*Assertiveness Training for Women.*	Book

Carrillo-Beron, Carmen   "The Effect of Group Process on   Ph.D. Thesis
                         Sex-Role Ideology in Chicano and
                         Anglo Adolescents."

PUBLIC HEALTH

Rahman, Shafiqur   "A Comparative Study of the   Ph.D. Thesis
                         Factors Affecting the Choice of
                         Intra-Uterine Device and Oral
                         Contraceptives."

Supannatas, Somjit   "Some Psychological, Social, and   Ph.D. Thesis
                         Cultural Factors Affecting the
                         Non-Acceptance of a Birth Con-
                         trol Method among Thai Married
                         Women Who Already Have Two
                         Children at the Post-partum Period."

RHETORIC

Sullivan, Nell   "The Female Voice in Gothic   Ph.D. Thesis
                         Fiction."

SLAVIC

Coote, Mary   "Women's Narrative Songs in   Article
                         Serbo-Croatian."

SOCIAL WORK

Nichols, Abigail   "The Determinants of the Labor   DSW Thesis
                         Force Participation of AFDC
                         Mothers."

Peskin, Tsipora   "Divorce and the Adult Life Style: DSW Thesis
                         A Longitudinal Study."

Moses, Alice   "On Avoiding the Straight-   DSW Thesis
                         Jacket: The Sex-Role Socialization
                         and Sex Role Behavior of Lesbian
                         Women."

Hochschild, Arlie   Sex Differences in Emotion-Work.   Book

Gaffin, Judith   "Manifestations of Gender Strat-   Ph.D. Thesis
                         ification in Interactions Between
                         Single Adults."

Gladieux, Johanna	"Pregnancy, The Transition to Parenthood: Satisfaction with the Pregnancy Experience as a Function of the Marital Relationships and Social Network."	Ph.D. Thesis
Horowitz, Diane	Role Induction in Pregnancy: The Social Creation of Motherhood."	Ph.D. Thesis
Micossi, Anita	"The Effects of Communal Living on Dyadic Intimacy."	Ph.D. Thesis
Raz, Maxine	"Adult Socialization: An Example from the Contemporary Women's Movement."	Ph.D. Thesis
Sells, Lucy	"Sex and Discipline Differences in Doctoral Attrition."	Ph.D. Thesis
Stroud, Janice	"Women's Employment, Life Patterns, and Psychological Functioning in the Middle Age."	Ph.D. Thesis
Polotnik, Margaret	The male definition of sexuality.	Research
Leffler, Anne	Non-verbal indicators of sex related differences.	Research
Morgan, Elizabeth	Parenting in the Black family.	Research
Joslyn, Kersten	The politics of volunteerism.	Research
Stueve, Ann	Old age and widowhood.	Research

STATISTICS

Scott, Elizabeth	Salary inequities, employment inequities, inequities in admissions of students, etc.	Articles, position papers
Davis, Amy	Inequities in admission of students.	Research
Marchat, Francoise	Inequities in salary.	Research

VI: Women's Caucus letter to Vice Chancellor Ira Michael Heyman

May 18, 1976
Ira Michael Heyman
The Vice Chancellor

University of California, Berkeley

Vice Chancellor Heyman:

The Comparative Literature Women's Caucus, composed of graduate women in Comparative Literature, would like to append this report to our department's self-evaluation. Since you stressed that the treatment of students should be the specific focus of this self-evaluation, we believe our evaluation of the Comparative Literature Department will be of interest to you.

According to the Comparative Literature Departmental report for 1974–75, women represent the majority of students on every academic level except the doctoral, where an equal number of male and female students received the doctorate. The Comparative Literature Women's Caucus continues to assert that sex discrimination does exist in our department as long as an equal number of men and women do not hold faculty positions. Men hold positions in the department in the ratio of 3:1, but the department continues to hire more men than women. Last year two men and one woman were hired in Comparative Literature. This policy promotes sex discrimination in our department. We believe that women should be hired exclusively until the ratio of men to women is equal. If the department committed itself to this affirmative action, female graduate students would eventually see women moving up the academic ladder and receiving tenure. At present only two women hold tenure in a faculty of twenty-four persons.

This imbalance is discouraging to women students, who feel that even though they are allowed to study literature and get degrees, they will be thoroughly discriminated against once they enter the job market. To promote the hiring of more women in the Department, the Women's Caucus believes that the Affirmative Action Committee should inform women students of its policies and include women students in its membership. The Caucus learned only recently that this committee existed.

The Comparative Literature Women's Caucus initiated an outstanding and highly successful program of Women's Studies courses which has become part of the University's overall Women's Studies Program. The Caucus feels that Comparative Literature has not made an effort to hire a woman in a ladder faculty position specializing in Women's Studies and Literature. As a result, the Department has recruited instructors who do not do research in Women's Studies to teach the upper division course in Women and Literature. This practice reflects the attitude towards Women's Studies which many faculty members take. Many professors do not consider Women's Studies a legitimate academic field. Women graduate students who are dealing exclusively with women authors and who present a feminist perspective in their research report that faculty members do not take their work seriously. Consequently, women in these areas of research are often actively or subtly discouraged from offering a new perspective on literature.

The Comparative Literature Women's Caucus recommends that the Department hire a woman faculty member who does research on women and literature and who would like to teach classes in this area. This affirmative act would prevent the Department from asking an instructor to teach the women's course solely because she is female, rather than because she has specialized in Women's Studies, and it would provide a competent and encouraging advisor for women students studying women's literature.

We also recommend that the Department eliminate night courses because women cannot commute to class safely at night. Several women in the required graduate introductory course reported that they were harassed and, in two cases, nearly raped when returning from this course.

Although statistics show women students to be in the majority on every academic level except the doctorate, these figures do not relate the real experience of female students in Comparative Literature. The psychological undermining of the female student's confidence and self-esteem is ritualized through sexist jokes and comments on exams and recommendations. Here are a few of the faculty comments reported by women students:

(1) One woman was told on her Ph.D. exam that she "thought like a woman," while another faculty member on the same exam told the woman she "thought like a man." Both comments were intended as criticisms, the first meaning that the woman was insufficiently logical and rational, the second meaning just the opposite, but implication that she was not "womanly" enough.

(2) Another woman was greeted by the chairman of her M.A. oral exam with the comment, "Would you like to sit in that empty chair there or in Mr. ___'s lap?"

(3) One woman reports that before her M.A. exam a male professor said to her: "My dear young lady, you overestimate your abilities. You are overambitious." She was so demoralized that she temporarily withdrew from the University. She is now a Ph.D. and a literature professor.

(4) Several female graduate students commented that faculty joke about women's appearance and clothing.

(5) Several women reported that faculty used words with sexist bias to evaluate their exams or dissertation research. Words and phrases like "naive" and "lacks intellectual rigor" were more frequent criticisms of female than male students. Evaluations also contained such statements as "she's a charming girl, but..."

(6) A female graduate student, consulting her male advisor, reported.

the following interchange. When she went to his office, he greeted her with "I'd kiss you, but I have a cold." He then saw a male colleague passing his door, and called out to him loudly, "I'd kiss her, but I have a cold."

(7) Women report that faculty members are often condescending to the secretarial staff in Comparative Literature.

Male faculty members expect women students to react to these critical, humiliating, and condescending comments and attitudes with humor and acceptance. If a woman does not react with a grin, she is considered "lacking in any sense of humor."

This patronizing of female students, in both its subtle and gross forms, impedes, if not destroys, intellectual exchange between female students and male faculty members (and female faculty members who have adopted the same posture). Women students feel male faculty members do not treat them as peers but rather as children, sex objects, mothers, muses (researchers), and menials (typists). Because the professor often holds a great deal of power over the student's career, his/her relationship with the student is essential to the student's future. Therefore, it is the professor's responsibility to avoid belittling a female student by treating her according to a sexist type. Professors should recognize they are affecting a person's self-image as well as her/his status in the department, and that a failure to treat someone as a serious student contributes to that person's inability to take her/himself seriously.

Because these attitudes make it difficult for women to establish good rapport with faculty members, female graduate students often avoid consulting faculty members when it is not absolutely necessary. Women see their male colleagues functioning more comfortably and effectively both in the mentor/protege (male professor/male student) model and in the old boy" system of mutual favors when they are looking for jobs. Even if the male graduate student is uncomfortable in his role, he at least has the assurance that once he passes his initiation rites, he will enter an establishment that welcomes his gender. The fact that he knows there are eighteen men and only six women on the Comparative Literature faculty gives him a psychological edge over women. The male graduate student recognizes his future place if his instructors, exam committees, and advisors are predominately male; the female graduate student realizes that she must either be exceptional or excluded.

It should be no surprise, then, that in 1974–75 Comparative Literature had 15 female and 5 male doctoral candidates, but only 3 female Ph.D.'s and 3 male Ph.D.'s. Although these figures require further documentation, they suggest what many women graduate students know: that seven to ten years of discrimination and overt and subtle psychological undermining discourage women from finishing their Ph.D.'s. Since both statistics and the experience of students indicate the discrimination of women in the Comparative Literature Department, the Caucus hopes that you will consider this report carefully and that the information will be useful to you.

Sincerely, The Women's Caucus
Department of Comparative Literature

Contributors

JOANNA BANKIER believes that having been born Jewish in Warszaw (Poland) in 1939 and having survived may have predestined her for a belief in the possibility of a life of narrow escapes and events out of the ordinary. Or maybe it was a matter of temperament which made her experience the revolution in consciousness of May '68 (Paris), if not as a norm at least as the way life should be, a perception which was confirmed in the following years in Marsha Hudson's women's caucus meetings and the heartwarming collaborative work with women graduate students–friends in Comparative Literature at UC Berkeley. These experiences also generated a heady sense of being able to shape things to correspond a little better to human desires and operated a radical break in the horizon of her everyday expectations, affirming that women and ordinary people could speak from a subject position. In the two anthologies, *The Other Voice*, 1975, and *Women Poets of the World*, 1982, Joanna Bankier collaboratively set out to articulate this new ontology and her subsequent work in translation studies, cultural studies and Jewish studies has continued to mix, in a similar way, scholarship with political and existential commitment. Her latest book, *Nyhetens Obehag* (Newness and Its Discontents), appeared in 2001 in Sweden, where she presently lives and teaches interdisciplinary courses in the humanities.

GLORIA BOWLES received her Ph.D. in 1976. She went on to be the founding Coordinator of Women's Studies at UC Berkeley, 1976–1985. She has taught Women's Studies at UC Santa Cruz, UC Davis, Stanford University, and UC Berkeley. She has been named Distinguished Woman Scholar (UC Davis, 1986) and was elected to Women's Hall of Fame at UC Berkeley in 1995. Among her numerous publications are *Theories of Women's Studies* (ed., with Renate Duelli-Klein), 1983; *Strategies for Women's Studies in the Eighties* (ed., 1984); *Louise Bogan's Aesthetic of Limitation* (1987); and presently in manuscript, *The Unsettled Self: Journals 1961–88*. Since 1986 she has been on the editorial board of Women's Studies International Forum.

BRIDGET CONNELLY is a folklorist who writes about rural and migrating peoples. An emerita professor of Rhetoric at the University of California,

Berkeley, she enjoyed a 22-year teaching career after receiving her Ph.D. in Comparative Literature (Arabic and French) in 1974. She worked at Cornell University as an assistant professor of Arabic, where she also taught French and Comparative Literature; as a Fulbright Teaching Fellow, she taught American Literature at the University of Besançon, France. For her work recording Arabic oral traditional narrative in Tunisia and Egypt, the Finnish Academy elected her a Folklore Fellow in Epic. Her first publication received the Arberry Prize in Arabic Literature (1974) at Cambridge University, and her book, *Arab Folk Epic and Identity* (California 1986), received the 1987 Chicago Folklore Prize as the best book worldwide in folklore. She has also translated Arabic and Provençal poetry *(Women Poets of the World,* Bankier and Lashgari, editors). In Dublin, her recent book, *Forgetting Ireland* (Borealis Books 2003), was named a "best book of 2003" by *The Irish Times.*

LAUREN COODLEY was born in Los Angeles where her maternal grandparents moved in 1920, five years after Upton Sinclair's arrival. She has been teaching at Napa Community College for her entire adult life, usually classes she created, including math anxiety, women's history, children's literature, and California history. She has just been re-elected president of the faculty, and received the Distinguished Teaching Award for 2003. Lauren will be publishing two books in the next year. She is editing a collection of Upton Sinclair's writings about California (including the story of Liberty Hill) for Heyday Books, and she is writing a history of the City of Napa which will focus on Napa's unknown labor history. She recently organized an eight month community campaign for locked out UFCW workers at one of Napa's last union wineries, and participated in the hiring of the new manager of KPFA/Pacifica radio.

NAOMI V. CUTNER graduated from UC Berkeley in 1970 with a double major in French and Comparative Literature and received her master's degree in Comparative Literature in 1974. In 1975 she moved to New York and worked in book publishing and journalism; in 1995 she received her MSW and began her career as a social worker and psychotherapist. She treats adults and children in an outpatient mental health clinic and in her private practice. In 2003 she completed five years of psychoanalytic training. She loves and partakes enthusiastically of all that her adopted city has to offer, though she left at least a piece of her heart in her native California.

DORIS EARNSHAW graduated from Middlebury College, Vermont, in 1946, majoring in political science and languages. After graduation she taught English for a year at Le College Cevenol in the south of France. There followed a long hiatus of family-centered time before she returned at age 45 to graduate school. In 1981 she finished a Ph.D. at U.C. Berkeley in Comparative Literature. She has held faculty positions at the University of California campuses at Berkeley, Irvine and Davis, and at universities in Ohio and Colorado. Retiring in 1993, she began a publishing business, Alta Vista Press, that published a *Women Speak* series in three volumes: *California Women Speak* (1994); *American Women Speak* (1995); and *International Women Speak, the Emergence of Women's Global Leadership* (2000). Other publications include: *The Female Voice in Medieval Romance Poetry*, Peter Lang, 1988; *The Other Voice, Twentieth Century Women Poets in Translation*, W.W. Norton, 1976; and reviews in *World Literature Today*, 1980–present.

OLIVIA EIELSON received her B.A. in English from Radcliffe College, her M.A. in English from the University of Minnesota, and her Ph.D. in Comparative Literature from U.C. Berkeley. She also studied painting, first with Morton Sacks (Boston/Cambridge) and then at Oskar Kokoschka's *Schule des Sehens* in Salzburg, Austria. She has taught English at several colleges, and for many years was an Academic Counselor at St. Mary's College in California. Although she has had verse published in various small magazines, her main work has been in painting. She has had many one-woman shows, and her paintings are in private collections across the U.S.

After receiving her Ph.D. from Berkeley in 1981, DEBORAH ELLIS went on to a distinguished career as a teacher and medieval scholar. She taught at Case Western Reserve for five years, then moved to Southwestern University where she was a key founder of the Women's Studies program as well as the Writing Center; she chaired the Faculty Affairs Council, served as acting chair of the English Department and as University Sexual Harassment Officer; she also brought a Phi Beta Kappa chapter to Southwestern's campus. Ellis was a member of the executive committee of the Arthurian Literature Group of the Modern Language Association. She co-authored *Phi Beta Kappa General Report* (Southwestern 1989) and co-edited *No More Stares* (Berkeley: Disability Research and Education Defense Fund 1981). Her scholarly work received many fellowships, including a National Endowment award, a Fulbright Fellowship to Great Britain, and a Brown Fellowship. Ellis published many scholarly articles on the domestic sphere and has written a book on the representation of the home in early English and Spanish literature. In October 1999 Debby Ellis died very suddenly of a heart attack. Her students at Southwestern University proposed the university honor their devoted and energetic teacher by naming the new writing center as a tribute to her: Today it is called the Debby Ellis Writing Center.

LISA GERRARD is a lecturer in the writing programs at the University of California, Los Angeles, and has published in women's studies, literature, rhetoric, and computers and composition. Her most recent work is "Beyond 'Scribbling

Women': Women Writing (on) the Web," edited by Sibylle Gruber (2002). In 2001, she was awarded the Technology Exemplar Award by the National Council of Teachers of English for her research, teaching, and service to the profession in the use of computer technology in English.

JENNIFER RUTH HOSEK is finishing her dissertation in Comparative Literature at Berkeley entitled "Imagining Cuba: German Representations of Exotic Utopia." The study analyzes German national identity as triangulated through representations of Cuba in German literature, film and cultural artifacts. She has published on East German literature and the intersections of critical theory and neuroscience. Jennifer is the recipient of numerous honors, including the Center for German and European Studies Research Fellowship, the Alexander von Humboldt Research Fellowship, the German Academic Exchange Research Fellowship (DAAD), and UC Berkeley's Outstanding Teaching Award. In addition to being an avid teacher, she has presented on and organized numerous academic panels and is involved in several professional organizations, notably and currently as a WiG Steering Committee member. Her extra-academic activism includes organizing and publishing on women's health and community infrastructure. After living on military bases in Germany until the age of 20, she completed a double BA *summa cum laude* and with Highest Distinction in German and Comparative Literature at the University of Illinois, Urbana-Champaign. In addition to English, Jennifer speaks German, French and Spanish.

MARSHA HUDSON received her B.A., M.A. and Ph.D. in Comparative Literature at the University of California, Berkeley. During her graduate school years she taught at UC Berkeley and at Santa Clara University. Upon completion of her doctoral work she developed a career in the financial services industry, rising to the level of senior vice president. She returned to part-time teaching in 1990 while she wrote a novel (unpublished) and served on the faculties of several community colleges in Southern California. She currently is on the faculties of UC Santa Cruz and Cabrillo College, and is a certified gestalt practitioner.

From a feminist perspective, MELANIE KAYE/KANTROWITZ's academic life was saved twice: once by J.J. Wilson, with whom she worked as a teaching assistant and who offered an example (then very rare) of an enormously talented woman teacher and scholar doing absolutely everything her own way; the second time was by the Comp. Lit. Women's Caucus. After completing her doctorate in Comparative Literature at Berkeley, and a Renaissance dissertation, Kaye/Kantrowitz reconstructed herself as a teacher of Women's Studies, Jewish Studies, and race theory, and as a writer. She is the author of several books, including *The Color of Jews* (to appear from South End Press in 2005), *The Issue Is Power: Essays on Women, Jews, Violence, and Resistance* (Aunt Lute, 1992), *My Jewish Face and Other Stories* (Aunt Lute, 1990), *Diaspora: a Novel* (seeking a publisher), and *Tales of Late Capitalism* (in progress). Her work is widely published in the feminist, gay and lesbian, and progressive Jewish press, and she reviews regularly for *The Women's Review of Books*, in which her essay originally appeared. She is also a long-time social justice activist, the former director and co-chair of Jews for Racial and Economic Justice in New York City, and is currently the director of the Queens College/City University of New York Worker Education Extension Center in Manhattan.

ROBIN TOLMACH LAKOFF received her A.B. (magna cum laude) from Harvard College in Classics and Linguistics; her M.A. from Indiana University in Linguistics and Classics; and her Ph.D. from Harvard University in Linguistics. She has been a faculty member in the Linguistics Department of the University of Michigan. Since 1972 she has been a member of the Linguistics Department of the University of California at Berkeley. She was a Fellow at the Center for Advanced Study in the Behavioral Sciences at Stanford University in 1971–72, and has been an NIMH Postdoctoral Fellow at M.I.T. and has been awarded a Guggenheim fellowship. Among her publications are *Abstract Syntax and Latin Complementation*, M.I.T. Press, 1968; *Language and Woman's Place*, Harper & Row, 1975; *Face Value: The Politics of Beauty* (with Raquel Scherr), Routledge & Kegan Paul, 1984; *When Talk Is Not Cheap* (with Mandy Aftel), Warner, 1985; *Talking Power: The Politics of Language* (Basic Books, 1991); *Father Knows Best: The Use and Abuse of Psychotherapy in Freud's Case of Dora* (with James Coyne), Teachers College Press, 1993; and *The Language War*, University of California Press, 2000. She has also published about 80 scholarly papers, reviews, and articles in newspapers and magazines, on topics including the semantics of modality; the relationship between *some* and *any;* language and law; language and gender; language in psychotherapy; advertising language; narrative in group and individual identity formation; and the analysis of political rhetoric.

DEIRDRE LASHGARI is professor of English at California State Polytechnic University, Pomona, where she specializes in ethnic and world literatures, as well as writing by women. She helped organize the student multicultural club MADILA, and served for a number of years as faculty sponsor. Earlier she taught English for a year at Sonoma State University, and (as a part-time lecturer) at Mills College in Oakland, San Francisco State University, and (six years) at UC Berkeley (in the Peace and Conflict Studies Program, the undergraduate seminar program Strawberry Creek College, and the Comparative Literature Department). She is co-editor of two international anthologies of poetry by women, *The Other Voice: Women's Poetry in Translation* (Norton, 1976) and

Women Poets of the World (Macmillan, 1983). She also edited and contributed two pieces to a volume of essays on women writers with the University Press of Virginia (1995) *Violence, Silence, and Anger Women's Writing as Transgression.* Currently, she is working on a volume of essays entitled *Reconceiving the World: Contemporary Global Poetry by Women.* In 1969, she spent a year in Iran on a Fulbright Fellowship studying Western and folk influences on modern Iranian poetry, as well as women's changing roles in urban and village life. She has translated both classical and modern Iranian poetry, and has written, published, and lectured on Iranian fiction and film as well as on women writers of fiction and poetry in Iran, China, India, Ghana, and the United States.

SHERYL ST. GERMAIN has taught creative writing at the University of Texas at Dallas, The University of Louisiana at Lafayette, Knox College, and is currently on the creative writing faculty at Iowa State University where she teaches both poetry and creative nonfiction, and directs the Center for Excellence in the Arts and Humanities. Her work has received several awards, including two NEA Fellowships, an NEH Fellowship, the Dobie-Paisano Fellowship, the Ki Davis Award from the Aspen Writers Foundation, and most recently the William Faulkner Award for the personal essay. Her poems and essays have appeared in numerous literary journals, including *TriQuarterly Review, Chatahoochee Review, New Letters, River Styx* and *Calyx.* Her books include *Going Home, The Mask of Medusa, Making Bread at Midnight, How Heavy the Breath of God,* and *The Journals of Scheherazade.* She has also published a book of translations of the Cajun poet Jean Arceneaux, *Je Suis Cadien.* A book of lyric essays, *Swamp Songs: The Making of an Unruly Woman,* was published in spring 2003 by the University of Utah Press.

SUSAN STERLING grew up in Connecticut and now lives in Waterville, Maine, with her husband, Paul Machlin, their children, Greg and Erica, and their dog, Maggie. Since receiving her Ph.D. in 1975 from the University of California, Berkeley, she earned an M.F.A. in fiction from the Program for Writers at Warren Wilson College in Asheville, North Carolina, and has taught writing and literature at Thomas College and at Colby College, where she also served for three years as acting director of the Writer's Center. Currently she is taking time off to complete a novel and serve as co-facilitator for a Survivors of Suicide bereavement group through Hospice Volunteers. Her stories and essays have appeared in *Best American Sports Writing 1998, The New York Times, The North American Review, The Christian Science Monitor,* the French journal *Etudes, The Marlboro Review, Blueline,* and *Jacaranda,* and are forthcoming in *Colby* and the *Larcom Review.*

JUDY WELLS was born in San Francisco, California. She received her B.A. from Stanford University in 1966 and her Ph.D. in Comparative Literature from UC Berkeley in 1976. She has six books of poetry to her credit: *I Have Berkeley; Albuquerque Winter; Jane, Jane; The Part-Time Teacher; The Calling: Twentieth Century Women Artists;* and *Everything Irish*. A seventh book, *Call Home*, is forthcoming from Scarlet Tanager Books. Her poetry has been reviewed in several issues of the French magazine *Femmes Artistes International* (Paris), edited by Laurence Moréchand-Peeraer, Docteur ès Lettres. Judy's essay, "Daddy's Girl," has appeared in several editions of *The Borzoi College Reader* (Alfred A. Knopf) and a recent Irish essay, "The Sheela-na-Gigs," was published in *Travelers' Tales Ireland,* 2000. In the early eighties, she worked as a free-lance writer in Albuquerque, New Mexico, and published articles in *Sister Lode, Daily Lobo,* and the *Albuquerque Journal,* including interviews with poets Joy Harjo, Paula Gunn Allen, and Judy Grahn, and reviews of the work of Susan Griffin and Judy Chicago. She taught composition, creative writing, women's poetry and fiction, and the Great Books at various Bay Area colleges, before a 15 year stint working with adults as an academic counselor in the School of Extended Education at St. Mary's College in Moraga, California. She is currently a faculty member of the Graduate Liberal Studies Program at St. Mary's and lives with her husband, poet Dale Jensen, in Berkeley.

ELIZABETH A. WHEELER is an associate professor of English at the University of Oregon and the author of *Uncontained Urban Fiction in Postwar America* (Rutgers University Press), which was selected by *Choice* magazine as one of the outstanding academic books of 2001. Her articles have appeared in *The Journal of Film and Video, Southern California Quarterly,* and *Essays in Postmodern Culture*. She received her Ph.D. in Comparative Literature from UC Berkeley in 1996 and her A.B. summa cum laude from Bowdoin College in 1981. In 1992–1993 she conducted dissertation research on a fellowship at the University of the West Indies, Kingston, Jamaica. She is co-director of the University of Oregon Literacy Initiative, which trains college students to do literacy volunteer work in the community while enrolled in English classes where they write about and reflect on their community experiences. Professor Wheeler simultaneously produced her first book and her first baby, Kevin. Tenure arrived just ahead of her second child, Bridget. Professor Wheeler's current research lies at the intersection of urban ecology and disability studies, literature and oral history. Examining hidden minority communities along Oregon riverbanks, she explores what kinds of landscape description presume what kinds of bodies in the landscape.

Chapter Notes

Preface

1. *The Feminist Memoir Project*, eds. Rachel Blau DuPlessis and Ann Snitow (New York: Three Rivers Press, 1998), p. 22.

2. Daddy's Girl Goes Mad: Ten Years at UC Berkeley, 1966–1976

1. Sylvia Plath, *Ariel* (New York: Harper & Row, 1966), p. 49.
2. *SCUM Manifesto*: Society for Cutting Up Men. An extremist one-woman diatribe by the writer who is mostly known for shooting Andy Warhol.
3. Plath, p. 51.
4. Judith Wells, "Daddy's Girl," *Libera* 1, Winter 1972, p. 44.
5. Phyllis Chesler, *Women and Madness* (New York: Doubleday, 1972), p. 56.

9. The Legacy: From Comp. Lit. 40 to Women's Studies

1. Deirdre Lashgari and Lauren Coodley, "Surfacing: An Oral History of 'Women in Literature' 1972–1990," Western Association of Women Historians Conference, Huntington Library, May 4–6, 1990, 3.
2. Marsha Hudson would tackle Muriel Rukeyser in her 1978 dissertation, "A Woman of Words."
3. *Theories of Women's Studies*, eds. Gloria Bowles and Renate Klein, Routledge and Kegan Paul, 1983; *Louise Bogan's Aesthetic of Limitation*, Indiana University Press, 1987.
4. For the rest of the story, see "A Quiet Struggle: Women's Studies at Berkeley," *Chronicle of the University of California 5* (Spring 2002), 69–92 and "From the Bottom Up: The Students' Initiative," *The Politics of Women's Studies: Testimony from Thirty Founding Mothers*, ed. Florence Howe, Feminist Press, 2000, 142–54.

10. Yours, in Sisterhood

1. Report of the Committee on Senate Policy, May 6, 1969.
2. Report of the Subcommittee on the Status of Academic Women on the Berkeley Campus, May 19, 1970, p. 2.
3. Ibid., 7–9.

4. League of Academic Women, Chronicle of League of Academic Women, University of California, Berkeley, 1971, amended 1972.

5. "Report to the Business Meeting, December 1970," *MLA Newsletter* 3, no. 1 (February 1971): 2–3.

6. Ibid., 3.

7. The letter, addressed to Robert Alter, chairman of the department, and L. Janette Richardson, vice chairman for graduate studies, was signed by the six Women's Caucus members at that time: Page du Bois, Melanie Kaye Persoff, Marsha Hudson, Susan Sterling, Shelley Parlante, Lisa Gerrard, and Judith L. Wells.

8. "Sexism in Letters of Recommendation," *MLA Newsletter* (September 1972): 5.

9. Office of the Chancellor, "Suggestions for Departmental Self-Evaluation," April 30, 1976.

12. From Student to Teacher, from Teacher to Student: A Pedagogical Matrilineage

1. Coodley and Lashgari, "Surfacing: An Oral History of 'Women in Literature' 1972–1990," Western Association of Women Historians Conference, Huntington Library, May 4–6, 1990.

2. Mary Field Belenky, Blythe McVicker Clinchy, Nancy Rule Goldberger, Jill Mattack Tarule, *Women's Ways of Knowing: The Development of Self, Voice, and Mind* (New York: Basic Books 1986).

14. From Women's Caucus to Coalition of Women in German

1. Clausen, Jeanette. "The Coalition of Women in German: An Interpretative History and Celebration." *Women in German Yearbook* 1 (1985): 1–28.

2. I would particularly like to thank Wiggies Jeanette Clausen and Jeannine Blackwell, as well as Marjanne Goozé, Dan Wilson and Chantelle Warner, for their input.

15. Liberation Studies Now

1. See my discussion of the Good White Knight, who positions her/himself as the only white "good" on racism, which s/he demonstrates by attacking and shaming other whites: "Anti-Semitism, Homophobia, and the Good White Knight," *off our backs* (May 1982). The "Good Knight" can manifest among any dominant group.

2. Tamar Lewin, "How Boys Lost Out to Girl Power," *New York Times Week in Review* (December 13, 1998): 3.

17. The Way We Were

1. Modeled on the Declaration of Independence, according to the same footnote in the *Norton Anthology* (2001), p. 2164.

2. What goes completely unacknowledged, however, is the comparative and global cast we strove to give our version of feminism. Within less than a decade other fem-

inisms and narratives of women's history other than the American and Anglo-Saxon have all but vanished from consciousness.

3. The graduate student who said the "e" word was of course me, and I would have found myself out in the cold if it had not been for the women in the department who convinced the professorial powers to give me another chance.

4. Stuart Hall, "Cultural Studies and Its Theoretical Legacies," *The Norton Anthology of Theory and Criticism*, General Editor, Vincent B. Leitch, New York: W.W. Norton, 2001, p. 1905.

5. Although the women's movement is not ended, there are already any number of ways of telling its story—the apologetic, the mock-serious, the satirical, the neo-heoric.

6. Joyce Appleby, Lynn Hunt, Margaret Jacob, *Telling the Truth about History*, New York: W.W. Norton, 1994, p. 26.

7. *New York Review of Books* 35: 21–22. Jan. 19, 1989.

8. Paul Berman, *Terror and Liberalism*, W. W. Norton, 2003, p. 195.

Index